AF647101

LITERARY AND HISTORICAL STUDIES IN INDOLOGY

BY

Mahāmahopādhyāya

DR. VASUDEV VISHNU MIRASHI, M.A., D. Litt.

Former Head of the Departments of Sanskrit, and Ancient Indian History and Culture, Nagpur University; Hon. Correspondent of Archaeological Survey of India; Fellow, Sahitya Akademi, etc.

MOTILAL BANARSIDASS

DELHI :: VARANASI :: PATNA

MOTILAL BANARSIDASS
Indological Publishers and Booksellers
Head Office : BUNGALOW ROAD, JAWAHARNAGAR, DELHI-7
Branches : 1. CHOWK, VARANASI (U.P.)
2. ASHOK RAJ PATH (OPP. PATNA COLLEGE),
PATNA-4 (BIHAR)

© Author

ISBN O 8426 960 1

First Edition : Delhi, 1975

Printed in India

BY SHANTILAL JAIN, AT SHRI JAINENDRA PRESS BUNGALOW ROAD, JAWAHARNAGAR, DELHI-7, AND PUBLISHED BY SUNDARLAL JAIN FOR MOTILAL BANARSIDASS, BUNGALOW ROAD, JAWAHARNAGAR, DELHI-7

Dedicated to the Memory

of

Dr. F. Kielhorn

as a token of reverence

CONTENTS

LIST OF PLATES

PREFACE

This is the fifth Volume of my research articles dealing with various problems of Sanskrit literature, ancient Indian history and culture, numismatics, art and architecture, written during the last ten years. It is being issued under a slightly different title.

The present Volume contains twenty-seven articles grouped under four Sections. The first Section has nine articles. The first of them attempts to fix a lower limit for the date of the original form of the *Harivaṁśa*, the *Khila-parvan* of the *Mahābhārata*. This *parvan* of the Great Epic received additions from time to time. A critical edition of it has recently been published by the Bhandarkar Institute. But the MS. evidence of its age does not go back to an earlier date than the 11th cen. A.D. It has now been proved on inscriptional and literary evidence that the Constituted Text of this *Khila-parvan* is at least as old as A.D. 200. One of the subsequent articles (No. III) adduces additional evidences for the identification of Kālapriyanātha mentioned by Bhavabhūti from that poet's own plays. The date of Dhanañjaya, the author of the *Dvisandhāna* or *Rāghavapāṇḍavīya Kāvya*, had long been a matter of keen controversy. It is now shown in Article No. IV that he flourished as early as the latter half of the eighth cen. A.D. Another work of this author, *viz.* the *Nāmamālā* is next shown to be earlier than the famous *Nāmaliṅgānuśāsana* or *Amarakosha*. The author and the date of the play *Kundamālā* had long become quite controversial. I have stated my views on them in the previous Volumes of my *Studies in Indology*. In the next (No. VI) article I have examined in detail the arguments advanced against them and shown them to be ill founded. The historical background of Rājaśekhara's *Viddhaśālabhañjikā* was variously interpreted. Article No. VII shows its correct interpretation. Soḍḍhala's *Udayasundarīkathā*, though published more than fifty years ago, had not received the attention it deserves from scholars. Article No. VIII gives detailed information about it. The last article in this Section discusses the real meaning of the technical term *mattavāraṇī* used in Bharata's *Nāṭyaśāstra*.

The second Section deals with some problems of ancient Indian history. It contains seven articles. The historicity of Rāmagupta has now been proved by unimpeachable evidence ; but some incidents in his career are still baffling. Article No. XI tries to clarify them. The next two articles (XII and XIII) discuss problems presented by some newly discovered copper-plate grants of the Traikūṭakas and the Vishṇukuṇḍins. It has almost been unanimously held that the Śilāhāra king of North Koṅkaṇ who was killed in the invasion of Someśvara I was Mummuṇi. Article No. XV shows that this is an erroneous view and that the king who succumbed to the attack was his elder brother Nāgārjuna. Finally, the last article (XVI) gives an incomplete but interesting copper-plate grant of the Yādava king Rāmachandra.

Section III contains six articles on the readings and interpretations of some newly discovered coins of the Sātavāhanas, Mahishas, Kshatrapas, Traikūṭakas and Vishṇukuṇḍins. They have yielded valuable information about the ancient history of Western Mahārāshṭra, Vidarbha and Andhra.

Section IV contains five articles. They deal with some questions which have recently become controversial such as the location of Rāvaṇa's Laṅkā, the religious affiliation of the caves at Dhārāśiva, and the age of the Mārkaṇḍī temples. The last article (XXVII) tears off the mask from the fake Sanskrit historical *kāvya Ayyaṇavaṁśacharita*.

Many of the articles in the present Volume were published from time to time in Felicitation Volumes and Research Journals, but some of them are new. I am thankful to the Editors of the Volumes and Journals where they were published, for permission to reprint them. My thanks are also due to M/S. Motilal Banarsidass, Delhi, for having undertaken the publication of the present Volume and having done it expeditiously.

Mahārāshṭra Day
1st May, 1975

V.V. Mirashi

ABBREVIATIONS

A.B.O.R.I.—Annals of the Bhandarkar Oriental Research Institute
A.S.W.I.—Archaeological Survey of Western India
A.R.A.S.I.—Annual Report of the Archaeological Survey of India
B.S.P.S.—Bombay Sanskrit and Prakrit Series
B.M.C.—Catalogue of Coins in the British Museum
Bom. Gaz.—Bombay Gazetteer
C.A.S.R.—Cunningham's Archaeological Survey Report
C.I.I.—Corpus Inscriptionum Indicarum
D.K.A.—Pargiter, Dynasties of the Kali Age
E.I. or *Ep. Ind.*—Epigraphia Indica
Ep. Carn.—Epigraphia Carnatica
G.O.S.—Gaekwad's Oriental Series
H.C.I.P.—History and Culture of the Indian People
I.A. or *Ind. Ant.*—Indian Antiquary
Ind. Cult.—Indian Culture
I.H.Q. or *Ind. Hist. Quart.*—Indian Historical Quarterly
J.A.S.Bom.—Journal of the Asiatic Society of Bombay
J.A.S.B.—Journal of the Asiatic Society of Bengal
J.B.B.R.A.S.—Journal of the Bombay Branch of the Royal Asiatic Society
J.B.O.R.S.—Journal of the Bihar and Orissa Research Society
J.N.S.I.—Journal of the Numismatic Society of India
J.O.I. or *Journ. Or. Inst.*—Journal of the Oriental Institute
J.R.A.S.—Journal of the Royal Asiatic Society
J.R.A.S.B.—Journal of the Royal Asiatic Society of Bengal
List—List of Brāhmī Inscriptions by Lüders
M.A.S.I.—Memoir of the Archaeological Survey of India
P.W.M.B.—Prince of Wales Museum Bulletin
Z.D.M.G.—Zeitschrift der Deutschens Morganländischen Gasellschaft

SECTION I

SANSKRIT LITERATURE

I. THE DATE OF THE ORIGINAL HARIVAṀŚA*

In 1919, on the occasion of the first session of the All-India Oriental Conference held at Poona, the Bhandarkar Oriental Research Institute resolved to undertake the preparation and publication of a Critical Edition of the *Mahābhārata*, and with the help of several scholars and munificent grants from the UNESCO, the Central and State Governments, the Universities and the generous public, completed the project in 1966. The *Harivaṁśa* is traditionally regarded as the *Khilaparvan* or Supplement of the *Mahābhārata* and so without its critical edition, the work on the Great Epic cannot be said to be complete. So Dr. P. L. Vaidya, the third and last Editor of the Critical Edition of the *Mahābhārata*, undertook the Critical Edition of the *Harivaṁśa* and has since published its first Volume containing the Introduction, Critical Text and Notes. The second volume will contain long passages interpolated in the *Harivaṁśa* from time to time.

Dr. Vaidya has based his Critical Edition on four printed editions and thirty-six manuscripts in eight different scripts collected from different parts of India. In constituting the Text he found the following five manuscripts most helpful—(1) A manuscript in the Śāradā script written on birch bark, nearly 500 years old. It represents the version current in North-West India. (2) A manuscript in the Newāri script written on palm-leaf and nearly as old as the eleventh century A.D. It represents the version current in North-East India. (3) Three manuscripts in the Malayālam script written on palm-leaf, which represent the version current in South India.

* *Prof. P. B. Desai Felicitation Volume*, pp. 425 f.

These three versions show remarkable agreement in contents and readings, and, therefore, form the basis of the Constituted Text. That text is the shortest among all versions of the *Harivaṁśa* and is corroborated by the *Bhāratamañjarī* of Kshemendra, a Kashmirian poet of the eleventh century A.D. The *Harivaṁśa* received several additions from time to time. Most of them are absent from the *Bhāratamañjarī* as they are from the three types of the manuscripts mentioned above.

The Constituted Text represents the shortest version of the *Harivaṁśa*. It has 118 *adhyāyas* and 6073 *ślokas* as against 318 *adhyāyas* and 18000 *ślokas* of its Vulgate. So it is nearly one-thrid of the Vulgate. Dr. Vaidya thinks that the original *Harivaṁśa* must have been still shorter. It probably contained only the first 98 *adhyāyas*. He has, however, included the subsequent *adhyāyas* because they are supported by the three types of the oldest manuscripts mentioned above.

Like the *Mahābhārata*, *Harivaṁśa* also received additions from time to time. They were mostly of following types :—

संग्रामश्च विवाहश्च स्तुतिर्वेववरादिकम् ।
प्रक्षेपकारणान्याहुः पञ्चमं च फलश्रुतिः ॥

The interpolations included the description of battles, and marriages, praises of gods and goddesses, the boons granted by them and their consequences, and finally, the *phalaśruti* (the merit accruing to the reciter and the listener of the religious work). Dr. Vaidya has discussed some important interpolations in the Introduction.

The Date of the Original Harivaṁśa

Dr. Vaidya says in one place (p. xv) in the Introduction that the original *Harivaṁśa* was composed at about A.D. 400, and at another (p. xxxix) that its Constituted Text was current at about A.D. 300. At that time it had only the first 98 adhyāyas. The next twenty *adhyāyas* came to be added in the period from A.D. 300 to A.D. 1050, since that part is noticed as summarised in Kshemendra's *Bhāratamañjarī*. Some other portions in the Vulgate appear to have been interpolated after A.D. 1050. They are to be given in the second Volume of the Critical Edition.

Dr. Vaidya has not cited any evidence for fixing the afore-mentioned date of the original *Harivaṁśa*, but it is easy to conjecture it. Several land-grants from the middle of the fifth century A.D. contain benedictory and imprecatory verses taken from the *Mahābhārata*. In the Kho copper-plate grant[1] of Śarvanātha dated A.D. 533-34, these verses are introduced with the following words :—

उक्तञ्च महाभारते शतसाहस्र्यां संहितायां पराशरसुतेन वेदव्यासेन व्यासेन ।

This refers to the *Mahābhārata* as a work of a hundred thousand *ślokas*. So the Great Epic must have attained this form before the fifth century A.D. Like the *Harivaṁśa*, the *Mahābhārata* also has received additions from time to time. If its extent in the fifth century A.D. was one hundred thousand *ślokas*, it must have then included the *Harivaṁśa*. Otherwise, this voluminous extent of the Great Epic would be inexplicable. The current North-Indian version of the Epic has 84000 *ślokas* up to the *svargārohaṇa parvan*. If we add 16000 ślokas of the North-Indian version of the *Harivaṁśa* to it, the number of the *ślokas* would be one hundred thousand as stated in the land-grant. In the South Indian version the number would go to one lakh and twenty thousand *ślokas*. The Critical Edition of the *Mahābhārata* contains about 73,000 *ślokas*. If we add 6073 *ślokas* of the Constituted Text of the *Harivaṁśa* to this number, it would not, of course, come to a lakh *ślokas*, but, Dr. Vaidya says, even this number of 80,000 *ślokas* under a single title is very large and so the *Mahābhārata* came to be regarded as a *Śata-sāhasrī Saṁhitā*.

This argument is evidently based on conjecture. It is, however, possible to adduce more definite evidence to prove even a higher antiquity for the original text of the *Harivaṁśa*.

The *Harivaṁśa* is mainly concerned with the genealogy and the life of Kṛishṇa. *Pārijāta-haraṇa* (removal of the Pārijāta tree from heaven) forms an important event in the life of

1. Fleet, *Gupta Inscriptions*, p. 137.

Kṛishṇa. So the latter is named 'Pārijāta' in the colophons of some *adhyāyas* of the *Harivaṁśa*. The incident is as follows :—

Narakāsura, the ruler of Kāmarūpa (modern Assam), had forcibly removed the *kuṇḍalas* (ear-ornaments) of Aditi, the mother of gods. So Indra sought the help of Kṛishṇa to regain them. Kṛishṇa then invaded Prāgjyotishapura (the capital of Naraka), killed the demon and released the daughters of the Gandharvas and Asuras imprisoned by him. Kṛishṇa was accompanied by Satyabhāmā in this expedition. They then went to heaven, presented the *kuṇḍalas* to Aditi and, on their way back, Kṛishṇa uprooted the heavenly Pārijāta tree, placed it on his vehicle Garuḍa and brought it to Dvārakā.

The story of *Pārijāta-haraṇa* has two forms in the Vulgate of the *Harivaṁśa*. One of them, which is shorter, occurs in *adhyāya* 64 of the *Vishṇu-parvan*, the second *parvan* of the *Harivaṁśa*.[1] After narrating the incidents up to the release of the Gandharva and Asura maidens as summarised above, the version describes the removal of the Pārijāta tree in the following words :—

स ददर्श महाबाहुराक्रीडे वासवस्य ह ।
दिव्यमभ्यर्चितं देवैः पारिजातं महाद्रुमम् ॥

नित्यपुष्पधरं दिव्यं पुण्यगन्धमनुत्तमम् ।
यमासाद्य जनः सर्वो जाति स्मरति पौर्विकीम् ॥

उत्पाट्यारोपयामास विष्णुस्तं गरुडोपरि ।
सोऽपश्यत्सत्यभामा च दिव्यमप्सरसां गणम् ॥

श्रुत्वा तं देवराजस्तु कर्म कृष्णस्य तत्तदा ।
अनुमेने महाबाहुः कृतकर्मेति चाब्रवीत् ॥

This version describes that on his way back from heaven, Kṛishṇa saw the ever-flowering and fragrant heavenly tree

1. The Vulgate of the *Harivaṁśa* has three *parvans*, viz., *Harivaṁśa-parvan*, *Vishṇuparvan*, and *Bhavishyaparvan*, and the *ślokas* in each are numbered separately. Though the Critical Edition mentions the three *parvans*, the stanzas there have been numbered consecutively from beginning to end.

Pārijāta in the Nandana-vana of Indra, uprooted it and brought it to Dvārakā. He was then accompanied by Satyabhāmā. When Indra came to know of it, he acquiesed in it as a *fait accompli.*

This version of *Pārijāta-haraṇa* is the older one and is given in *adhyāya* 92 (*ślokas* 63-67) of the Constituted Text. The same version is noticed in the following stanzas of the Critical Edition of the *Droṇaparvan* (*adhyāya* 10, *ślokas* 22-23) :—

वैनतेयं समारुह्य त्रासयित्वामरावतीम् ।
महेन्द्रभवनाद्वीरः पारिजातमुपानयत् ॥
तच्च मर्षितवान् शक्रो जानंस्तस्य पराक्रमम् ।
राज्ञां चाप्यजितं कञ्चित्कृष्णेनेह न नः श्रुतम् ॥

As stated above, the Critical Edition of the *Harivaṁśa* bears remarkable agreement with the *Bhāratamañjarī* of Kshemendra. It is noticed in this respect also. The latter describes the incident in the following *ślokas* :—

ददर्श नन्दनोत्तंसं सर्वकामप्रदं सदा ।
पारिजातं सुधाजातमभिजातमिवेश्वरम् ॥
तं दृष्ट्वा नयनानन्दबान्धवं माधवः स्वयम् ।
समुत्पाट्य जहाराशु तच्चामन्यत वृत्रहा ॥

This shorter version of *Pārijāta-haraṇa* thus occurs in the oldest MSS. of the *Harivaṁśa*, the *Droṇa-parvan* of the Critical Edition of the *Mahābhārata* and the *Bhāratamañjarī* of Kshemendra. It is, therefore, the older version of the episode and has, consequently, been given in the Constituted Text of the *Harivaṁśa*.

The other or longer version of the episode occurs in *Vishṇu-parvan, adhyāya* 65-71 of the Vulgate. It may be summarised as follows :—

Once upon a time Kṛishṇa went to the Raivataka mountain (near Girnar in Kathiawad), together with his wives, sons and other relatives for the *vratodyāpana* of Rukmiṇī. While he was sitting with Rukmiṇī in the assembly, there came the heavenly sage Nārada, who presented a flower of the heavenly tree Pārijāta to him. The latter presented it to Rukmiṇī. This greatly enhanced her beauty. Nārada congratulated her and said, "This flower will return to heaven after a year. Since Kṛishṇa has presented it to you, you appear to be his second self." Some servants of Satyabhāmā communicated the incident to her. She was greatly upset and was terribly enraged against Kṛishṇa. When the latter came to know of it, he hurried to her apartment and tried to appease her. But she would not listen to him and spoke harsh words, rebuking him for his partiality to Rukmiṇī. Then Kṛishṇa asked her forgiveness for presenting the celestial flower to Rukmiṇī and said :—

पारिजातकपुष्पाणि यदीच्छस्यतिकोपने ।
तदा दातास्मि सुश्रोणि सत्यमेतद्ब्रवीमि ते ।
स्वर्गास्पदादानयित्वा पारिजातं द्रुमेश्वरम् ।
गृहे ते स्थापयिष्यामि यावत्कालं त्वमिच्छसि ॥

(If you want those flowers, I would present them to you. I shall uproot the tree from heaven and plant it near your mansion. It will remain there as long as you may desire.)

Thereafter, Kṛishṇa honoured Nārada. The latter said, "The tree was created by Kaśyapa for the ornamentation and diversion of his wife Aditi. The latter donated it to me for the attainment of religious merit and then took it back after paying its price. The same was done by Śachī, the wife of Indra, Rohiṇī, the consort of the Moon, and Ṛiddhi, the spouse of Kubera." Then, as he was leaving for heaven, Kṛishṇa sent through him the following message to Indra, "My wives want to make a gift of the Pārijāta. So you should send it here." Then Nārada told him, "Indra is not likely to comply with your order. The tree came out of the ocean when it was churned by gods and demons. It was then presented by Śiva to Indra for the sake of his wife Śachī. None but Śiva, Pārvatī and myself can enter the garden of Nandana where it stands." Then Kṛishṇa replied, "I have vowed to present it to Satyabhāmā. If Indra does not accept my request to part with it, I shall strike his breast with my mace."

When Nārada communicated Kṛishṇa's message to Indra the latter said, "O Great Sage, please convey my reply to

Kṛishṇa. You have incarnated yourself for reducing the burden of the earth. When you will return to heaven after fulfilling the purpose of incarnation, I shall present you with the Pārijāta. It would not be proper to remove a valuable thing to the earth for flimsy reasons." Nārada tried to persuade Indra to part with the Pārijāta, but the latter would not yield. He said to Nārada, "Please tell my message to Kṛishṇa—

पलाशपत्रार्धमपि त्वयाजितो
न पारिजातस्य तव प्रदास्यति ॥

(Unless I am defeated, I shall not give you even half a leaf of the Pārijāta).

When Nārada told Indra's message to Kṛishṇa, the latter said, "I am going to attack Indra's city Amarāvatī tomorrow. Please warn him." When Indra heard of Kṛishṇa's resolve, he consulted Bṛihaspati about the matter. The latter said, "O Indra, you with your son should oppose Kṛishṇa. I shall also try to solve this question in a just manner." Then Bṛihaspati went to Kaśyapa and told him what had happened. The latter approached Śiva and praised him for winning his favour. (*Vishṇuparvan*, *adhyāya* 72, *ślokas* 29-60). Śiva said, "Formerly, Indra coveted the wife of a sage. This is the result of that misbehaviour. Kṛishṇa will surely take away the Pārijāta. You should repair there together with Aditi. Ultimately, there would be an amicable settlement between Indra and Kṛishṇa."

Kṛishṇa, taking Sātyaki with himself, mounted Garuḍa and attacked the garden of Indra. His son Pradyumna followed him. Kṛishṇa uprooted the Pārijāta in defiance of the guardians of the Naṇḍanavana and placed it on Garuḍa. In the meanwhile Indra came to know of it and marched against him. Then Indra fought with Kṛishṇa, and Jayanta with Pradyumna. Indra's friend Pravara, who had previously studied under Paraśurāma, tried to snatch away the Pārijāta, but Sātyaki prevented him.

When Indra began to cut off the wings of Garuḍa one after another, Kṛishṇa asked Pradyumna to go to Dvārakā and get his chariot there together with the charioteer Dāruka. Thereafter, he, in that chariot, proceeded to the Pāriyātra mountain, where Indra, mounted on the Airāvata, was expecting him. Pradyumna and Sātyaki also followed him to guard the Pārijāta tree. Just then the sun set. So at the suggestion of Kṛishṇa, fighting was stopped for the night. Indra then repaired to Pushkara, where Brahmā, Kaśyapa, Aditi, Aśvins, Āditya, Rudra and other gods soon assembled. Kṛishṇa, however, stayed at Pāriyātra. The Gaṅgā soon came there as he desired. Kṛishṇa bathed in its water and worshipped Śiva with the water of the Gaṅgā and the leaves of the Bilva tree. He then praised him (*Viṣṇuparvan, adhyāya* 54, *ślokas* 22-34). Śiva became pleased and gave him a boon. Since then the temple of Śiva on that hill became known as Bilvodakeśvara. Kṛishṇa spent the night on the Pāriyātra mountain and gave it the boon that those who would climb it and have his *darśana* would attain the merit of the gift of a thousand cows.

Then commenced a terrible fight between Kṛishṇa and Indra. Just then there arrived Kaśyapa and Aditi as advised by Brahmā. On seeing them, both stopped fighting. Then Aditi said to Kṛishṇa, "You may take the Pārijāta to Dvārakā. After Satyabhāmā's performance of the Puṇyaka vow, it should be replanted in the Nandana garden."

Then Kṛishṇa returned to Dvārakā along with Pradyumna and Sātyaki. Kṛishṇa then planted the tree in the courtyard of Satyabhāmā[1]. As soon as Kṛishṇa thought of Nārada, the latter appeared there. Satyabhāmā then tied Kṛishṇa to the tree and gave him away to Nārada together with gold, jewels etc. Then Nārada jocularly said to Satyabhāmā, "If you would give me a brown cow with a calf, a pot filled with sesamum and gold, I would release Kṛishṇa." That being done, Kṛishṇa called together all his relatives including Bhīshmaka and the Pāṇḍavas and showed them the Pārijāta

1. A later form of the story states that when Rukmiṇī became displeased as the Pārijāta tree was presented to Satyabhāmā, Kṛishṇa pacified her by assuring her that though the tree was in the courtyard of Satyabhāmā, its flowers would fall in her own courtyard. See Śrīdhara's Marāṭhī *Harivaṁśa, adhyāya* 26, verses 206 f.

tree. As soon as the year was over, he sent it back to Indra. The next (77th) *adhyāya* describes the *Puṇyakavrata*.[1]

This second version of *Pārijātaharaṇa* is after the manner of the Purāṇas. Its purpose seems to have been to glorify the Bilvodakeśvara temple on the Pāriyātra mountain and the holy *tīrtha* of Pushkara, lying in its vicinity. Dr. Vaidya conjectures that it must have been borrowed from some Purāṇa.

The two versions of *Pārijātaharaṇa* are poles apart. The version in the Critical Edition is given in only five *ślokas* (adhyāya 92, ślokas 63-67). The episode is narrated in a simple unembellished manner. On the other hand, the second version in the Vulgate occupies as many as thirteen *adhyāyas* (*Vishṇuparvan,* adhyāyas 64-76, comprising 751 *ślokas*). The description evokes different *rasas* such as Vipralambha-Śṛiṅgāra, Vīra and Adbhuta. We shall now proceed to show when the episode attained this second elaborate form.

The great rhetorician Ānandavardhana says in his *Dhvanyāloka*,[2] "If a poet chooses a historical story for his work, he should omit all incidents in it which would be opposed to the intended sentiment; for the object of the poet is not to teach history. That is done by historical works." To illustrate his view Ānandavardhana cites the works of Kālidāsa and the *Harivijaya* of Sarvasena. Ānandavardhana has not stated what incidents were omitted and new ones added by Sarvasena in the story of the *Harivijaya,* but here his commentator Abhinavagupta comes to our help. He states that the *Harivijaya* has for its theme the removal of the Pārijāta tree from heaven which was done by Kṛishṇa for the appeasement of his wife (evidently Satyabhāmā), though this is not stated in history.[3]

1. The Pārijāta tree is no longer seen on the earth. What goes by the name of Pārijāta in Mahārāshṭra, is really the Śephālikā tree, the flowers of which have been described as follows in Bhāsa's *Svapna-Vāsavadatta*— ते (शेफालिकागुल्मका:) कुसुमिता नाम प्रवालान्तरितैरिव मौक्तिकलम्बकैराचिता: कुसुमै: ।

2. इतिवृत्तवशायातां कथञ्चिद्रसाननुगुणां स्थितिं पुनरुत्प्रेक्ष्याभीष्टरसोचितकथोन्नयो विधेय: यथा कालिदासप्रबन्धेषु । यथा च सर्वसेनविरचिते हरिविजये ।

3. हरिविजये कान्तानुनयाङ्गत्वेन पारिजातहरणादि निरूपितमितिहासेष्वदृष्टमपि । ध्वन्यालोकलोचन, तृतीयोद्योत.

Ānandavardhana has cited some *gāthās* from the *Harivijaya* which show that the work was composed in the Mahārāshṭrī Prakrit. Bhoja, the author of the *Sarasvatīkaṇṭhābharaṇa*, has cited two *gāthās* from the *Harivijaya*, without stating their source. Of these, the first (v. 264) states that Satyabhāmā alone, in the midst of all other wives of Kṛishṇa, got enraged by humiliation (when the Pārijāta flowers obtained from heaven were presented by Kṛishṇa to Rukmiṇī) because of her great love for Kṛishṇa. The second *gāthā* (V. 288) is even more important. It runs as follows :—

सुरकुसुमेहिं कलुसिअं जइ तेहिं चिअ पुणो पसाएमि तुमं ।
तो पेमस्स किसोअरि अवराहस्स अ ण मे कअं अणुरूअं ॥

(सुरकुसुमैः कलुषितां यदि तैरेव पुनः प्रसादयामि त्वाम् ।
ततः प्रेम्णः कृशोदरि अपराधस्य च न मे कृतमनुरूपम् ॥)

Bhoja has not given the context of this verse, but it is evidently addressed by Kṛishṇa to Satyabhāmā. Says he, "If I appease you, who are enraged by the presentation of flowers (to Rukmiṇī), by presenting the same flowers to you, it would not be in keeping with either my love for you or my offence against you. Hence I intend to present the Pārijāta tree itself to you." This *gāthā* also was evidently taken from the *Harivijaya* and corroborates the statement of Abhinavagupta that the theme of the work was the removal of the Pārijāta tree from heaven for the appeasement of Satyabhāmā.

The *Harivijaya* is not extant now, but from the *gāthās* cited from it by Ānandavardhana and Bhoja and the statements of Hemachandra in his own commentary on his *Alaṅkārachūḍāmaṇi*, we can gather the following bits of information about the Prakrit *Kāvya*.

The *Harivijaya* was throughout written in one metre, *viz*. *Skandhaka*. The last *gāthā* of each canto contained the word *utsāha*. Its theme, as stated above, was the forcible removal, by Kṛishṇa, of the Pārijāta tree from heaven for the appeasement of Satyabhāmā after subjugating Indra. It seems that Kṛishṇa first sent Sātyaki as a *nisṛishṭārtha-dūta* (Commissioner with full powers of negotiation) to Indra. Like Sanskrit *Mahākāvyas*, the *Harivijaya* contained the description of a city (Dvārakā), the hero (Kṛishṇa), a season (spring), sunset, horses and elephants, drinking parties and so forth. Kṛishṇa invaded heaven, defeated Indra, and forced him to part with the Pārijāta tree, which he presented to Satyabhāmā to appease her anger.

The date of the *Harivijaya* was uncertain until we fixed it nearly twenty-five years ago. That its author flourished before Ānandavardhana (ninth century A.D.) was known from the citations in the *Dhvanyāloka*, but nothing more was known about him. We drew attention for the first time to the following verse occurring in the introduction to the fragmentary prose work *Avantisundarī-kathā* of Daṇḍin, published in the Dakshiṇa-Bhāratī Grantha-mālā—

राज्ञा श्रीसर्वसेनेन . . . . ।
. . . . विजयं हरेः ॥

Only one manuscript of this work has been found, from which the work has been edited. It was greatly damaged. So several words in the above verse have been lost, but fortunately, its most important portion has been preserved. It shows that the author of the *Harivijaya* was a king named Sarvasena. The order in which the several authors have been praised in the introduction of the *Avantisundarī-kathā* seems to be chronological. In these verses Sarvasena, the author of the *Harivijaya*, is mentioned after Bhāsa and before the author of the *Setu* and Kālidāsa. So Sarvasena seems to have preceded Kālidāsa.

Until 1939 nothing was known about king Sarvasena. In that year a copper-plate grant of the Vākāṭakas was discovered at Bāsim in the Akolā district of Vidarbha. It has been subsequently edited by us in the *Epigraphia Indica* (Vol. XXVI, pp. 139f). It mentions Sarvasena as a son of the powerful Vākāṭaka *Samrāṭ* Pravarasena I and as the founder of the Vatsagulma (modern Bāsim) branch of the Vākāṭaka family, Sarvasena was also mentioned in the inscription in Ajaṇṭā

Cave XVI, but as that record is very much abraded, the name was wrongly read as *Rudrasena*, who was identified with the first Vākāṭaka prince of that name. In our edition of that record we have shown where the name of Sarvasena occurred in it.

There is only one prince named Sarvasena in Indian history. He belonged to the Vākāṭaka family and flourished from *c.* A.D. 330 to A.D. 355. He is evidently the author of the afore-mentioned Prakrit *kāvya Harivijaya*.

From Ānandavardhana's statement cited above, it is clear that the original story of *Pārijātaharaṇa* was simple and unembellished as in the Critical Edition of the *Harivaṁśa*. When Sarvasena used it as the subject of his *kāvya*, he seems to have made several changes in it, omitting some incidents and adding others, but the story in the *Harivaṁśa* remained unaffected by his Prakrit *kāvya* as is evident from its version given by Kshemendra.[1] Thereafter, some poet seems to have changed it on the model of the *Harivijaya kāvya*. The new version shows that Kṛishṇa invaded Indra's city to obtain the Pārijāta tree for the appeasement of Satyabhāmā. That version differed from the *Harivijaya* in certain respects. For instance, the latter *kāvya* states that Kṛishṇa sent Sātyaki as his *nisṛishṭ-ārtha dūta* to Indra. In the new version Nārada was entrusted with the negotiation. There must have been other changes as well, but as the *Harivijaya* has not been recovered till now, it is not possible to state them definitely.[2]

As stated above, the story of *Pārijātaharaṇa* in the *Harivaṁśa* was a simple, unembellished one as in the Critical Edition till the time of Sarvasena. That the *Harivaṁśa* was then included in the *Mahābhārata* has already been shown. So the *Mahābhārata* and the *Harivaṁśa* must have both attained the

1. The story occurs as in the Critical Edition in the *Bhāgavata Purāṇa* (10th cen. A.D.). See X, 59, 39-40.

2. There are other instances of Sanskrit classical works having been drawn upon in the Purāṇas. We have shown in our *Kālidāsa* (pp.139 f. and 305 f.) that the *Śivapurāṇa* has borrowed some incidents and expressions from the *Kumārasambhava*, and the *Padmapurāṇa* from the *Śākuntala*.

form in their Critical Edition at least a hundred and fifty years before. In other words, the *Harivaṁśa* must have been composed before A.D. 200 at least. This is the lower limit of its date. Its story is as old as the age of Patañjali (middle of the second century B.C.), but the upper limit of the *Harivaṁśa* cannot be definitely fixed in the present state of our knowledge.

II. A NOTE ON THE SUBHĀSHITARATNAKA-RAṆḌAKAKATHĀ OF ĀRYAŚŪRA*

The *Subhāshitaratnakaraṇḍakakathā* has recently been published as an Appendix to the *Jātakamālā* of Āryaśūra (No. 21 of the Bauddha Saṁskṛita Granthāvali).[1] The work has been edited by Dr. A.C. Banerjee from a single Nepāli manuscript. It contains twenty-eight chapters called *kathās* containing verses from two to forty-three, preaching the various *pāramitās* (perfections). The work is generally ascribed to Āryaśūra, the well-known author of the *Jātakamālā*, but both Dr. P.L. Vaidya, who has edited the *Jātakamālā*, and Dr. Banerjee are of the opinion that the author of the work under consideration is not the famous Āryaśūra who flourished in the fourth century A.D., but some other namesake of his who lived in a later age, which neither of them has tried to determine. In this note it is proposed to show that the *Subhāshitakaraṇḍakakathā* also is an early work and may have been from the pen of the famous Āryaśūra.

The editor has given the name of the work as *Subhāshitakaraṇḍakakathā*, but it does not occur in the colophon of the work in the Nepāli manuscript, which gives the name as *Subhāshitaratnakakaraṇḍaka*. The name given to the present work is said to occur in the Tibetan version. I have not been able to verify this. But if the word *kathā* formed a part of the title, the latter may have been *Subhāshitakathāratnakaraṇḍaka*; for it contains collections of verses called *kathās* (*e.g.* Puṇya-protsāhana-kathā, Dharma-śravaṇa-protsāhana-kathā. etc.).

As for the lower date of the work, I invite attention to the citation of the verse *Lakshmī-niketam* etc. (v. 6 of the first *kathā*) in two copper-plate grants of the Maitrakas of Valabhī, namely, (1) the Valabhī grant of Guhasena, dated Gupta year 248 (A.D. 567-68) and the Valabhī grant of Dharasena II, dated

* The Adyar Literary Bulletin, Vol. XXV, pp. 304 f

Gupta year 269 (A.D. 588-89). Generally, at the end of a copper-plate grant there are benedictory and imprecatory verses usually ascribed to Vyāsa or Rāmchandra. Such verses occur both in the earlier and later grants of the Maitrakas of Valabhī. But those who drafted the two grants mentioned above seem to have drawn upon the *Subhāshitakathāratnakaraṇḍaka* which contains didactic verses, for one of them. The earlier of the two grants, in which the verse *Lakshmī-niketaṁ etc.* occurs, does not introduce it with the usual words *api cātra Vyāsa-gītāḥ śloka bhavanti*, being evidently aware that it occurred not in the *Mahābhārata* but in a Buddhist work, *viz.* the *Subhāshitakathā-ratna-karaṇḍaka*. In course of time, however, this work seems to have gone out of use, and so in the second grant, namely, the Valabhī copper-plate grant of Dharasena II, the benedictory and imprecatory verses including the verse in question are introduced with the words *uktaṁ cha bhagavatā veda-vyāsena Vyāsena*. Its author evidently did not know that the verse was taken from a Buddhist work.

The citation of the verse *Lakshmī-niketaṁ etc.* in the earlier of the two Valabhī grants shows that the work *Subhāshitakathā-ratna-karaṇ ḍaka* was composed at least before A.D. 550. We know of no Buddhist writer named Āryaśūra who flourished before this date except the well-known author of the *Jātakamālā*. It is not, therefore, unlikely that the *Subhāshitakathā-ratna-karaṇḍaka* also was the work of Āryaśūra who flourished in the fourth century A.D.

The verse occurs in a very corrupt form in both the aforementioned Valabhī grants. In the earlier grant it is cited as follows :—

लक्ष्मीनिकेतं यवपाश्रयेण प्राप्तोसि..................।
पक्षंन्येव च पुण्यान्यभिवाद्धा यथा न कर्शनीयो ह्युपकारिपक्षः ॥

In the other grant the wording is :—

लक्ष्मीनिकेतं यवपाश्रयेण प्राप्तो...कोभिमतं नृपार्थम् ।
तान्येव पुण्यानि विवर्धयेथा न हापनीयो ह्युपकारिपक्षः ॥

Owing to the corrupt form the verse was not properly understood by the editors of the grants. Dr. Banerjee has given us the following correct form .—

लक्ष्मीनिकेतं यदुपाश्रयेण प्राप्तोऽसि लोकाभिमतं प्रभुत्वम् ।
तान्येव पुण्यानि विवर्धयेथा न कर्षणीयो ह्युपकारिपक्षः ॥

The verse, therefore, means : "The religious merit by virtue of which you have obtained (*this*) lordship respected in the world, which is the abode of royal fortune, should be augmented; the obliging ally (*i.e.* your religious merit) should not be abandoned."

In the first *kathā* or collection of didactic verses which preach the augmentation of religious merit, there is nothing more appropriate for citation in a copper-plate grant than the verse in question.

We need not doubt, as Dr. Vaidya and Dr. Banerjee have done, Āryaśūra's authorship of the *Subhāshita-kathā-ratna-karaṇḍaka*. The verses are composed in elegant Sanskrit. As all of them are didactic, there is no scope for any flight of fancy. But the work has certainly sufficient merit to justify our ascribing it to Āryaśūra, who has been praised for his chaste expression.

III. FRESH LIGHT ON THE IDENTIFICATION OF KĀLAPRIYANĀTHA

It is well known that all the plays of the great Sanskrit poet Bhavabhūti were staged at the fair of the god Kālapriyanātha. Several Sanskrit commentators and almost all editors of Bhavabhūti's plays identify this god with Mahākāla of Ujjayinī. Thus, Tripurāri, an old commentator of the *Mālatīmādhava*, says कालप्रियनाथस्य महाकालास्पदस्य शम्भोः । "Kalapriyanātha is god Śiva in the temple of Mahākāla." Some other commentators like Vīrarāghava, though they have not made such an explicit statement as this, still identify the god Kālapriyanātha with Śiva. Vīrarāghava, for instance, who first adopts the reading *Kālapriyānātha*, says, कालप्रियानाथस्य कालप्रियानामिकाम्बिकापतेः । (Kālapriyānātha means Śiva, the husband of Kālapriyā *i.e.* Ambikā.) He shows further that even with the reading *Kālapriyanātha* the same meaning is intended. Dr. Belvalkar[1], Dr. Kane,[2] Prof. Todar Mall[3] and Prof. Karmarkar[4] also have accepted the view that Kālapriyanātha was a name of Śiva. But while Dr. Belvalkar and Dr. Kane identify him with Mahākāla of Ujjayinī[5] Prof. Karmarkar thinks that he is identical with Suvarṇabindu of Padmāvatī, mentioned by Bhavabhūti in the *Mālatīmādhava*. M. V. Lele, who located the temple of Kālapriyanātha at Kālpī, also thought that the god was none other than Śiva.[6]

From references in the Purāṇas and inscriptions I showed several years ago that Kālapriyanātha was a name of the Sun,

1. See his translation of the *Uttararāmacharita* (Harward Oriental Series), p. 15, n. 1.
2. See his edition of the *Uttararāmacharita*, Notes, p. 3.
3. See his edition of the *Mahāvīracharita*, Introd., p. xxiv.
4. *Bhavabhūti*, p. 6.
5. Belvalkar would, however, like to keep this question open. *Op. cit*, p. xxxvii.
6. *Loc. cit.*

and that there was a famous temple of that god at Kālpī on the Yamunā. There is still an artificial mound at Kālpī known as *Kālapadeva kā ṭīlā* (the mound of Kālapadeva), which probably marks the site of the temple of Kālapriyanātha. Dr. Kane raised some objections against this identification in his recent edition of the *Uttararāmacharita*. They have been critically examined and shown to have no weight in my *Studies in Indology*. Vol. IV, pp. 72 f. In the present note I intend to draw the attention of scholars to some new evidence that has recently come to my notice.

I have recently been engaged in bringing out a new edition of Bhavabhūti's *Mālatīmādhava* critically edited by Dr. R. G. Bhandarkar. While reading the proofs of the new edition, I noticed an important extract from an old manuscript of the work given in a foot-note by Dr. Bhandarkar. It has a bearing on the present question.

In the *prastāvanā* of the *Mālatīmādhava* the Sūtradhāra after giving information about the ancestors of Bhavabhūti and about his learning, says,[1] अतो यदस्माकमर्पितं प्रियसुहृदा तत्रभवता काश्यपेन भवभूतिनाम्ना ब्राह्मणेन प्रकरणं स्वकृतं मालतीमाधवं नाम तदेव भगवतः कालप्रियनाथस्य सकलजगदेकचक्षुषो विश्वात्मनः सूर्यस्य पुरतो यथाप्रयोगेण प्रख्यापयितुमहमुद्यतः। This passage occurs in a Ms. in the collection of Bhau Daji.

From inquiries I learn that an identical passage occurs also in another manuscript deposited in the Bhandarkar Oriental Research Institute, which was not collated by Dr. Bhandarkar.[2]

Though all the plays of Bhavabhūti state that they were first staged at the fairs of Kālapriyanātha, they give no description of that god. So almost all commentators and editors of the plays have identified Kālapriyanātha with Śiva. The passage cited above from two manuscripts of the *Mālatīmādhava* shows, however, that Kālapriya was a name of the Sun-god;

1. *Mālatīmādhava*, ed. by R.G. Bhandarkar (second ed.), p. 17, notes 50-52.

2. I owe information about this manuscript to the courtesy of Dr. A.D. Pusalkar, Curator, Bhandarkar Institute, who has supplied me an extract from it.

for he is described therein as the soul of the world and the sole eye of the entire universe. This description suits no god except the Sun. So at the time of these manuscripts of the *Mālatīmādhava* at least, Kālapriyanātha was regarded as a name of the Sun.

Dr. Bhandarkar had collected manuscripts from all parts of India for his critical edition of the *Mālatīmādhava*. The manuscript from which he gave the above extract was in the collection of Dr. Bhau Daji, a well-known researcher of Bombay. From Dr. Bhandarkar's remarks it seems to have been deposited in the Library of the Bombay Branch of the Royal Asiatic Society (now Asiatic Society of Bombay). It may still be there. It bears the date Saṁvat 1765, Nabhasyāmāvāsyāyām 'the new-moon day of Bhādrapada in the (Vikrama) Saṁvat 1765.' It is thus more than 250 years old. The other manuscript which also gives the above passage about Kālapriyanātha is deposited in the Bhandarkar Institute. It is No. 437 of 1887-91. It bears the date in a chronogram[1] which signifies Saṁvat 1703. It is, therefore, older than the previous manuscript by 62 years. So the extract given above is not likely to have been recently interpolated in the two manuscripts.

The extract in question is also not likely to have been inserted in the two manuscripts in the years cited therein, because for several hundred years past people have forgotten that Kālapriyanātha was a name of the Sun-god. From some passages in the *Varāha* and *Bhavishya Purāṇas* I have shown that there was in ancient time a famous temple of the Sun at Kālapriya (modern Kālpī) on the bank of the Yamunā, where the Sun was believed to be present at mid-day.[2] These purāṇas are at least a thousand years old. Again, Kālapriyanātha is mentioned in the plays of Bhavabhūti, who flourished in the

1. ज्वलनगगनभूभृद्भूमिभिर्भावितेऽब्दे
शुचिबहुलदशम्यां वासरे तिग्मरश्मेः ।
उदयपुरपुरेऽब्दः पुस्तकं संप्रपूर्णं
लिखितमलघुविद्यारामभट्टेन भव्यम् ॥

2. See my *Studies in Indology*, Vol. I (second ed.), p. 17,

first quarter of the eighth century A.D. We next get a reference to the temple of Kālapriya in the Cambay plates in the description of the Rāshṭrakūṭa King Indra III's invasion of Kanauj, which probably occurred in A.D. 918.[1] From the description there we learn that the temple of Kālapriyanātha had an extensive courtyard, which could accommodate the entire army of Indra III. The next reference to Kālapriya occurs in the *Kāvyamīmāṁsā* of Rājaśekhara, from which we learn that it was situated to the south of Kanauj.[2] Rājaśekhara flourished in the first half of the tenth century A.D. We have not come across any references to Kālapriyanātha in later works. So none is likely to have inserted the aforecited description of Kālapriyanātha in the manuscripts of the *Mālatīmādhava* after the eleventh century A.D.

It is not unlikely that the aforecited passage about Kālapriyanātha being the soul of the world and the sole eye of the entire universe is from the pen of Bhavabhūti himself. In the Introduction to his edition of the *Mālatīmādhava* Dr. R. G. Bhandarkar has remarked.[3] "Looking to the fact that the groups (of manuscripts) give readings which are intelligible enough and often equally good, though a shade of difference can be discovered, which renders one preferable to the other, the conviction forced itself upon me that these changes were made by the poet himself at different times and some Mss. have preserved the earlier form and others the later." This was also the opinion of Todar Mall, who has critically edited the *Mahāvīracharita*. After referring to the aforecited remarks of Dr. Bhandarkar, he says,[4] "I am inclined to think that the same remark applies to the Mss. of the *Mahāvīracharita*. It is likely that before completing this drama Bhavabhūti had his Ms. circulated among his contemporary poets and critics, who however, did not show much appreciation of it. This threw the poet into a rage, to which he gave open utterance in his *Mal.* I, 8. The incomplete text (ending with V. 46) is, I hold,

1. *Ep. Ind.* Vol. VII, pp. 36f
2. *Kāvyamīmāṁsā* (Gaikwad's Or. Series), p. 94.
3. *Mālatīmādhava* (second ed.), Preface, p. vi.
4 *Mahāvīracharita*, Introd , p. viii.

preserved in the Mss. of the Southern Group. Sometime afterwards, Bhavabhūti not only completed the text to the end of Act V, but also went through the original. This revised text travelled to the North, where it now appears in the Mss. of the Northern Group."

It seems likely, therefore, that the description of Kālapriyanātha as the Sun-god noticed in the aforementioned two old Mss. of the *Mālatīmādhava* was inserted by Bhavabhūti himself. In any case, it leaves no doubt now that Kālapriyanātha was the name of the Sun-god and not of Śiva at Ujjayinī or any other place.

IV. THE DVISANDHĀNA OR RĀGHAVAPĀṆḌAVĪYA KĀVYA OF DHANAÑJAYA

Sanskrit rhetoricians have classified *kāvyas* into three categories, *viz.* (1) the *Dhvanikāvya*, in which the suggested sense is more charming than the expressed sense, (2) the *Guṇībhūtavyaṅgyakāvya*, in which the former is subordinated to the latter, and (3) the *Chitrakāvya*, in which the former is either nonexistent or is negligible. The first of these is regarded as the best type, and the last lowest. It is common experience that what is suggested is more charming than what is directly expressed. So the *Dhvanikāvya* is regarded as the best type of poetry. Sentiments such as Śṛiṅgāra (the Erotic) are always suggested, never directly expressed. The works of Kālidāsa, which abound in the delineation of *rasas* (sentiments) are examples of the best type of poetry. On the other hand, those *kāvyas* in which stress is laid on the use of *alaṅkāras* (figures of speech) based on the poet's *tour de force* are regarded as of the lowest type.

Kālidāsa's *kāvyas* are the best examples of the *Dhvanikāvya*. He has indeed indulged in the use of *śabdālaṅkāras* (figures of word) such as *anuprāsa* (alliteration) and *yamaka* (rhyme) in the ninth canto of the *Raghuvaṁśa*, but has not carried them to excess. His successors such as Bhāravi[1] and Māgha[2] have not observed such restraint. They have given

1. Verse 14 of Canto XV of the *Kirātārjunīya* is composed only of one letter *n*. See—

न नोननुन्नो नुन्नोनो नाना नानानना ननु ।
नुन्नो नुन्नोऽननुन्नेनो नानेना नुन्ननुन्ननुत् ॥

Canto XV, verse 12 contains the *gomūtrikābandha*.

2. Verse 114 of the *Śiśupālavadha* (Canto *XIX*) is composed only of the letter *d*.

us examples of the *Chitrakāvya* by the use of such figures as *Ślesha*, the use of one, two or three consonants only in certain verses and of such syllables as could be arranged into figures like the *Sarvatobhadra*, *Muraja*, *Chakra*, *Gomūtrikā* and other *bandhas*. Their intention in this was evidently to gain applause from their readers by such *tour de force*. In course of time the more obscure a *kāvya* was on account of such devices, the better it was regarded to be.

The *Dvisandhāna kāvya* is an instance of such *Chitra kāvyas*. When the wording of a verse is capable of being understood in two different ways as descriptive of two different stories, it is an instance of a *dvisandhāna kāvya*. Poet Kavirāja, who has described the stories of the two epics, the *Mahābhārata* and the *Rāmāyaṇa*, in the same words, says of such *kāvyas* :—

रम्या रामायणी यैषा भारती सैव भारती ।
अर्धनारीश्वरमयी मूर्तिरेकत्र शोभताम् ॥

He says that separate images of Śiva and Pārvatī are fashioned and they are indeed very beautiful, but there is a rare charm in the joint image of the two. So is the *Dvisandhāna Kāvya* in which the stories of the *Rāmāyaṇa* and the *Mahābhārata* are combined and narrated in identical words.

Dhanañjaya, the author of the *Dvisandhāna Kāvya*, is an early poet, though he may not be the first who wrote such a *kāvya*. There are diverse opinions about his identity and date even among scholars. Though his work was published as early as 1895 in the Kāvyamālā of the Nirṇayasāgar Press, it is rarely read and has not yet been critically studied. Dr. K.B. Pathak's view stated in the *Indian Antiquary*, Vol. XIV (pp. 14 f.) as far back as 1895 that he was identical with the Jaina *Muni* Śrutakīrti Traividya[1] who received a grant from Gaṇḍarāditya, the Śilāhāra king of the Kolhāpur branch (A.D. 1105-1140), has been accepted and cited in their histories of Sanskrit literature by such savants as Winternitz,[2] Keith[3] and S. K. De.[4] It is, however, erroneous as will be shown in the sequel.

1. *Traividya* means proficient in *āgama* (sacred texts), *nyāya* (logic) and *vyākaraṇa* (grammar).

2. *Geschichte der indischen Litteratur*, Vol. III, p. 75.

3. *History of Sanskrit Literature*, p. 137.

4. *History of Sanskrit Literature*, p. 340.

My attention was drawn to this problem recently as I was studying the inscriptions of the Śilāhāras of Kolhāpur; for it is believed that Dhanañjaya *alias* Śrutakīrti-Traividya was patronized by a Śilāhāra king (*viz.* Gaṇḍarāditya). The aforementioned edition of the *Dvisandhāna-kāvya* has long been out of print. So I had to get its copy from the Bhandarkar Institute of Poona. I have discussed the problem here from the material available to me.

Different Views about the Date of Dhanañjaya—I—Dr. K. B. Pathak's View—*circa* A:D. 1125.

Dhanañjaya has not given information about his place and date in his *kāvya*. The work consists of eighteen cantos. In the last verse of the last canto we learn that his father was named Vāsudeva, mother Śrīdevī and teacher Daśaratha. It does not name the *kāvya*. However, from the colophons of cantos we learn that it was named *Dvisandhāna* and also as *Rāghavapāṇḍavīya*. The first of these two names seems to have been current in the earlier age of Bhoja and Rājaśekhara as shown later. There were some other *kāvyas* also of the name *Rāghavapāṇḍavīya*, one of which, *viz.* that of Kavirāja, is still extant. Dhanañjaya was a Jaina by religious faith, while Kavirāja was a Hindu. So their stories of Rāghava (*i.e.* Rāma) and the Pāṇḍavas vary in several respects.

The Kannaḍa poet Nāgachandra *alias* Abhinava-Pampa[1] states in his *Rāmachandra-charita* or *Pampa-Rāmāyaṇa* that the Jaina *Muni* Śrutakīrti Traividya caused surprise to learned men by composing his *Rāghavapāṇḍavīya-kāvya* in the *gata-pratyāgata* manner. In an epigraph dated A.D. 1163 and incised on a pillar of a Jaina temple at Śravaṇa Beḷgoḷ in the Karnāṭaka State the aforementioned two verses eulogising Śrutakīrti Traividya[2] have been cited in praise of a homonymous disciple of Māghanandī, a famous Jaina *Muni* of Kolhāpur. Again, the latter is mentioned in a stone inscription dated Śaka

1. His predecessor Pampa (called Ādi-Pampa) had written his *Vikrmārjunavijaya* or *Pampa-Bhārata* in A.D. 943. So Nāgachandra is called Abhinava-Pampa.

2. *Epigraphia Carnatica* (*Ep. Carn.*), Vol. II, Translation, p. 18.

Śaṁvat 1045 (A.D. 1123) in a Jaina temple at Terdāḷ in the former Sāngli State.[1] He is described there as a disciple of Māghanandi-Saiddhāntika of Kollagiri (Kolhāpur).[2] There is a Jaina temple of Pārśvanātha near the Śukravāra gate of Kolhāpur, which a Sāmanta of the Śilāhāra king Gaṇḍarāditya had built and named Rūpanārāyaṇa, which was a *biruda* of that king.[3] A stone inscription deposited in the courtyard of the temple there mentions Śrutakīrti Traividya, who was evidently the officiating priest of that temple. It is dated Śaka Saṁvat 1058 (A.D. 1135).

The aforementioned Terdāḷ inscription, though it describes Śrutakīrti Traividya, does not mention his authorship of the *Rāghavapāṇḍavīya*. So K. B. Pathak, who edited that inscription, conjectured that Śrutakīrti Traividya must have written it after A.D. 1123, the date of the record; for both the *Pampa-Rāmāyaṇa* and the Śravaṇa Beḷgoḷ inscription state explicitly that Śrutakīrti Traividya was the author of the *Rāghavapāṇḍavīya*. As neither of these mentions the name of Dhanañjaya in connection with that *kāvya*, Pathak conjectured that Śrutakīrti Traividya must have published it under that pseudo-name. The work must have been composed between Śaka Saṁvat 1045 (A.D. 1123), the date of the Terdāḷ inscription, and Śaka Saṁvat 1076 (A.D. 1154), the known date of Pampa.[4] Pampa evidently knew of this pseudo-name Dhanañjaya of Śrutakīrti Traividya. So he has mentioned the latter as the author of the *Rāghavapāṇḍavīya*. But others did not know it. Hence the *Rāghavapāṇḍavīya* is known as the work of Dhanañjaya, the real name of the author (Śrutakīrti Traividya) having passed into oblivion.

Examination of Pathak's View

The aforementioned view of Pathak about the identity and date of Dhanañjaya has been accepted by Winternitz, Keith and S.K. De, but that it is erroneous was first shown conclusively by A. Venkatasubbiah in his article in the *Jour-*

1. *Ind. Ant.*, Vol. X, pp. 14 f.
2. *Ibid.*, p. 23.
3. *Ep. Ind.*, Vol. XIX, pp. 30 f.
4. Pampa is, however, proved to have flourished before A D. 1100

nal of *the Bombay Branch of the Royal Asiatic Society,* Vol. III (New Series, 1928), pp. 134 f. His arguments were as follows :—

(1) Śrutakīrti Traividya, mentioned by Pampa as the author of the *Rāghavapāṇḍavīya,* was different from the homonymous Jaina priest of the Kolhāpur Jaina *Basadi,* though both bore the epithet *Traividya* (proficient in *āgama, tarka* and *vyākaraṇa*); for their *guru-paramparās* were different. The *guru-paramparā* of Śrutakīrti Traividya, the author of the *Rāghava-pāṇḍavīya* mentioned by Pampa, was—Bālachandra-Meghachandra-Śubhakīrti-Vāsupūjya-Śrutakīrti, while that of Śrutakīrti Traividya, the priest of the Kolhāpur Jaina temple, was Kulabhūshaṇa-Kulachandra-Māghanandī-Śrutakīrti.

(2) Pampa flourished in *circa* A.D. 1100; for an extract from his *Rāmāyaṇa* has been cited in praise of the Jaina *Muni* Meghachandra in a Śravaṇa Beḷgoḷ inscription, dated A. D. 1115.[1] So the Śrutakīrti Traividya described by him must have lived considerably prior to A.D. 1100. On the other hand, the inscriptions of the time of the Śrutakīrti of Traividya of Kolhāpur are dated Śaka Saṁvat 1045 and 1058. He was a contemporary of the Śilāhāra king Gaṇḍarāditya (*circa* A.D. 1105-1140). His successor Māṇikyanandī Paṇḍita was officiating as the priest of the Kolhāpur *Basadi* in Śaka Saṁvat 1065 (A.D. 1143).[2] So Śrutakīrti Traividya seems to have officiated as priest of the Kolhāpur temple from A.D. 1120 to 1140. Therefore, he was undoubtedly different from his namesake described by Pampa.

(3) The *Rāghavapāṇḍavīya* mentioned by Pampa seems to have been different from the extant *kāvya* of that name composed by Dhanañjaya. The former, according to Pampa's description was of the *gatapratyāgata* type. R. Narasimhachariar a well-known Archaeologist of Mysore, interpreted this to mean that its verses when read from left to right, gave the story of Rāma, and when read from right to left, narrated that of the Pāṇḍavas.[3] But this does not seem to be a correct inter-

1. *Ep Carn* . Vol. II, Inscr,No. 127.
2. *Ep. Ind.*, Vol. XIX, p. 31.
3. See Narasimhachariar's Introduction to Nāgavarman's *Kāvyāvalokana*. *J. B.B.R.A.S.* (New Series), Vol. III, p. 138.

pretation of the term *gatapratyāgata.* It seems to mean the same as *Anulomapratiloma* illustrated by Mamma a in the Tenth Ullāsa of his *Kāvyaprakāśa.* It signifies that one gets the same wording of the verse whether it is read from left to right or *vice versa.* An instance of this in Dhanañjaya's *Dvisandhāna-kāvya* is as follows :

ततसारतमास्थासु सुमावानमितारधीः ।
धीरताभिनवामासु सुस्थामा तरसातत ॥
(द्विसन्धान, १८, ४३)

The first hemistich of this verse gives the whole *śloka* if we read it first from left to right and then the same hemistich from right to left. Similarly, the second hemistich also gives the same *śloka* if it is first read from right to left and then the same from left to right.

The meaning of the verse is as follows :—

"Vishṇu, whose sharp intellect has mastered (all *śāstras*) (अमितारधीः) and who is valiant (सुस्थामा), expressed with force (तरसा) his noble intentions (सुभावान्) in his detailed vows (ततसारतमास्थासु) which appeared even more important by his serenity (धीरताभिनवाभासु)." From this instance readers can have a fair idea of the obscurity of this *kāvya.*

The *Dvisandhāna-kāvya* has two more instances of such *gatapratyāgata* type (XVIII, 138 and 139). It has, besides, some quarters (XVIII, 58) and hemistichs (XVIII. 30) of the same type. But the whole *kāvya* has not been composed in the *gatapratyāgata* manner. So it is not likely to have been intended by Pampa.

II—Venkatasubbaiah's View—Tenth Century A.D.

Venkatasubbiah has written a lengthy article in the *J.B.B.R.A.S.*, Vol. III (New Series), pp. 134-160, on "the Authors of the *Rāghavapāṇḍavīya* and *Gadyachintāmaṇi*'. In that article he has put forward the suggestion that Dhanañjaya, the author of the *Rāghavapāṇḍavīya Kāvya* was the same as the Jaina *Muni* Hemasena, mentioned in the inscription No. 67 at Śravaṇa Beḷgoḷ. He was a very learned man and had the title of *Vidyā-Dhanañjaya.* In his *Pārśvanāthacharita* Vādirāja has praised several Jaina authors including Dhanañjaya, the author of the *Rāghavapāṇḍavīya*. All of them were Jaina *Munis*. So Dhanañjaya also must have been a Jaina *Muni*. This Hemasena *alias* Vidyā-Dhanañjaya flourished in *circa* A.D. 985, which appears to be the date of the author of the *Rāghavapāṇḍavīya*.

Examination of this View

Vādirāja has eulogised his predecessors such as Deva (Pūjyapāda), Akalaṅka, Jinasena *etc*., one of whom is Dhanañjaya, but it is not cogent to suppose that he was a Jaina *Muni*. We have no indication of this *munitva* in the *Rāghavapāṇḍavīya*. He names his teacher as simple Daśaratha. He does not call him *Muni*.[1] So he also was only a *Śrāvaka* (lay disciple), not a *Muni*. Besides, as shown below, he has been mentioned by Rājaśekhara (first half of the tenth century A.D.). So he could not have been as late as A.D. 985.

The Date of Dhanañjaya

What is then the date of Dhanañjaya ? To answer this question, we must collect references to him and to his *kāvya* chronologically.

(1) The Kannaḍa poet Durgasiṁha (*circa* A.D. 1025) says in his *Pañchatantra* that by his *Rāghavapāṇḍavīya* Dhanañjaya became the lord of Sarasvatī. Durgasiṁha was a contemporary of the Later Chālukya king Jayasiṁha II (or Jagadekamalla I) (A.D. 1015-1042). So Dhanañjaya must have flourished before A.D. 1000.

(2) Vādirāja has the following verse about Dhanañjaya in his *Pārśvanāthacharita* (I, 26)—

अनेकभेदसन्धानाः खनन्तो हृदये मुहुः ।
बाणा धनञ्जयोन्मुक्ताः कर्णस्येव प्रियाः कथम् ।

This verse has several *śleshas*. It means—

How can the words of Dhanañjaya, which convey several senses and require pondering over in the mind, be dear to the ear ? Were the arrows of Arjuna, which hit several marks simultaneously and pierced deeper and deeper into the heart, pleasing to Karṇa ?

Vādirāja composed this work in Śaka Saṁvat 947, Kār-

1. See Nathuram Premi's *Jaina Sāhitya aur Itihāsa* (second ed.).

ttika śu. di. 3 (27th October A.D. 1026). Dhanañjaya must have flourished sometime before him, *i.e.* before A.D. 1000.

(3) King Bhoja of Dhārā has referred to the *Dvisandhāna kāvya* of Dhanañjaya in some places in his *Śṛiṅgāraprakāśa*. One of the references is as follows[1]—तृतीयस्य (द्विसन्धानप्रकारस्य) उदाहरणं यथा दण्डिनो धनञ्जयस्य वा द्विसन्धानप्रबन्धौ रामायणभारतावनबध्नीतः । Bhoja flourished from A.D. 1015 to 1055. So Dhanañjaya must be earlier than A.D. 1000. His contemporary Prabhāchandra has mentioned a *Dvisandhāna kāvya* in his *Prameyakamalamārtaṇḍa*, but whether it was of Daṇḍin or of Dhanañjaya is not clear.

(4) In one of his stray verses Rājaśekhara has described Dhanañjaya as follows—

द्विसन्धाने निपुणतां स तां चक्रे धनञ्जयः ।
यथा जातं फलं तस्य सतां चक्रे धनं जयः ।

(Dhanañjaya as also Arjuna attained such proficiency in the composition of a *Dvisandhāna-kāvya* and in piercing two targets that they obtained, in the assembly of good people, wealth and victory respectively.

Rājaśekhara was a court-poet of the Pratīhāra kings Mahendrapāla and Mahīpāla and also of the Kalachuri king Yuvarājadeva I.[2] He, therefore, flourished from *circa* A.D. 900 to 940. Dhanañjaya must have flourished before the close of the ninth century A.D.

(5) The following verse giving the different senses of the indeclinable *iti*, which occurs in Dhanañjaya's *Anekārthanāmamālā*, has been cited in the commentary *Dhavalā* of Vīrasena, the *guru* of the well-known Jaina author Jinasena. The commentary was written in Vikrama Saṁvat 873 (A.D. 816). So Dhanañjaya must have flourished before A.D. 800.[3]

(6) Another work of Dhanañjaya called *Nāmamālā* gives synonyms of Sanskrit words. It appears to be one of the earliest Sanskrit lexicons. It gives the names of several Hindu gods and goddesses such as Śiva, Vishṇu, Brahmā and Kārttikeya, but makes no mention of Gajānana. It seems, therefore,

1. Raghavan, *Bhoja's Śṛiṅgāra-prakāśa*, p. 838.
2. Mirashi, *Inscriptions of the Kalachuri-Chedi Era* Introd., pp. lxcivf.
3. Shaṭkhaṇḍāgama, Introd., p. 62.

to belong to the age before Gajānana found recognition as a god in Hindu society. We find that the god gradually gained recognition at the close of the sixth century A.D. He does not find mention as a god in some works composed in the seventh century A.D. 750-800 may therefore, be the approximate date of Dhanañjaya.

(7) In his *Nāmamālā* Dhanañjaya mentions Akalaṅka's work on the *pramāṇas* and the grammar of Pūjyapāda as the best works of their kind like his own *Dvisandhāna*. The dates of these authors are not settled. Some place Akalaṅka in A.D. 720-750, and Pūjyapāda-Devanandī, the author of the Jainendra Vyākaraṇa, about the end of the sixth century A.D. These *pramāṇas* seem to point to A.D. 800 as the approximate date of Dhanañjaya, the author of the *Dvisandhāna-kāvya*. He cannot, therefore, be identical with Śrutakīrti Traividya (A.D. 1050), eulogised by Abhinava Pampa as the author of the *Rāghavapāṇḍavīya*, nor with the Jaina *Muni* Śrutakīrti Traividya of the Kolhāpur Jaina *basadi* who lived in the first half of the twelfth cen. A.D.

The Works of Dhanañjaya

Besides the *Dvisandhāna-kāvya*, Dhanañjaya wrote *Nāmamālā*, *Anekārthanāmamāla*, *Vishāpaharastotra* and *Yaśodharacharita*. The first of these gives synonyms of Sanskrit words as in the *Amarakosha*. It belongs, however, to a much earlier age than the latter. His *Anekārthanāmamālā* has forty-four verses, containing vocables giving more than one sense. The verse giving the different meanings of *iti* has been cited above. The *Vishāpaharastotra* has 39 verses in the *Indravajrā* metre. Its recitation is supposed to cure one from the effects of poisoning. Hence its name.

The aforementioned works of Dhanañjaya are still available, but his *Yaśodhara-charita* is known only from its mention in the work of that name of Bhaṭṭāraka Jñānakīrti, composed in Vikrama Saṁvat 1650. As this work has not yet been traced it is not possible to say whether its author Dhanañjaya was the same as the homonymous author of the aforementioned works.[1]

1. Nathuram Premi. *Jaina Sāhitya aur Itihāsa* (second ed.), p. 100.

The Dvisandhāna kāvya of Daṇḍin

Dhanañjaya is probably not the earliest known poet who composed a *Dvisandhāna-kāvya*. Daṇḍin, who was probably his predecessor, also wrote a *kāvya* of the same type as shown below. Rājaśekhara states that Daṇḍin composed three works which have become famous in the three worlds :—

त्रयोऽग्नयस्त्रयो वेदास्त्रयो धर्मास्त्रयो गुणाः ।
त्रयो दण्डिप्रबन्धाश्च त्रिषु लोकेषु विश्रुताः ॥

What these works are has been a matter of keen controversy among scholars for a long time; but from recent researches they appear to be the following :—(1) the *Kāvyādarśa*, a well-known work on rhetoric; (2) *Avantisundarikathā*, a romance in prose, of which a few pages have been recovered and published. The *Daśakumāracharita* seems to have been an abridgment of that work. It is not one of the three works of Daṇḍin as supposed by some scholars; for it is written in a different style. (3) The third work is the *Dvisandhāna-kāvya*. That Daṇḍin wrote a *Dvisandhāna-kāvya* is known from Bhoja's *Śṛiṅgāraprakāśa*. The relevant extract from Bhoja's work has been given above. Bhoja has not only mentioned that *kāvya* but has also cited the following verse from it :—[1]

उदारमहिमारामः प्रजानां हर्षवर्धनः ।
धर्मप्रभव इत्यासीत्ख्यातो भरतपूर्वजः ॥

This verse, by virtue of *Ślesha*, describes Rāma and Yudhishṭhira in the same words as stated below.

(1) The *Rāmāyaṇa*—Rāma, who enhanced the delight of the subjects, was endowed with great nobility and was the elder brother of Bharata, became renowned as one who laid down rules of religious conduct.

(2) The *Mahābhārata*—Yudhishṭhira, the son of Dharma (Yama), who enhanced the delight of the people, was endowed with great nobility, and was a descendant of Bharata, attained (great) renown.

Daṇḍin seems to be the earliest Sanskrit poet who wrote a *Dvisandhāna-kāvya*. It is not extant now, but from the example

1. Raghavan, Bhoja's *Śṛiṅgāraprakāśa*, p. 838.

cited above, it seems to have been lucid like his *Kāvyādarśa*, not obscure like the *kāvya* of Dhanañjaya.

As shown by Dr. Kane, Daṇḍin's literary activity probably lay in the period A.D. 660-690. Dhanañjaya may have flourished slightly later.

Dhanañjaya's *Dvisandhāna-kāvya* has eighteen cantos. He has woven *Dhanañjaya* in the last verse of his *kāvya*. This was an ancient custom. Bhāravi has inserted *Lakshmī*, and Māgha *śrī* similarly in the last verse of every canto of their *kāvyas*, the *Kirātārjunīya* and the *Śiśupālavadha* respectively. Prakrit poets also did the same. The Prakrit *kāvya Harivijaya* of the Vākāṭaka king Sarvasena is not now extant, but we learn from Hemachandra's *Alaṅkārachūḍāmaṇi* that it had the word *utsāha* as the poet's mark in the last verses of its cantos.[1] The *Setubandha*, another Prakrit *kāvya* composed by Pravarasena, has the word *anurāga* used similarly. This mode of inserting a particular word as the poet's mark continued down to the thirteenth century A.D.; for Kavirāja, who flourished then, has used his patron's name *Kāmadeva* in the same manner. Dhanañjaya has used his own name for the same purpose. See the following last verse of the first Canto of his *Dvisandhāna-kāvya* :—

को वा कविः पुरमिमां परमार्थवृत्त्या
शक्नोति वर्णयितुमत्र विनिर्णयेन ।
नित्यं विधिः सततसंनिहितो विभूति-
मन्याहृशं सृजति यत्र धनंजयाय ॥

See also the following hemistichs of the last verses of the next two cantos—

Canto II

व्यसनरहितराजराज्यभारः
स्वमुपचिकाय यशो धनंजयेन ॥

Canto III

न हि श्रुतवतां नामासाध्यं
धनञ्जयमिच्छताम् ॥

In a *Dvisandhāna-kāvya*, the poet narrates two stories in identical words. How this becomes possible, is stated by the

1. Mirashi, *Studies in Indology*, Vol. I (second ed.), p. 116.

poet Kavirāja, who composed his *Rāghavapāṇḍaviya* in a later age :—

प्रायः प्रकरणैक्येन विशेषणविशेष्ययोः ।
परिवृत्त्या क्वचित्सद्भुपमानोपमेययोः ॥
क्वचित्पदैश्च नानार्थैः क्वचिद्वक्रोक्तिभागिभिः ।
विधास्यते मया काव्यं श्रीरामायणभारतम् ॥

Kavirāja says, "I have used the following devices in narrating the stories of the *Rāmāyaṇa* and the *Bhārata* in the same words :—In some places, where the incidents (*e.g.* going into exile) are identical, the same description applies to both; in some other cases, the *viśeshaṇas* of one narrative (*e.g. bibhīshaṇa, duryodhana*) become the *viśeshyas* of the other; similarly the *Upameya* and the *Upamānas* can be interchanged. In some cases this becomes possible by the use of *Śleshas* and *Vakroktis*." Dhanañjaya also has used all these devices in his *kāvya*.

Dhanañjaya was a Jaina by religious faith. He has, therefore, prayed to the Tīrthaṅkara Neminātha in the first or *maṅgala-śloka* of his *kāvya* :—

श्रियं जगद्बोधविधौ विहायसि व्यदीपि नक्षत्रमिवैकमुद्गतम् ।
स यस्य वस्तीर्थरथस्य सुव्रतः प्रवर्तको नेमिरनश्वरीं क्रियात् ॥

(May that Neminātha grant you eternal bliss !—who, when he attained enlightenment, found the (whole) world as clear as a single constellation shining in the sky and who, like the rim of a chariot, propagated the sacred religion.)

The stories of Rāma and the Pāṇḍavas in the Jaina tradition are different in some respects from those in the Hindu epics. So those described in Dhanañjaya's *Kāvya* have been briefly given below. That work has in several places become obscure by the use of *Śleshas* and the persistent attempt to narrate both stories in identical words. The commentary *Padakaumudī* of Nemichandra proves very helpful in such cases. Badarīnātha Śāstri has summarised it in the edition of Dhañanjaya's work in the Kāvyamālā.

Dhanañjaya has himself described in a rather humorous way how a poet gets perplexed in composing a *dvisandhāna*-

kāvya by comparing him with a lover approaching his lady-love in the context of Rāvaṇa entering Laṅkā together with Śītā, and Yudhishṭhira Dvārakā :—

वक्रोक्तिमुत्प्रेक्षणमङ्गबन्धं श्लेषं स्मरन्कालबलातिमूढः ।
द्विसन्धिचिन्ताकुलितो विषण्णः कविर्वियोगीव जनोऽभ्यसर्पत् ॥

(As a poet proceeding to compose a *dvisandhāna-kāvya* becomes perplexed with the thought of inserting *vakroktis* (equivocal expressions), *utprekshās* and various *bandhas*, the lover separated from his beloved proceeded to meet her, engrossed in the thought of how to talk equivocally to her, how to cast side glances at her and how to indulge in various gesticulations and embraces.)

A short synopsis of Dhanañjaya's Dvisandhāna-kāvya[1]

Canto I—After eulogising Tīrthaṅkara Neminātha and Sarasvatī, the poet describes the cities of Ayodhyā and Hastināpura in identical words.

Canto II—King Daśaratha was ruling in Ayodhyā and Pāṇḍu in Hastināpura. Description of their queens Kausalyā and Kuntī respectively.

Canto III—Daśaratha had four sons, *viz*. Rāma, Lakshmaṇa, Bharata and Śatrughna, born to him, while Pāṇḍu had five, Yudhishṭhira and others. Dhṛitarāshṭra had Duryodhana and others.

Canto IV—Having become very old, the king (Daśaratha and Pāṇḍu) crowns his son (Rāma and Yudhishṭhira), after giving instruction to him in political science. This enrages Kaikeyī and Duryodhana. (A) Rāma and others are sent into exile. (B) Yudhishṭhira loses to Duryodhana in gambling and goes into exile with his brothers. They both reach the Narmadā (v. 42).

Canto V (A)—Rāma goes to the Daṇḍakāraṇya. (B) Yudhishṭhira reaches the Virāṭa country. (A) Lakshmaṇa cuts down the forest of *kīchakas* (bamboos). (B) Draupadī is seen by Kīchaka. (A) Śūrpaṇakhā becomes enamoured of Lakshmaṇa and (B) Kīchaka of Draupadī. (A) Khara,

1. Incidents in the story of Rāghava (Rāma) are shown by *A* and those in that of the Pāṇḍavas by *B*. Other description is common to both.

espousing the cause of Śūrpaṇakhā, and (B) Duryodhana, seeking to avenge the murder of Kīchaka, come to fight. Description of the battle.

Canto VI–(A) Rāma kills Khara and Dūshaṇa. (B) The Pāṇḍavas prevent the capture of Virā a's cows (*go-grahaṇa*).

Canto VII–Description of the Śarad season. (A) Śūrpaṇakhā goes to meet Rāvaṇa. (B) Yudhishṭhira goes to Dvārakā to meet Kṛishṇa. (A) Rāvaṇa abducts Sītā. (B) Yudhishṭhira resolves to win back his kingdom. They both go to the sea-shore—(A) Rāvaṇa to the shore of the Southern Sea, and Yudhishṭhira to that of the Western Sea near Dvārakā.

Canto VIII—Description of the sea. Description of town-ladies flocking to see (A) Sītā in Laṅkā and (B) Yudhishṭhira in Dvārakā. (A) Rāvaṇa and (B) Yudhishṭhira discuss political measures with others.

Canto IX—(A) Vālī comes out of his city to fight with Sugrīva. (B) Kṛishṇa comes out of Dvārakā together with Balarāma and the Pāṇḍavas to fight with the army sent by Jarāsandha. (A) After the battle Sugrīva offers his daughter Kalyāṇī to Rāma and (B) Kṛishṇa offers his sister Subhadrā to Arjuna.

Canto X—(A) Lakshmaṇa rebukes Sugrīva and (B) Jarāsandha's envoy Purushottama rebukes Kṛishṇa.

Canto XI—(A) Sugrīva, Hanumān and Jāmbavān and (B) Kṛishṇa, Balabhadra, Yudhishṭhira and Bhīma discuss measures to be adopted in the circumstances.

Canto XII—(A) Lakshmaṇa leaves for the site of the *Koṭi-śilā* (B) Kṛishṇa together with Balarāma also leaves for the same place. Indra had brought that *śilā* (slab) from the Meru mountain for the coronation of Jina. (A) Lakshmaṇa and (B) Nārāyaṇa (Kṛishṇa) assume a larger form than the *śilā* and, having lifted it, they place it in its proper place.

Canto XIII—Hanumān, the envoy of Rāma, approaches Rāvaṇa, and Śrīśaila, that of Kṛishṇa, goes to Jarāsandha. They address them. (A) Hanumān moves about in search for Sītā and (B) Śrīśaila for Sundarī. Having met them, they assure them about their rescue by (A) Rāma and (B) Kṛishṇa.

Canto XIV—Description of the invasion of the enemy's country by (A) Rāma and (B) by Kṛishṇa and the Pāṇḍavas. (A) Rāma and others reach the shore of the Southern Sea and (B) Kṛishṇa and the Pāṇḍavas reach the bank of the Gaṅgā.

Canto XV—Description of *jala-krīḍā* (sporting in water) of (A) the monkeys and (B) the Yādavas.

Canto XVI—(A) Rāvaṇa issues out of Laṅkā and (B) Jarāsandha comes out of Rājagṛiha to fight. (A) Bibhīshaṇa seeks refuge with Rāma and (B) Sātyaka, an ally of Duryodhana, with Yudhishṭhira. Description of the battle.

Canto XVII—Description of the fight of (A) Rāma and Rāvaṇa and (B) Kṛishṇa and Jarāsandha. Lakshmaṇa falls down, being struck by a *śakti*. Hanumān revives him by means of the medicinal herbs fetched from Droṇa-giri. (B) The Pāṇḍavas are encouraged to fight by the speech of Kṛishṇa. Description of an evening.

Canto XVIII—Description of the fight of (A) Rāma and Rāvaṇa, and (B) of Kṛishṇa and Jarāsandha. (A) After Rāvaṇa is killed, Sītā meets Rāma. (B) After killing Jarāsandha Kṛishṇa bestows the kingdom of the earth on the Pāṇḍavas. Then (A) Rāma leaves for Ayodhyā and (B) Kṛishṇa and the Yādavas for Dvārakā. Description of Kṛishṇa's excellent administration.

From the brief synopsis given above, readers will have an idea of the nature of a *Dvisandhāna-kāvya*. Every verse in such a *kāvya* does not have two meanings. Every *Mahākāvya* was expected to contain the descriptions of some common subjects such as those of a city, a season, sporting in water, a morning or an evening, battles *etc*. So verses descriptive of them convey only one meaning. Besides, some incidents such as going into exile may be common to both the narratives. In other respects, the poet tries to convey two meanings by means of *Ślesha* (*double entendre*). *Duryodhana*, *e.g.*, may mean either (a) Dhṛitarāshṭra's son of that name or (b) invincible. Similarly, *dhṛitarāshṭra* can be understood either in the sense of (a) the Kaurava king of that name, or (b) one who governs his kingdom.

The story of Rāma in Dhanañjaya's *kāvya* is mostly as

in Vālmīki's epic. We say 'mostly', because there are some differences also. See *e.g.* Sugrīva's offer of his daughter Kalyāṇī to Rāma. But there are many more variations in the story of the Pāṇḍavas. They are represented to have fought not with the Kauravas but with Jarāsandha to gain their kingdom. There are several geographical errors. The Pāṇḍavas need not have crossed the Narmadā to reach Dvārakā. Similarly, they could not have repaired to Virāṭa's country after crossing that river; for the latter was situated near modern Jaipur in Rājasthāna.

Dhanañjaya, being of the Jaina faith, has unneccessarily inserted the incident of the lifting of the *Koṭi-śilā* in the present *kāvya*. The poet describes that both Rāma in his march on Laṇkā and Kṛishṇa and others in their invasion of Jarāsandha's kingdom noticed it. So its location is uncertain. Jaina writers also are not unanimous in regard to this. Some locate it in Kaliṅga, others in Magadha and some others near the Daśārṇa mountain.[1] It was so called because a *koṭi* (crore) of Jaina *Munis* attained salvation while sitting on it. It is believed that it was a *yojana* in expanse. It is regarded as sacrosanct in Jainism, but its description in the present *kāvya* is irrelevant.

Dhanañjaya's *kāvya* has become extremely artificial and obscure in several places by the use of *Ślesha*. Besides, he has indulged in several feats of *tour de force* by composing verses or their parts in one or two consonants only as well as by such figures as *Samapādayamaka*, *Vishamapādayamaka*, *Pādādiyamaka*, *Pādamadhyayamaka*, *Pādāntayamaka*, *Śṛinkhalāyamaka*, *gatapratyāgata etc.* as well as by arranging syllables so as to form various *bandhas* such as *Aśvapluta*, *Samudgaka*, *Gomūtrika*, *Muraja* and so forth. One cannot but regret such misplaced intellectual labour.

Dhanañjaya has in many places imitated Kālidāsa. See *e.g.* the following descriptions :—

(1) *Kālidāsa*—

विवं मरुत्वानिव मोक्ष्यते भुवं
दिगन्तविश्रान्तरथो हि तत्सुतः ।

1. Nathuram Premi, *Jaina Sāhitya aur Itihāsa*, pp. 447-448.

अतोऽभिलाषे प्रथमं तथाविधे
मनो बबन्धान्यरसान् विलङ्घ्य सा ॥

(रघु. ३, २४)

Dhanañjaya—

जाने हि मृत्स्नाभ्यवहारमात्रं
मातुः प्रकाश्य छलमन्तरात्मा ।
समुद्रवेलाजलसिक्तसीमां
गर्भस्थितः स ग्रसते स्म भूमिम् ॥

(द्विसन्धान, ३, ७)

(2) Kālidāsa—

शुद्धान्तदुर्लभमिदं वपुराश्रमवासिनो यदि जनस्य ।
दूरीकृताः खलु गुणैरुद्यानलता वनलताभिः ॥

(शाकुन्तल, १, १७)

Dhanañjaya—

यदीदृशमिदं रूपं स्याद्वनेऽन्तःपुरेण किम् ।
किमुद्यानलताक्लेशो रम्या वनलतास्ति चेत् ॥

(द्विसन्धान, ७, ८६)

(3) Kālidāsa—

पत्तिः पदातिं रथिनं रथेश-
स्तुरंगयायी तुरगाधिरूढम् ।
यन्ता गजस्याभ्यपतद्गजस्थं
तुल्यप्रतिद्वन्द्वि बभूव युद्धम् ॥

(रघु., ७, ३७)

Dhanañjaya—

रथो वरूथस्य हयस्य वाजी
गजः करेणोः पदिकः पदातेः ।
दुर्मन्त्रितं ध्यानमिवात्मबिम्बं
स्वस्यैव संनद्धमिवाग्रतोऽभूत् ॥

(द्विसंधान, १६,७)

Though Dhanañjaya's *kāvya* has become obscure in several places by the use of *Ślesha* and the attempt to form *bandhas*, it is not altogether devoid of fresh ideas and lucid descriptions. See *e.g.* the following illustrations :—

(1) See the following description of mountain streams flowing through thickets of forest-creepers in Summer—

इह भान्ति मण्डलभुवः सलताः सवितर्दिका गिरिपतत्सलिलाः ।
वनदेवताभिरपविश्य मिथः पथिकान् प्रपा इव शुचौ रचिताः ॥

(द्विसन्धान, १२, २५)

The poet describes the streams as *prapās* arranged by sylvan deities for thirsty travellers in summer.

(2) See the following description of warriors causing several wounds on the chests of their enemies by their arrows :—

ध्रुवस्य शौर्यायतनस्य कर्तुं राज्ञा शिलाशासनमिच्छतेव ।
वक्षः स्वनामाक्षरमार्गणाङ्कं परोवरस्याक्रियताखिलेन ॥

(द्विसंधान, १७, १८)

When one erects a temple, he gets an inscription incised on a stone placed nearby, recording that event. The wounds caused on the enemy's chest are so to say an inscription recording his valorous deeds.

We come across such fresh ideas in this *kāvya* here and there. It is indeed a matter for regret that the poet should have misdirected his poetic talent in composing an obscure *dvisandhāna-kāvya*.

Dhanañjaya's *kāvya* was also known as *Rāghavapāṇḍavīya*. Two other *kāvyas* of this name are known. One of them was composed by Śrutakīrti Traividya as stated in Abhinava-Pampa's *Rāmachandrapurāṇa*. We have shown above that this poet lived some time before A.D. 1100 and, therefore, he cannot be identical with the homonymous *Bhaṭṭāraka* of the Pārśvanātha temple near the Śukravāra gate in Kolhāpur. The verses in the Śravaṇ Beḷgoḷ inscription ascribing the *kāvya* to the latter have been erroneously quoted from Abhinava-Pampa's work.[1] There is no evidence to show that he also composed a *kāvya* named *Rāghavapāṇḍavīya*.

The second *kāvya* of this name was composed by a Hindu poet named Kavirāja. It was published by the Nirṇayasāgar Press in 1897 and is now out of print. Its author is known to many from the following verse in it (I, 41) :—

1. This is discussed in detail below.

सुबन्धुर्बाणभट्टश्च कविराज इति त्रयः ।
वक्रोक्तिमार्गनिपुणाश्चतुर्थो विद्यते न वा ॥

Of the poets mentioned here as adept in *Vakrokti* (equivocal description), Subandhu is the author of the prose romance *Vāsavadattā*. He boasts in that work that he has used *Ślesha* on every *akshara* of it.[1] Bāṇa is well known as the author of the *Harshacharita* and the *Kādambari*. Kavirāja claims that he should be ranked with them as he has composed the *Rāghavapāṇḍaviya* full of *Ślesha*.

Diverse opinions have been expressed about his date. According to Macdonell, he flourished about A.D. 800. R.G. Bhandarkar thought that as his work is more lucid than Dhanañjaya's he must have lived earlier, between A.D. 896 and 1141. K.B. Pathak placed the composition of his *kāvya* between A.D. 1182 and 1197. Venkatasubbiah showed that Kavirāja was patronized by the Kadamba king Kāmadeva II and his *Rāghavapāṇḍaviya* was composed between A.D. 1236 and 1307. Further, he has stated that Pathak's view that the poet's real name was Mādhavabhaṭṭa and *Kavirāja* was only a title conferred on him is unacceptable. As his work is not the subject of the present article, we do not go into this question.

Kavirāja's *Rāghavapāṇḍaviya* is written in a comparatively lucid style. See *e.g.* the following verse (I, 85) from it :—

प्रतीपदर्शिनी सैषा विचचारास्य यत्पथि ।
ततो गुरुगिरा तस्या जीवितेशो बभूव सः ॥

This verse describes the following incidents in the *Rāmāyaṇa* and the *Mahābhārata*—(1) Rāma killed Tāṭakā by the bidding of Viśvāmitra and (2) Bhīma accepted Hiḍimbā as his wife by the bidding of Yudhishṭhira. In this verse there is a pun (*Ślesha*) on *jīviteśa* meaning (1) Death and (2) a husband. The *Rāghavapāṇḍaviya* of Kavirāja narrates the story of the *Rāmāyaṇa* from the reign of Daśaratha to the coronation of Rāma and that of the *Mahābhārata* from the rule of Pāṇḍu to the crowning of Yudhishṭhira in identical words.

1. See—

सरस्वतीदत्तवरप्रसादाच्चक्रे सुबन्धुः सुजनैकबन्धुः ।
प्रत्यक्षरश्लेषमयप्रबन्धविन्यासवैदग्ध्यनिधिर्निबन्धम् ॥

The following *Dvisandhāna-kāvyas* of other poets have come down to us[1] :—

(1) *Pārvatī-Rukmiṇīya* or Vidyāmādhava—This describes the marriage of Śiva and Pārvatī, and of Krish a and Rukmiṇī in the same words. This poet lived during the reign of the Later Chālukya king Someśvara I.

(2) The *Rāghava-Naishadhīya* of Haradattasūri—This poet flourished after Bhaṭṭoji Dīkshita. Only two cantos and 148 verses of the third have been recovered. They describe the lives of Rāma and Nala.

(3) *Rāmacharita* of Sandhyākaranandī—This is a *kāvya* of historical importance. It describes the life of Rāma and the reign of the Pāla king Rāmapāla (11th cent. A.D.) in the same words.

(4) *The Dvyāśraya-kāvya* of Hemachandra—This is a *dvisandhāna* of a different type. It describes the life of Kumārapāla a Chaulukya king of Aṇahilavāḍ (*circa* A.D. 1145-1171) in Sanskrit and Prakrit and illustrates rules of grammar.

Trisandhāna, Chatuḥsandhāna and *Pañchasandhāna kāvyas* are also known.

* * *

After this article was completed I came to know from a casual reference in my friend Dr. A. N. Upadhye's letter that the *Dvisandhāna-kāvya* of Dhanañjaya has recently been published with an Introduction by Dr. H.L. Jain and himself and a Hindi translation by Prof. K. C. Gorawala in the Jñānapīṭha Granthamālā. The learned authors of the Introduction have independently come to the same conclusion as myself except in one respect. They identify Śrutakīrti Traividya mentioned as the author of the *Rāghavapāṇḍavīya* in Abhinava-Pampa's *Rāmachandracharitapurāṇa* with the homonymous *Bhaṭṭāraka* of the Rūpanārāyaṇa Jaina temple in Kolhāpur and place him in A. D. 1100-1150.[2] I do not agree with this view. This matter must be discussed here in some detail.

1. See Viraraghavacharya's article in the *K.B. Pathak Commemoration Volume*, pp. 324 f.
2. See Introd. of the edition, pp. 10-11.

The hierarchical lists of Jain Munis, like those of Hindu Śaṅkarāchāryas, contain the same names again and again, and their titles like *Traividya* are also found repeated. So one cannot identify Jaina Munis merely on the evidence of the identity of their names and titles. Other evidence also must be taken into account. The Śrutakīrti Traividya mentioned by Abhinava-Pampa as the author of the *Rāghavapāṇḍaviya* cannot be identified with his namesake who was the priest of the Rūpanārāyaṇa Jaina temple in Kolhāpur for the following reasons :—

(1) Difference in dates—Śrutakīrti Traividya mentioned by Pampa must have flourished considerably before A.D. 1100. An extract from Pampa's *Rāmāyaṇa* has been cited in Inscription No. 127 at Śravaṇa Beḷgoḷ dated A.D. 1115.[1] So Pampa must have flourished before A.D. 1100, and Śrutakīrti Traividya mentioned by him much before. On the other hand, Śrutakīrti Traividya of the Rūpanārāyaṇa temple lived in the period A.D. 1120-1140; for he is mentioned as the contemporary priest of that temple in the Kolhāpur inscription dated Śaka Saṁvat 1058 (A.D. 1136) and the Terdāḷ inscription dated Śaka Saṁvat 1045 (A.D. 1123). So his period of activity must have been A.D. 1120 to 1140.

(2) Difference in the *Guru-paramparās*—The *Guru-paramparā* of Śrutakīrti mentioned by Pampa was Bālachandra-Meghachandra-Śubhakīrti (Vāsupūjya)—Śrutakīrti, while that of the Śrutakīrti of the Rūpanārāyaṇa temple was Kulabhūshaṇa-Kulachandra-Māghanandī-Śrutakīrti. So the two Śrutakīrtis were not identical .

(3) Non-mention of the *Rāghavapāṇḍavīya* in the inscriptions of the time of Śrutakīrti-Traividya of Kolhāpur—This Śrutakīrti Traividya was fairly well known in his age. If he had composed a *kāvya* of the name of the *Rāghavapāṇḍavīya* it would surely have been mentioned in his eulogy. But neither in the inscriptions of his own time nor in those of a later time in Kolhāpur and its neighbourhood do we notice any reference to his authorship of that *kāvya*. It may be

1. *Ep. Carn.* Vol. II, Transl., p. 54, f.n. 3,

objected that this is an *argumentum ex silentio*. So we proceed to state another.

Though the Śilāhāra king Gaṇḍarāditya describes himself as having had the favour of a boon from Mahālakshmī of Kolhāpur, he was favourably inclined towards Jainism. He had a queen named Karṇādevī of the Jaina faith. He as well as his Sāmantas erected Jaina temples in his reign. Some of them were given the names of his *birudas*. For instance, the *Rūpanārāyaṇa* besadi at Kolhāpur was erected by his Sāmanta Nimbarasa and named after the King's *biruda*. It was dedicated to Pārśvanātha. Another Jaina temple dedicated to the Tīrthaṅkara Chandraprabha was erected at Kolhāpur and named Tribhuvanatilaka which also was a *biruda* of Gaṇḍarāditya.

The Kannaḍa poet Karṇapārya who was connected with the latter Jaina temple wrote the *Nemināthapurāṇa* in the reign of Vijayāditya, the son and successor of Gaṇḍarāditya (A.D. 1140-1165). This work was published by the Madras University in 1940 and is now out of print.

In the beginning of his work *Nemināthapurāṇa*,[1] Karṇapārya has eulogised his predecessors such as Ponna, Ranna, Pampa and Nāgachandra-kavīndra (Abhinava-Pampa), but he makes no mention of the *Rāghavapāṇḍavīya* of Śrutakīrti. If the Jaina *Muni* Śrutakīrti Traividya of Kolhāpur had composed a *kāvya* like the *Rāghavapāṇḍavīya*, Karṇapārya, who wrote his work in Kolhāpur itself, would not have failed to mention it and its author in the introduction of his *kāvya*; but there is absolutely no reference to it in Karṇapārya's work.

But then, one may ask, how is it that this Śrutakīrti Traividya of the Rūpanārāyaṇa temple at Kolhāpur is described as the author of the *Rāghavapāṇḍavīya* in the Śravaṇ Beḷgoḷ inscription No. 64 (A.D. 1163)? It is not difficult to answer this question. This eulogy of Śrutakīrti Traividya is in the form of an extract from Abhinava-Pampa's *Rāmāyaṇa*. The drafters of inscriptions at Śravaṇa Beḷgoḷ used to draw upon Abhinava-Pampa's *Rāmāyaṇa* in composing eulogies of Jaina *Munis*. There is another instance of this. The inscription

1. For information about this Kannaḍa *kāvya* I am indebted to Dr. A.N. Upadhye.

No. 127 (dated A.D. 1115) at Śravaṇa Beḷgoḷ contains a similar eulogy of the Jaina *Muni* Meghachandra in the form of another extract from Abhinava-Pampa's work (Āśvāsa I, v., 10). So this eulogy of the Śrutakīrti Traividya of Kolhāpur at Śravaṇa Boḷgoḷ is not a trustworthy proof of his authorship of the *Rāghavapāṇḍavīya*.

The *Rāghavapāṇḍavīya* mentioned by Abhinava-Pampa has not come down to us. We do not even know whether it was written in Sanskrit or in Kannaḍa;. Since the other poets praised by Abhinava-Pampa in the introduction to his *Rāmāyaṇa* were authors of Kaṇnaḍa works, this Śrutakīrti Traividya eulogised by him as the author of the *Rāghava-pāṇḍavīya* may have written that *kāvya* in Kannaḍa, not in Sanskrit.

V. THE NĀMAMĀLĀ OF DHANAÑJAYA

The *Nāmaliṅgānuśāsana*, popularly known as *Amarakosha*, of Amarasiṁha is generally regarded as the oldest Sanskrit lexicon, but the author himself states in the beginning of his work that he has compiled it after collecting, abridging and codifying the lexicons of his predecessors. Keśava, in his *Kalpadruma-kosha* enumerates the Sanskrit lexicographers in the following verse :—

कात्यवाचस्पतिव्याडिभागुर्यमरमङ्कलाः ।
साहसाङ्कमहेशाद्या विजयन्ते जिनान्तिमाः ।

This verse mentions the following authors of lexicons :— Kātya, Bṛihaspati, Vyāḍi, Bhāguri, Amara (evidently Amarasiṁha), Maṅkala, Sāhasāṅka (Vikramāditya), Maheśa, and, finally, Jina. The works of most of these are not extant now, as they were eclipsed by the excellent *Amarakosha* even as the works of early grammarians were thrown into the background by the great *Ashṭādhyāyi* of Pāṇini; but some of them were current till the time of Kshīrasvāmin (the second half of the eleventh century A.D.), who has cited them. It is proposed to give information here about another lexicographer who also probably flourished before Amarasiṁha.

Dhanañjaya is his name. His work *Nāmamālā* has recently been published in the Bhāratīya Jñāna-pīṭha Series. It consists of 203 *ślokas*. As stated in the preceding article, Dhanañjaya was a Jaina by religious faith. The work opens with two *maṅgala ślokas*, the first of which is as follows :—

तन्नमामि परं ज्योतिरवाङ्मनसगोचरम् ।
उन्मूलयत्यविद्यां यद् विद्यामुन्मीलयत्यपि ॥

There is nothing peculiarly Jainistic in this verse. It can as well occur in a Vedantic work. The second verse, however, specifically mentions Jina :—

1. See the edition of Kshirasvāmin's com. by K. G. Oka, Introd. pp. 4 f.

द्वयं द्वितयमुभयं यमलं युगलं युगम् ।
युग्मं द्वन्द्वं यमं द्वैतं पादयोः पातु जैनयोः ॥

The author next proceeds to give vocables. Unlike Amarasiṁha, he does not give them under *vargas* (groups). He goes from one group of synonyms to another connected or suggested by it. Thus, after invoking the protection of the feet of Jina, he proceeds to give the synonyms of *muni*, because the Jina was a *muni*. Next come the synonyms of his disciples and then his *Siddhānta*. The *muni* roams about on the earth. So we get next the synonyms of the earth (*bhūmi*). This leads the author to the word *bhū-dhara*, which has three meanings—(1) a mountain, (2) a king and (3) a tree. So we next get the synonyms of a mountain, its table-land etc.; then those of a king, and lastly, of a tree. The tree leads the author to the monkeys that live on it, then to the forest, and lastly to the mountaineers, foresters, hunters and fowlers dwelling in it. We next get the synonyms of water, and then, of the fish, the cloud and the lotus, and next the ocean connected with it. Next we come to the man (*manushya*), his lord (the king), his servant, his wife, other types of women such as *kulaṭā* (an unchaste woman), *Abhisārikā*, *Gaṇikā etc.*, then, the lover and his beloved, members of the family such as the father, the mother, the son and the daughter, next, other relatives, male and female *etc*.

The foregoing analysis of the earlier part of the work will have given the reader a fair idea of the method followed by the author in collecting vocables and giving their synonyms in the present work. As a result of it, important vocables such as gods and goddesses, whose synonyms are given by Amara in the beginning of his *Kosha*, are relegated to a later part. The author of the present work was a Jaina. Yet he introduces Jina only incidentally after the synonyms of the world (*jagat*) whose lord he is :—

विष्टपं भुवनं लोको जगत् तस्य पतिर्जिनः । ११३

The author does not enumerate the names of all the Jinas anywhere. He mentions only Mahāvīra in v. 115. Hindu gods and goddesses fare better. Brahmā, Vishṇu, Śiva,

Indra, Lakshmī, Sarasvatī and so forth are mentioned, though incidentally, and their synonyms are given. The story of Kṛishṇa appears to have been fully developed. His brother Balarāma and his wife Revatī are mentioned. Among sons of gods, we have Madana and Kārttikeya, but we do not get any reference to Gajānana. After giving the names of Kārttikeya together in one place, the author mentions another name of his (*viz.* Guha) incidentally in connection with the peacock (*mayūra*):

मयूरो बर्हिणः केकी शिखी प्रावृषिकस्तथा ।
नीलकण्ठः कलापी च शिखण्डी तत्पतिर्गुहः ॥२२॥

So he could have mentioned Gajānana in connection with *gaja* (the elephant). His silence in this respect is significant and throws light on his date.

Some of the words and their meanings given by the author are interesting. He gives *Devānām-priya* in the sense of an ignorant person, and *mattavāraṇa* in the sense of *apāśraya* (a railing or gallery)—

(१) स देवानाम्प्रियोऽप्राज्ञो मन्दो धीनामवर्जितः ।१६६॥
(२) निर्व्यूहो मत्तवारणः ॥१३४॥

Dhanañjaya says at the end that his purpose in making this lexicon was only to guide the people in regard to the meanings of Sanskrit words. In this connection he gives the traditional story noticed in the initial *āhnika* of Patañjali's *Mahābhāshya* about Indra not being able to learn all words though Vāchaspati was his teacher.

Dhanañjaya has not included homonyms in his *Nāmamālā*. He has done this in a separate work called *Anekārthanāmamālā*. In the beginning of this work he has paid obeisance to Jinendra and says that he has compiled this work for the benefit of poets (कवीनां हितकाम्यया). And surely he must have felt the need of it while writing his *Dvisandhānakāvya*. We have shown before what light is thrown on his date by one verse (No. 39) in it about the meanings of the particle *iti*, cited in the commentary *Dhavalā*.

If we compare the contents of the *Nāmamālā* of Dhanañjaya with those of the *Nāmaliṅgānuśāsana* of Amara, we shall conclude that the former belongs to an earlier age. The latter work is not only more comprehensive but is also much better planned. It has given not only vocables (*nāmans*) but also their genders (*liṅgas*). Hence its name *Nāmaliṅgānuśāsana*. The genders of the vocables cited are nowhere mentioned in Dhanañjaya's work. Again, Amarasiṁha's work gives homonyms also. It is more systematic. It is divided into three *kāṇḍas* (sections). The first *kāṇḍa* contains the *vargas* (groups of words) in a certain order, *viz.*, Heaven, Sky, Dik, Kāla, *etc.*, then Pātāla and Naraka. The second *kāṇḍa* deals with the earth, towns, mountains, trees and creepers, animals and lastly men, their four castes and so forth. The third *kāṇḍa* contains adjectives, homonyms, indeclinables *etc.* Though this arrangement is not perfectly faultless, it is much better than the one followed by Dhanañjaya, in which words of all kinds are jumbled together without any classification. It is inconceivable that Dhanañjaya would have written his work in this manner if he had the *Nāmaliṅgānuśāsana* before him. So his work is much anterior to the *Amarakosha*.

Another evidence of the priority of Dhanañjaya's work to the *Amarakosha* is afforded by the non-mention of Gajānana in it, whereas the god appears in a fully developed form in the *Amarakosha*. The verse about him in that work runs as follows:

विनायको विघ्नराजद्वैमातुरगणाधिपाः ।
अप्येकदन्तहेरम्बलम्बोदरगजाननाः ॥

The name *Dvaimātura* in this *śloka* shows that Gajānana was regarded not only as a god but also as an adopted son of Pārvatī in the time of the *Amarakosha*. This points to a later stage in the mythological conception about him.

What light does this throw on the date of Dhanañjaya? The date of the *Amarakosha* has not yet been definitely fixed. The verse in the *Jyotirvidābharaṇa*[1] which makes Amara (the author of the *Amarakosha*) one of 'the gems' of Vikramāditya's court is now proved to be spurious. Max Müller long ago stated that the *Amarakosha* was translated into Chinese by

1. Mirashi and Navlekar, *Kālidāsa*, pp. 25f.

Guṇarāta of Ujjayini in the sixth cen. A.D., but he himself recanted it later.[1] Still his opinion is cited in some modern works on the *Amarakosha*.[2] But the *Amarakosha* is not so old. Winternitz places Amara between the 6th and 8th centuries A.D.[3] The reason he has stated for this view, *viz.*, that Amara must have lived before the decline of Buddhism began in the eighth cen. A.D. is not very cogent. The earliest quotation from the *Amarakosha* is supposed to occur in the *Nyāsa* of Jinendra-buddhi, who is said to have flourished in the beginning of the eighth cen. A.D., but this evidence also is proved to be uncertain.[4] A reference to the *Amarakosha* has also been traced in the *Amoghavṛtti* of Śākaṭāyana, which was written in the reign of the Rāshṭrakūṭa king Amoghavarsha I (A.D. 814-867). So Amara may have lived in the first half of the ninth cen. A.D. at the latest. Dhanañjaya, whose work is much inferior and therefore earlier than his, may be referred to About A.D. 750-800 as shown in the previous article.

A clue to the upper limit of Dhanañjaya's date is afforded by his mention of the work on the *pramāṇas* by Akalaṅka and that on grammar by Pūjyapāda in the following verse which occurs in the *Nāmamālā*[5] (v. 201):

1. *India, What can it teach us* ?, (first ed. 1883), p. 328. However, in a note on p. 376, Max Müller stated on the authority of Bunyiu Nanjio that the name of the original work was *Koshaśāstra-hetu-pratyaya-vastu* (not *Amarakosha*), and that the name of the translator may be Kulanātha, not Guṇarāta. He further remarked, "It shows how careful we ought to be in using the statements even of our best Chinese scholars." The statement is omitted in later editions of *India etc.*

2. See e.g. *Amarakosha* ed. by A.A. Ramanathan (Adyar Library) p. xx.

3. *History of Indian Literature* (English tr. pub. by Motilal Banarsi-dass), Vol. III, part ii, p. 456.

4 It has been pointed out by Srish Chakravarti in the Introd. to his edition of the *Kāśikāvivaraṇapañjikā* that the passage अथवा तन्त्रं सिद्धान्तै । 'तन्त्रं प्रधानं सिद्धान्ते' इत्यमरः । occurs only in one MS. of the work from the Deccan College (now Bhandarkar Institute). It is not noticed in the Bengali MS deposited in the Varendra Research Society, Rajshahi, nor in the MS. in the Malayalam characters in the Library of the Trivandrum Govt.

5. See the *Nāmamālā* (pub. by the Bhāratīya Jñānapīṭha), p. 92.

प्रमाणमकलङ्कस्य पूज्यपादस्य लक्षणम् ।
द्विःसन्धानकवेः काव्यं रत्नत्रयमपश्चिमम् ॥

There are two views about the date of Akalaṅka. Some scholars like A.N. Upadhye and Kailashachandra Shastri place him about the middle of the seventh century A.D.,[1] while others like R.G. Bhandarkar and Satishchandra Vidyabhushana place him in the middle of the eighth century A.D.[2] In his edition of *Akalaṅka-grantha-trayam* (Singhi Jainagranthamālā) Pandit Mahendrakumara Shastri has examined the question of Akalaṅka's date at great length and has shown that he flourished in *circa* A.D. 720-780.[3] So Dhanañjaya, who praises his work on the *pramāṇas* cannot be placed earlier than *circa* A.D. 750.

As for Pūjyapāda, the second author praised by Dhanañjaya, the tradition that makes him a *guru* of the Gaṅga king Durvinīta (A.D. 540-650) may be correct.[4] Dhanañjaya flourished much later.

The foregoing discussion substantiates our previous view that Dhanañjaya flourished in the period A.D. 750-800.

This date agrees with the non-mention of the synonyms or even the name of Gajānana in the *Nāmamālā*. As I have shown elsewhere, the god began to come into prominence at the end of the Gupta period. The verse describing his iconography in Varāhamihira's *Bṛihatsaṁhitā* is proved to be an interpolation.[5] He is no doubt mentioned as *eka-danta* (having only one tusk) by Bāṇa[6] (first half of the seventh cen. A.D.)

1. See *Akalaṅka-grantha-trayam*, Introd. by Mahendrakumara Shastri, p. 13.

2. *Loc. cit.*

3. *Ibid.*, pp. 13f. He has shown that Akalaṅka has criticised the views of Bhartṛihari (A.D. 600-650), Kumārila (A.D. 600-680), Dharmakīrti (A.D. 620-690), Dharmottara (A.D. 650-720), Prajñākara (670-725), Karṇagomin (A.D. 690-720), and Śāntarakshita (A.D. 705-760). He, therefore, places Akalaṅka in A.D. 720-780.

4. V.S. Agrawala places Pūjyapāda in the second half of the fifth cen. A.D. See his Introd. to the *Jainendra Vyākaraṇa*.

5. A.M. Shastri, *India as seen in the Bṛihatsaṁhitā of Varāhmihira*. p. 148.

6. *Harshacharita*, uchchhvāsa IV, v. 2.

and is prayed to by Bhavabhūti[1] (first half of the eighth cen. A.D.), but the latter mentions him only as a *gana* of Śiva, not as a son of Śiva and Pārvatī. The mythology that makes him an adopted son of Pārvatī was not then developed. It must have taken about a century to develop. Again, the Hindu god may have obtained recognition in other religions like Jainism a little later. So it is no wonder that his name is not noticed in the *Nāmamālā*. The *Amarakosha*, in which he appears as a full-fledged god with all mythological details, may, therefore, be referred to the first half of the ninth century A.D. This date is in keeping with the fact that a commentary on it called *Amoghavṛitti* was written by Śākaṭāyana, who flourished during the reign of the Rāshṭrakūṭa king Amoghavarsha I (*circa* A.D. 814-867).

There was another work named *Nāmamālā* which has been cited by Kshīrasvāmin in his commentary on the *Amarakosha*. Its author is not known; but from the quotations in the commentary it appears to be a lexicographical work different from the *Nāmamālā* of Dhanañjaya. See *e.g.* the following hemistichs cited by Kshīrasvāmin :[2]

(१) निकषा रक्षसां माता । p. 13.
(२) निखर्वः खट्टूरः खर्वः । p. 49.
(३) पाणिः शमः शयो हस्तः । p. 104.

None of these portions of the verses occurs in Dhanañjaya's work.

As stated before, Dhanañjaya has not collected homonyms in his *Nāmamālā*. These he has reserved for another work significantly named *Anekārthanāmamālā*. It gives important homonyms in forty-four verses. The work opens with a verse mentioning Pūjyapāda and Chailāchāryā Sivāyana. The homonyms are not arranged on any alphabetical basis as in some later lexicons of homonyms.

1. *Mālatī-Mādhava*, Act I, verse 1.
2. See *Amarakosha* with Kshīrasvāmin's Com. ed. by K.G. Oka.

VI

THE AUTHOR AND THE DATE OF THE KUNDAMĀLĀ —SOME OBJECTIONS CRITICALLY EXAMINED*

In my *Studies in Indology,* Vol. I (second ed., 1968, pp. 56-65), I put forward some new evidence to show that Dhīranāga, not Diṅnāga, was the author of the *Kundamālā,* and that his date lies between the seventh and the eleventh century A.D. When I brought my article to the notice of Dr. K.K. Dutt and asked for his comments, he very kindly drew my attention to certain objections that can be raised to my views. As the questions are important and similar objections are likely to be raised by others also, I am critically examining them here, though he has not put them forward in any published article.

(A) *The Author of the Kundamālā*

Objections to the view that Dhīranāga was the author of the *Kundamālā*—

Objection I—*Tarko'pratishṭhaḥ etc.* is an ancient floating verse, but when Vallabha ascribes it to Diṅnāga, is it not possible that at least according to the belief of Vallabha, there was a non-Buddhist poet Diṅnāga prior to his time ?

Answer—Yes. Vallabha may have believed that there was such a poet, but Vallabha is a very late anthologist. No verses of Diṅnāga have been cited as such in any other anthology—neither from the *Kundamālā* nor from any other literary work ascribed to him. Vallabha's ascribing of the aforementioned verse to Diṅnāga must, therefore, be treated as due to some mistake.

Objection II—Vidyākara anonymously quotes the verse *Jvāl-ev-ordhva etc.* from the *Kundamālā,* but ascribes the verse *Dyūte paṇaḥ etc.* from the same play to Dhīranāga. Had he any direct acquaintance with the play, he could have easily ascrib-

* *Samarpita Ardhaśatī* (Pandit D P. Mishra Felicitation Volume), pp. 535 f

ed both the verses to Dhīranāga. Does this not betray his dependence on hearsay ? So his evidence does not appear to be thoroughly reliable.

Answer—This is noticed not only in Vidyākara's *Subhāshitaratnakosha* but also in almost all anthologies; but we do not, on that account, treat their ascriptions as based on hearsay. For instance, Vidyākara cites 31 verses of Bhavabhūti, mentioning his name, and 13 others without it, but some of these latter occur in his extant plays. Are we to suppose that the plays in which these anonymously cited verses occur were not known to him ? This argument has, therefore, no force. We must utilise all positive references, checking them where possible, and leave the rest. Now, of the two verses cited by Vidyākara from the *Kundamālā*, one is definitely ascribed to Dhīranāga, while no verse from that play is anywhere ascribed to Diṅnāga. This evidence combined with the fact that the Tanjore manuscripts explicitly mention Dhīranāga as the author of the *Kundamālā* should clinch the issue.

Objection III—The *Prasannasāhityaratnākara* quotes the aforementioned verses, but ascribes the former to Vīranāga and the latter to Hanūmat. It is obvious that such evidences based on any thing but first-hand knowledge cannot be treated as reliable evidences.

Answer—All anthologies, no doubt, contain some wrong references, but we should utilise their evidence after verification and should not ignore it altogether. Now, as regards the name Vīranāga, I have shown that it is due to the writer's wrong reading of the name Dhīranāga in the manuscript from which he copied. As I have shown, the letters *va* and *dha* were closely similar in the 10th and 11th centuries A.D.; *va* had a short horizontal stroke at the top, which was absent in *dha*. In the thirteenth century A.D. *dha* developed a horn on the left, which distinguished it from *va*. So it is very likely that the writer of the manuscript of the *Kundamālā* wrongly read Dhīranāga as Vīranāga in the manuscript from which he copied. As for the other ascription to Hanūmat, we must reject it as due to some mistake. The verse must have been taken in the *Hanūmannāṭaka* from the *Kundamālā*. The author of the *Prasannasāhityaratnākara* evidently noticed it there, but failed to note that it occurs in the *Kundamālā* also. But this mistake cannot negative the evidence of Vidyākara's *Subhāshitaratnakosha* and of the Tanjore Mss.

Objection IV—The old palm-leaf manuscript of Mysore in its *prastāvanā* has the name of the playwright written as *Diṅ..*, which evidently leads to the reading Diṅnāga, but the paper manuscript of the same library corrupts it, and this manuscript is very recent. The Tanjore manuscripts, on the other hand, read in the colophon *Anūparājasya kaver-Dhiranāgasya*. Is the latter set more reliable than the former ? The problem can, therefore, be solved if any new reliable manuscript comes to our rescue and not otherwise.

Answer—The fragmentary reading *Diṅ...*, no doubt, suggests the poet's name as *Diṅnāga*, but its evidence is opposed to that of the Tanjore manuscripts. The latter are supported by the explicit mention of Dhīranāga by Vidyākara. Besides, it is only Dhīranāga (not Diṅnāga) whose *subhāshitas* are cited in the anthologies. Even if new manuscript evidence is discovered, it cannot shake the already available strong evidence.

In my opinion there is sufficient evidence to enable us to accept Dhīranāga as the name of the author of the *Kundamālā*.

(B) *The Date of the Kundamālā*

We shall next take up the second problem of the date of the *Kundamālā*. To show that the *Kundamālā* is not as early as the fifth century A.D. I had drawn attention to the occurrence of the *Nāndī* verse in praise of Heramba (the elephant-faced god). I pointed out that there is no obeisance to that god in any Gupta inscription. The image of the god in a cave of the Gupta period at Udayagiri near Bhilsā is crude. Later, from the image of the god at Bhumrā (*c.* A.D. 450-500) it appears that the worship of Gajānana came into vogue at the end of the Gupta period. To this view the following objections have been raised:—

Objections—References to Gajānana occur in several early works. So merely on account of the *Nāndī* verse in praise of Heramba, we should not date the *Kundamālā* later than the fifth century A.D. See *e.g.* the following:

(I) References to the elephant-faced god in early Vedic works—

The *Śatarudriya* text of the *Maitrāyaṇī Saṁhitā* (ed. by Leopold von Schroeder, Leipzig, 1903) (II.9.1) gives a *Gāyatrī-mantra* of Dantin who is Hastimukha and Karāṭa[1] (*Karaṭa* ?). The *Kāṭhaka* text (17, 11), the *Taittirīya Āraṇyaka* (X. 1. 5) and the *Mānavaśrautasūtra* (XI, 5) (Rudrajapa Section) also repeat the same *mantra*.

Answer—The *Maitrāyaṇī Saṁhitā* has, no doubt, a *gāyatrī-mantra* in praise of Hastimukha and it is often adduced to prove the antiquity of the worship of Gajānana. The controversy about this question arose in Vidarbha nearly forty years ago, in connection with which the late Pandit Krishnashastri Ghule of Nagpur adduced some important evidence to prove that the section of the *Maitrāyaṇī Saṁhitā* in which the *gāyatrī-mantra* about Gajānana occurs is interpolated. His arguments are not as well known to scholars as they deserve to be as the controversy was carried on in the Marathi monthly *Vāgīśvarī* of Nāgpur (Vol. III, pp. 276 f.). I shall briefly state his arguments, supplementing them with my own observations.

If one reads the section in the *Maitrāyaṇī Saṁhitā* (X, 9, 1), one will notice that most of thirteen *gayatris* included in it are about later Paurāṇic deities not mentioned in the Vedic texts. The following gods are, for instance, invoked therein—Kumāra Kārttikeya; Karāṭa-Hastimukha; Dantī; Chaturmukha (four-faced) Brahmā; Keśava-Nārāyaṇa-Vishṇu; Paramātmā-Vainateya. These gods are *not* Vedic. They are not praised or even mentioned in these forms in genuine Vedic literature. Their worship came into vogue only later. And this is corroborated by later secular literature and inscriptions. Again, the cognate *Kāṭhaka* and *Kapishṭhala-Kaṭha*

1. तत्कराटाय विद्महे हस्तिमुखाय धीमहि ।
तन्नो दन्ती प्रचोदयात् ॥

Saṁhitās do not contain these *gāyatri-mantras*. The *Kāṭhaka Saṁhitā* contains only the Rudra-gāyatrī; the *Kapishṭhala-Kaṭha Saṁhitā* does not contain even that. Besides, the word-forms and accents in them show several irregularities. See e.g. *paramātmāya*.[1] Notice also the accent of *prachodayāt*. As this word does not occur in a relative clause, it should not be accented,[2] but it has the *udātta* accent on the third syllable. The interpolater has evidently formed these verses on the model of the famous *gāyatri-mantra* (*Tat savitur vareṇyaṁ etc.*) in praise of the Sun,[3] but has bungled in respect of accents.

The *Taittirīya Āraṇyaka*—The *gāyatri-mantras* occur in several places in this Āraṇyaka. See pp. 699, 754-55 and 796-799 (Ānandāśrama ed.). Sāyaṇa was not sure about their genuineness. While commenting on the first of these in X. 1, he has remarked as follows—

इत ऊर्ध्वं तेषु तेषु देशेषु श्रुतिपाठा अत्यन्तविलक्षणाः । तत्र विज्ञानात्मप्रभृतिभिः पूर्वैर्निबन्धकारैर्द्राविडपाठस्यावृतत्वात्तद्वयमपि तमेवावृत्य व्याख्यास्यामः । तत्र षड्भिर्गायत्रीभिरात्मप्राप्तिद्वारभूता देवताविशेषाः प्रार्थ्यन्ते ।

This shows that there were several varying recensions of these *gāyatrīs*. Sāyaṇa comments here on six only, *viz.* Sahasrāksha Mahādeva, Mahādeva Rudra, Vakratuṇḍa Dantin, Suvarṇapaksha Garuḍa, Kanyākumārī Durgā and Vāsudeva Vishṇu. Other recensions had probably more *gāyatrīs*. Again, the same *Āraṇyaka* later (X, 1) invokes as many as twelve deities including, in addition to the six mentioned above, six more, *viz.* Chakratuṇḍa-Nandī, Mahāsena-Shaṇmukha, Hiraṇyagarbha-Brahmā, Tīkshṇadaṁshṭra Narasiṁha, Mahādyutikāra Āditya and Vaiśvānara Agni.

The *Mahānārayanīya Upanishad* belonging to the *Taittirīya-Śākhā*, which has a considerable portion in common with the Āraṇyaka, has as many as eighteen *gāyatrīs* invoking, besides those mentioned above, some more deities

1. *Maitrāyaṇī Saṁhitā*, X. 9. 1.
2. See Pāṇini, VIII. 1. 28.
3. The editor of the *Mahānārāyaṇīya Upanishad* says that two more *gāyatrīs* in praise of Hiraṇyagarbha Brahmā and Tīkshṇadaṁshṭra Narasiṁha are noticed in some manuscripts of the Upanishad.

such as Saptajihva Vaiśvānara, Divākara Sūrya, Sahasrakiraṇa Bhānu, Vakrapāda Vṛishabha, Bhagavatī Māhādurgā, Kāmamālinī Gaurī, Chaturmukha Brahmā and so forth.

It will be thus noticed that these *gāyatri-mantras* invoking different deities, some of whom came into vogue only in later times, were composed from time to time as sectarian interests required and were interpolated in some works of the Vedic literature. No reliance can, therefore, be placed on their evidence.

Objection—The *Sāmavidhāna Brāhmaṇa* has a *Vaināyikī Saṁhitā* for the propitiation of the god Vināyaka, who is not a demi-god as he is excluded from the list of demi-gods given in Ch. II.

Answer—That Vināyaka seems to be of the same type as that described in the *Yājñavalkya Smṛiti* (II, 271-294). He had not then assumed the later benignant form of Gajānana.

II—*References in the Purāṇas*—The *Vishṇudharma*, assigned to prior than the fourth century A.D. by Dr. R.C. Hazra, refers to the worship of Gaṇeśa.

Answer—There have been so many interpolations in the Purāṇas that it is impossible to rely on any portion in them as of a particular date.

III—Hāla's *Gāthāsaptaśatī* (ed. by R.G. Basak) refers to Gaṇapati with a trunk and his worship (IV, 72; V, 3).

Answer—I have shown (*Studies in Indology*, Vol. I, second ed., pp. 88-101) that the *Gāthāsaptaśatī* has gone through several recensions. Weber has proved that there are as many as seven recensions of it, only 430 verses being common to all. I have shown that some of the verses now included in it were composed by the Vākāṭaka kings Sarvasena and Pravarasena and the poet Vākpatirāja, a contemporary of Bhavabhūti. These poets flourished several centuries after Hāla (1st cen. A.D.). So unless we know definitely the date of any particular *gāthā* in it, it is better not to cite its evidence for any view.

I have shown so far that none of the arguments advanced to prove the antiquity of Gajānana worship have any weight. I have also shown from archaeological evidence how the god gradually rose into prominence at the end of the fifth cen. A.D. Secular works also corroborate this view.

There is no mention of the god in any secular Sanskrit literary work of the early centuries of the Christian era. He is not mentioned in the *Mahābhāshya* of Patañjali, the *Arthaśāstra* of Kauṭilya, the plays of Bhāsa and the works of Kālidāsa. This is not *argumentum ex silentio*; for Patañjali mentions the images of Skanda and Viśākha, and Kauṭilya says that tamples of certain gods such as Śiva, Vaiśravaṇa, Jayanta *etc.* should be erected. Images of Skanda, Viśākha *etc.* appear on Kushāṇa and Gupta coins, but we see nowhere any image of Gajānana. I may quote here the following significant passage from a private letter of the late Dr. V. S. Agrawala—"For the earliest representation of Gaṇeśa in the Śaka-Kushāṇa period, please refer to Dr. Coomarswamy's book entitled, *Yakshas*, pt. I. He is represented there not as a deity, but as an elephant-headed Yaksha. I think the idea originated that way. Perhaps many of our other deities got mixed up with the popular cults of Yaksha worship. At Mathurā there is an architectural panel of the Kushāṇa period, which shows a row of elephant-headed figures, again, I think, of the Yakshas. It is only in the late Gupta period that we have come across images of corpulent dancing Gaṇeśa, a good example being deposited in the Mathurā Museum."

Aśvaghosha also mentions some elephant-faced Yakshas in the army of Māra when he attacked Gautama Buddha.[1] The worship of Gajānana seems to have gradually come into vogue at the end of the Gupta period. The author of the *Kundamālā* in which Heramba (Gājānana) is described as in the classical form, could not have flourished in that age.

1. *Buddhacharita*, XIII, 13-21.

VII. IDENTIFICATION OF VĪRAPĀLA IN THE VIDDHAŚĀLABHAÑJIKĀ

The *Viddhaśālabhañjikā* of Rājaśekhara is one of the few plays in Sanskrit literature which have a historical setting. Like the *Svapnavāsavadatta* of Bhāsa and the *Mālavikāgnimitra* of Kālidāsa, it mentions a historical event in the last Act, but it has been variously interpreted. The play was staged first at Tripurī (near Jabalpur) during the reign of king Karpūra-varsha, whom Hultzsch was the first to identify with the Kalachuri king Keyūravarsha, also known as Yuvarājadeva I (A.D. 915-945). The plot of the play may be summarised as follows :

"The king Vidyādharamalla *alias* Karpūravarsha of Tripurī receives at his court Vīrapāla *alias* Chaṇḍamahāsena, the lord of Kuntala, who has been deprived of his kingdom by his relatives, and falls in love with his daughter Kuvalaya-mālā. His minister Bhāgurāyaṇa, however, comes to know from astrologers that the king who would marry Mṛigāṅkā-valī, the daughter of king Chandravarman of Lāṭa would be the sovereign of the whole world. He, therefore, contrives to bring about the marriage of his lord Karpūravarsha with Mṛigaṅkāvalī. Chandravarman, her father, had no son, and so, since her childhood, he has brought her up as a boy under the name Mṛigāṅkavarman. None but Bhāgurāyaṇa knows of this secret. He manages to have the pretender crown-prince of Lāṭa brought to Tripurī to stay at the Kalachuri court. Karpūravarsha's chief queen Madanasundarī, who, though a niece of Chandravarman, is shown to be ignorant of the personation, occasionally dresses the pretender boy in a female garb. When the king sees her in a dream, he falls in love with her. The queen, in order to play a practical joke on the king, induces him to marry a sister of the pretender boy. This sister is none other than Mṛigāṅkāvalī herself, though the queen, who is ignorant of her real sex, takes her to be Mṛigāṅkavarman in a female garb. The king agrees and the marriage is performed. In the meanwhile news comes from Chadravarman that a son has been born to him. He, therefore, requests his niece, the Kalachuri queen, to bestow his daughter Mṛigāṅkāvali, whom he has brought up as a son, on a worthy consort. The queen realises her mistake when it is too late. To make the best of the situation, however, she bestows both Mṛigāṅkāvalī and Kuvalayamālā, the Kuntala princess, on the king. Just then comes a massenger from the king's General Śrī-Vatsa with the following letter:

"Through the power of Your Majesty, who is an ornament of the Kalachuris, and the policy of the Minister Bhāgurāyaṇa, all the mighty kings of the east, west and north have already been subdued. Only those of the south did not submit. Vīrapāla, the lord of Kuntala, who had been deprived of his kingdom by his relatives, sought your Majesty's protection. By Your Majesty's order, we placed Vīrapāla at our head and encamped on the bank of the Payoshṇī." The General then describes how his forces fought with a confederacy of several kings, viz. those of Karṇāṭa, Siṁhala, Pāṇḍya, Murala, Āndhra, Kuntala, Koṅkaṇa and others, defeated them and placed Vīrapāla on the throne. Bhāgurāyaṇa then declares that the Kalachuri kīng reigns supreme over the whole country."

The historical event mentioned in the *Viddhaśālabhañjikā* has been variously interpreted. Dasharath Sharma identified the Kuntala king with the Rāshṭrakūṭa king Baddiga-Amoghavarsha III, and thought that the battle in which the Kalachuri forces obtained a decisive victory was fought on the bank of the Tāptī (mentioned as Payoshṇī in the play).[1] When I wrote on the problem nearly forty years ago,[2] I thought that the identification of Vīrapāla with Baddiga-Amoghavarsha was not possible, because the play states that the

1. *Ind. Ant.*, Vol. LX. pp. 61f.
2. *Ibid.*, Vol. LXIII, pp. 36f.

Kalachuri king married the former's daughter, which was manifestly impossible as Baddiga-Amoghavarsha (represented by Vīrapāla in the play) was his own son-in-law. If what the play states did actually take place, the Kalachuri king would be marrying the daughter of his own son-in-law. I, therefore, proposed to identify Vīrapāla of the play with some other claimant for the throne of Kuntala, perhaps Bappuva, whom Baddiga-Amoghavarsha's son Kṛishṇa III is known to have killed soon after his father's accession. Altekar, however, supported Dasharath Sharma's view. As for the difficulty caused by Vīrapāla's daughter marrying the Kalachuri king, he thought that it was a mere poetic invention intended to complicate the love affair in the play.[1] Subsequent study of the political events of the times convinced me that Altekar's view was the correct one and so I adopted it in *C.I.I.*, Vol. IV, pp. lxxxi f.

Buddha Prakash has recently opened the question.[2] He says, "It is highly improbable that Yuvarājadeva married the daughter of his own son-in-law which would be the position if Baddiga-Amoghavarsha is identified with Chaṇḍamahāsena-Vīrapāla...The very idea of such a marriage must have been so abhorrent and revolting to the conscience of the courtiers and other people, associated with the Kalachuris of Tripurī, that no person in his senses could conceive of presenting it on the stage. It utterly passes comprehension as to what could be that unavoidable necessity of introducing such an obnoxious episode in the play which compelled the poet to throw overboard all sense of decency and decorum."

Buddha Prakash thinks that Vīrapāla of the *Viddhaśālabhañjikā* represents the Eastern Chālukya king Bhīma, called Chālukya Bhīma II, who bore the *birudas Rājamārtaṇḍa*, and *Chaṇḍamahendra*. He overthrew Yuddhamalla (A.D. 928-934), who was ruling with the support of the Rāshṭrakūṭas. He was a claimant for the throne of Veṅgī occupied by Yuddhamalla. He was making preparations for gaining the throne and

1. *The Rāshṭrakūṭas and Their Times* (first ed.) p. 110.
2. *Dr. Mirashi Felicitation Volume*, pp. 406 f.

eventually succeeded in getting it in A.D. 934. He sought the Kalachuri king's help by giving him his daughter in marriage. His *biruda Chaṇḍamahendra* corresponds to *Chaṇḍamahāsena*, the *biruda* of Vīrapāla in the *Viddhaśālabhañjikā*. Since Yuddhamalla was only a nominal ruler and the Rāshṭrakūṭas were supreme at Veṅgī, the Kalachuri force headed by Bhīma fought with the Rāshṭrakūṭas on the bank of the Pūrṇā or the Paingaṅgā. On the eve of the battle the Rāshṭrakūṭa king Govinda IV died and consequently his army was routed. Then Bhīma Chaṇḍamahendra was installed on the throne of Veṅgī in A.D. 934. On the death of the Rāshṭrakūṭa king Govinda IV, the feudatories offered the throne to Baddiga-Amoghavarsha, who was staying at Tripurī. The Kalachuri king Yuvarājadeva I thus attained the position of the most powerful monarch of his time. But soon after the accession of Baddīga-Amoghavarsha, his son Kṛishṇa III undertook to terminate the paramountcy. He avenged the defeat of his dynasty by marching against the Kalachuris and inflicted a defeat on them as stated in the following verse :[1]

रामहतसहस्रभुजो भुजद्वयाकलितसमदरामेण ।
जननीपत्नीगुरुरपि येन सहस्रार्जुनो विजितः ॥

Consequently, the traditional Kalachuri friendship with the Rāshṭrakūṭas came to an end. The Kalachuris, thereafter, allied themselves with the Chālukyas of Kalyāṇī, who supplanted the Rāshṭrakūṭas.

Buddha Prakash has reiterated his theory recently.[2] So it is necessary to examine it critically. There are several insuperable difficulties in accepting his theory. They may be stated briefly as follows:

(1) Buddha Prakash identifies Vīrapāla with the Eastern Chālukya king Bhima II, because the latter's *biruda Chaṇḍamahendra* is similar to the *biruda Chaṇḍamahāsena* of the former mentioned in the *Viddhaśālabhñjikā*.

1. See Karhāḍ plates of Kṛishṇa III, *Ep. Ind.*, Vol. IV, pp 278 f.
2. *Umesh Mishra Commemoration Volume*, pp. 371 f.

But the correct *biruda* of Bhīma II was not *Chaṇḍamahendra*, but *Gaṇḍamahendra*. Buddha Prakash has wrongly read the *biruda* in Yazdani's *Early History of the Deccan*, Vol.II, p. 500. The correct *biruda* given there from the Pāganavaram plates of Chālukya Bhīma II is *Gaṇḍamadendra*.[1] See *Ind Ant.*, Vol. XIII, pp. 213 f.

(2) Vīrapāla is described in the play as a claimant for the throne of Kuntala. The General Śrī-Vatsa says that after the battle of the Payoshṇī he placed him on the throne of Kuntala. On the other hand, Chālukya Bhīma II was a king of Āndhra and not of Kuntala. His capital was Veṅgī, which at no time was included in Kuntala.

Buddha Prakash is in great straits in explaining this discrepancy. He says that in its widest extent Kuntala meant the whole of the Kanarese country. But this does not help his theory; for Veṅgī was never included in the Kanarese country. Next Buddha Prakash makes the desparate statement that when Rājaśekhara uses Kuntala in the plural, he understands thereby the states of South India in general. He gives no example to support his statement. Does he not know that in Sanskrit the names of countries are always used in the plural unless some word like *deśa* is affixed to them ?[2] Kuntala in the singular means the king of Kuntala.[3] There is not even a shred of evidence to show that Kuntala ever included the country round Veṅgī.

(3) There is no evidence to show that Chālukya Bhīma II had gone to Tripurī to seek the help of the Kalachuri king Keyūravarsha. It is a mere conjecture of Buddha Prakash.

(4) There is no reason why the Rāshṭrakūṭa prince

1. See line 45 in the facsimile of the Pāgavaram plates between pages 214 and 215 in *Ind. Ant.*, Vol. XIII.

2. See e.g. the following—

(i) अस्ति दक्षिणापथे विदर्भेषु पद्मनगरं नाम नगरम् ।

Mālatīmādhava ed. by R.G. Bhandarkar, p. 11.

(ii) पञ्चालास्तव पश्चिमेन त इमे वामा गिरां भाजनम् ।

Bālarāmāyaṇa, X, 86.

3. See e.g. the following—

कुन्तलः कुन्तशाली । *Viddhaśālabhañjikā*, IV, 19.

न कुन्तलः कुन्तलतामवाप । *C.I.I.*, Vol. IV, p. 293.

Kṛishṇa III should have felt offended if the Kalachuri Yuvarājadeva installed Chālukya Bhīma II on the throne of Veṅgī as supposed by Buddha Prakash. As a matter of fact the relations of the Rāshṭrakūṭas and the Kalachuris were not at all strained as a result of the battle of the Payoshṇī. Kṛishṇa III did not defeat a Kalachuri king as wrongly supposed by Buddha Prakash. The verse रामहतसहस्रभुजो etc. cited above does not mention any victory of Kṛishṇa III over a Kalachuri king. It only states that Kṛishṇa III surpassed Sahasrārjuna, the eponymous ancestor of his mother and wife. The root *ji* means here to excel or to surpass. I have pointed out another instance of the use of the root in this sense from Bagumrā plates of Indra III, which had baffled scholars for a long time.[1] The relations of the two families continued to be cordial after the battle of the Payoshṇī. I have drawn attention to some verses in an unpublished commentary of a Śaiva work which state explicitly that Baddiga came back and stayed at Tripurī in the Chedi court while his son Kṛishṇa III was governing the country as *Yuvarāja* from the capital Mānyakheṭa[2]

(5) Even supposing that Vīrapāla of the play represents Chālukya Bhīma II, why should the Kalachuri army meant to instal him on the throne of Veṅgī proceed to the south-west from Tripurī (near Jabalpur) and reach the Payoshṇī (the Pūrṇā) instead of proceeding direct to Veṅgī through South Kosala (Chhattisgaḍh)? The latter was the route followed by both Samudragupta in the fourth century A.D.[3] and later by

1. *Studies in Indology*, Vol. IV, pp. 115 f.

2. गतवति शककाले षड्ग्रसेष्वष्टसंख्ये शरदि विशदपक्षे चाश्विने शुक्रवारे । उडुनि सुरपतीशे योग आयुष्मतीयं तिथिरपि च गतानां पञ्चमी यत्र शुद्धा ॥ चेदिकुलराजधान्यां गतवति श्रीबद्दिगे निहत्यारीन् । तच्छासनेन वसुधां परिरक्षति कृष्णराजेऽपि ॥

The *tithi* Friday, Āśvina śu di 5, Śaka 858, regularly corresponds to the 23rd September A.D. 936. I obtained this extract from an ancient manuscript in the possession of Dr. S.N.Sen, Keeper of the Nepal Museum, and personally verified it at Hyderabad at the Session of the All-India Oriental Conference held there in 1941. The manuscript deserves to be published.

3. *CII.*, Vol. III, p. 7. Samudragupta passed through Kosala (Chhattisgadh) and Mahākāntāra (Bastar District of M.P.) before invading Pishṭapura and other territories on the eastern coast.

Īśānavarman Maukhari in the sixth century A.D.[1] to reach the countries on the eastern coast like Āndhra.

There is thus not even an iota of evidence to support this novel theory of Buddha Prakash that Vīrapāla, the dispossessed king of Kuntala, was Bhīma II of the Eastern Chālukya dynasty.

On the other hand, there is ample evidence to show that Vīrapāla was meant to represent the Rāshṭrakūṭa king Baddiga-Amoghavarsha. We know that he was a claimant for the throne of Mānyakheṭa. He was residing at the Kalachuri court of Tripurī as stated in the Kuḍlur[2] and Sudi plates.[3] He celebrated the marriage of his daughter Revakannimaḍī with the Gaṅga prince Permāḍi Būtuga there. His son Kṛishṇa III had married a Kalachuri princess. It is not, therefore, surprising that the Kalachuri king Keyūravarsha (Yuvarāja-deva I) espoused his cause and helped him in gaining the throne. The route to Mānyakheṭa from Tripurī lay through Vidarbha. The army was opposed by the Rāshṭrakūṭa ruler of Achalapura named Karkara, who owed allegiance to Govinda IV. A sanguinary battle was fought on the bank of the Payoshṇī (Pūrṇā), which flows at a distance of only ten miles from Achalapura. The *Viddhaśālabhañjikā* tells us that Vīrapāla accompanied the army and we know from a verse in a Śilāhāra grant in praise of Amoghavarsha III that he had defeated Karkara (evidently the ruler of Achalapura).[4] Thus, there is

1. *Ep. Ind.*, Vol. XIV, pp. 115 f

2. See the following said of the Gaṅga prince Būtuga —

तस्यानुजो निजभुजार्ज्जितसंपदर्थं भूवल्लभं समुपगम्य डहालदेशे । श्रीवद्दिगं तदनु तस्य सुतां सहैव वाक्कन्यया व्यवहदुक्तविधिस्त्रिपुर्याम् ॥

An. Rep, of Mysore Arch Deptt, 1921, p 11.

Būtuga later took part in the battle near Achalapura. See—

किं चात: किनु नागादचलपुरपति: कक्कराजोऽन्तकास्यम् etc. *Loc, cit.*

3. *Ep. Ind.*, III, p. 179.

4. श्रीमत्कर्करराष्ट्रकूटकटकेऽसह्यंश्नसंघर्षतो
रौद्रद्रोहदवप्रतापशमनं निस्त्रिणवाराजलै: ।
येनाकारि समुद्धतेन्द्रधनुषा भूषाश्मभिर्विद्युता
भाति श्रीमदमोघवर्षसुघनोऽसद्धूलिविध्वंसनात् ॥

Altekar, *The Rāshṭrakūṭas etc.*, p. 110.

ample evidence to support the view that Vīrapāla of the *Viddha-śālabhañjikā* represents Baddiga-Amoghavarsha III.

But then, how to explain the obnoxious marriage of the Kalachuri king with the daughter of Vīrapāla if the latter was his own son-in-law ? As suggested by Altekar, it was meant to complicate the love-story of the play. This is not surprising in a work of Rājaśekhara. He is guilty of several other indiscretions, though not of such magnitude. He had little sense of propriety. He was a chatter-box who took delight in incongruous situations and statements. We shall notice here a few of them.

(1) In the *Bālarāmāyaṇa* (Act III) Rājaśekhara shows that several kings of the contemporary dynasties attended the *svayaṁvara* of Sītā, viz. the king of Chedi ruling at Tripurī, the Chaulukya king of Lāṭa, the lord of Marahaṭṭa (Mahārāshṭra), the Śaka king etc. He is not conscious of any anachronism in that scene.

(2) In the fourth Act of the same play Śatānanda gives the following advice to Sītā :—

निर्व्याजा दयिते ननान्दृषु नता श्वश्रूषु भक्ता भव
स्निग्धा बन्धुषु वत्सला परिजने स्मेरा सपत्नीष्वपि ।
पत्युर्मित्रजने सनर्मवचना खिन्ना च तद्द्वेषिषु
स्त्रीणां संवननं नतभ्रु तदिदं कान्तौषधं भर्तृषु ॥

This verse is evidently in imitation of the well-known *śloka* in Kālidāsa's *Śākuntala*, giving Kaṇva's advice to Śakuntalā. Rājaśekhara, however, is not conscious of any incongruity in asking Sītā to speak smilingly to her co-wives. Did he not know that Sītā had no co-wives either before or after her marriage ? He had no qualms of conscience in describing this advice to Sītā.

(3) In the eighth act of the *Bālarāmāyaṇa* Rājaśekhara describes the journey, through air, of the aerial car of Rāma and Sītā from Laṅkā to Ayodhyā. Rājaśekhara describes that they saw on their way the Himālaya, Kailāsa, the Mānasa lake, and Indra's Amarāvatī and the countries, mountains and rivers on the earth such as the Tāmraparṇī, the Godāvarī, Bhīmeśvara, thereafter Āndhradeśa, Kāverī, etc. irrespective

of their geographical position. He sees no incongruity in that description.

(4) In the fourth act of the *Viddhaśālabhañjikā*, the queen of Karpūravarsha says that she had previously arranged the marriage of her husband with the princesses of Magadha, Mālava, Pāñchāla, Avanti, Jālandhara and Kerala.[1] Can we say that these marriages had actually taken place ? Was the king of Mālava then different from that of Avanti ?[2] This will show that Rājaśekhara's statements are not to be taken seriously. Karpūravarsha's marriage with the daughter of Vīrapāla is of the same type.

(5) In the *Karpūramañjarī* also Rājaśekhara describes the marriage of Chaṇḍapāla (the Pratīhāra king Mahīpāla of Kanauj) with the princess of Kuntala. Again, he tells us that the princess was of the Rāshṭrakūṭa family and was staying at Vachchhoma (Vatsagulma).[3] Now, Vatsagulma was situated in Vidarbha, not in Kuntala. Again, such a matrimonial alliance of the Pratīhāras and the Rāshṭrakūṭas was very unlikely, because the Pratīhāra king Mahīpāla had been put to flight by the Rāshṭrakūṭa king Indra III, when he invaded and devastated Kanauj as stated in the copper-plate grants of his son Govinda IV.[4] This marriage with a Kuntala princess mentioned in the *Karpūramañjarī* is as unlikely as that in the *Viddhaśālabhañjikā*. We must not take these marriages seriously.

(6) In the description of the conquests of his patrons Rājaśekhara is carried away by his love for alliteration, not caring to see whether the conquests were possible. Thus in

1. See—

किञ्च पुन: परिणायित एवार्यपुत्रो मया । तद्यथा मगधाधिपस्य सुतामनङ्गलेखां मालवेन्द्रस्य दुहितरं रत्नावलीं प्रियदर्शनां च पाञ्चालनाथस्य तनयां विलासवतीमवन्तीश्वरसुतां केलिमतीं जालन्धरेशकुमारिकां लीलावतीं केरलराजपुत्रीं पत्रलेखामिति ।

2. The Paramāras had been established in Malwa towards the close of the 8th cen. A.D.

3. See—

अत्थि एत्थ दक्खिणावधे वच्छोमं णाम णअरं ।

Karpūramañjarī. ed. by Konow, p. 26.

and आत्थि दक्खिणावधे कुन्तलेसुं सअलजणवल्लहो वल्लहराओ णाम राआ ।

Ibid. p 33.

4. See the Sāngli and Cambay plates of Govinda IV.

describing the conquests of the Pratīhāra king Mahīpāla, he says :—

नमितमुरलमौलिः पाकलो मेकलानां
रणकलितकलिङ्गः केलितः केरलेन्दोः ।
अजनि जितकुलूतः कुन्तलानां कुठारो
हठहृतरमठश्रीः श्रीमहीपालदेवः ॥

In this verse Mahīpāla is credited with the conquests not only of the adjacent country of Kulūta in North India but also of such distant countries as Kerala, Murala and Kaliṅga. The only basis for this description seems to be alliteration. These conquests of Mahīpāla appear incredible in the political conditions of that age.

Rājaśekhara is very garrulous. While some of his *muktaka* verses have given interesting information about ancient poets, others have created insoluble problems for scholars. See *e.g.* the verses about three Kālidāsas[1] and three works of Daṇḍin.[2] He is quite unreliable. The more I study his works, the greater is my conviction that his statements must be taken not with the proverbial grain of salt but with a ton of it. It seems to me that he has unnecessarily complicated the plot of the *Viddhaśālabhañjikā* by mentioning the marriage of Kuvalayamālā, the daughter of Vīrapāla, with Karpūravarsha, the hero of the play. This was apparently in imitation of similar incidents at the end of the plays of Bhāsa and Kālidāsa. But that marriage is as fanciful as the others mentioned by his queen with the princesses of Magadha, Kerala *etc*.

The foregoing discussion will have shown that there is not a shred of evidence in favour of the theory that Vīrapāla of the *Viddhaśālabhañjikā* represents the Eastern Chālukya king Chālukya-Bhīma II. On the other hand, indisputable inscriptional evidence indicates that he must be identified with the Rāshṭrakūṭa king Baddiga-Amoghavarsha III.

1. See—
एकोऽपि जीयते हन्त कालिदासो न केनचित् ।
शृङ्गारे ललितोद्गारे कालिदासत्रयी किमु ॥
2. See—
त्रयोऽग्नयस्त्रयो वेदास्त्रयो धर्मास्त्रयो गुणाः ।
त्रयो दण्डिप्रबन्धाश्च त्रिषु लोकेषु विश्रुताः ॥

VIII. THE UDAYASUNDARĪKATHĀ OF SOḌḌHALA*

The *Udayasundarikathā* of Soḍḍhala was edited by Krishnamacharya from a single manuscript found in the Pārśvanātha-bhāṇḍāra at Pāṭaṇ in the former Baroḍā State, in the Gaekwāḍ's Oriental Series in 1920. It can be reckoned among the best *Champū Kāvyas* in Sanskrit and contains much valuable information for the history of Sanskrit literature. Still, it does not seem to have attracted the attention of scholars it deserves. Historians of Sanskrit literature have given no information about it beyond mentioning its author and determining its date.[1] Some have not even mentioned its name.[2] It is, therefore, proposed to give here some detailed information about it.

Several *Champūs* with imaginary themes are still extant, the earliest example of the type being the *Nalachampū* of Trivikramabhaṭṭa. Several of these *Champū-kāvyas* were written by Jaina poets, some of them being mentioned by Soḍḍhala's present work.

Sanskrit authors rarely give information about their family, date and place. But Soḍḍhala is, fortunately, an exception. He has written the present work partly on the model of Bāṇa's *Harshacharita*. As Bāṇa has done in the *Harshacharita*, Soḍḍhala has given considerable information about himself in the beginning and at the end of the *Udayasundarīkathā*. He was born in a Kāyastha family of Valabhī. This place (now known as Valā in Saurāshṭra) was the famous capital of the Maitraka dynasty for several centuries in the mediaeval age. Soḍḍhala gives the following traditionary or rather imaginary account of his family :—

* Prof. K. A. Nilakanta Sastri Felicitation Volume, pp 423 f.

1. Keith, *History of Sanskrit Literature*, p. 336.

2. S. K. De has not referred to the *Udayasundarikathā* in his *History of Sanskrit Literature*

"There lived in Valabhī a king named Śīlāditya. He had a brave and learned younger brother named Kalāditya. He defeated the king's enemy, Dharmapāla by name, and made him submit to him. Once upon a time the Rāja-lakshmī (Goddess of Royal Fortune) appeared in a dream before the king who was greatly worried on receiving a report from his spies that his ministers and other officers were scheming against him, and told him as follows :—"A *gaṇa* (attendant of Śiva) known as Kāyastha, as he always resided in water which is the *kāya* (body) of Śiva, lifted me up as I was sinking in the water of the ocean, having come out of it when it was churned by gods and demons with the help of the Mandara mountain. He then made me over to the gods. In the Kāyastha family descended from that Kāyastha *gaṇa*, your younger brother Kalāditya has been born. Give him this Garuḍa seal and entrust him with the administration of your realm." The king did as he was instructed. From that Gaṇa of Śiva, the Kāyastha family of Valabhī has descended."

We know of several such imaginary stories about the origin of the Kāyastha caste.[1] There were, however, as many as seven kings of the name of Śīlāditya in the Maitraka family of Valabhī, who ruled in the seventh and eighth centuries A.D. The poet evidently knew about them from tradition and so he has connected his family with them.

So ḍhala has given considerable information about his ancestors, fellow-students, friends and contemporaries in the present work. His family originally belonged to Lāṭa (Southern Gujarat). It held the important office of the Dhruva (Revenue-collector like the Mālguzār of modern times) of the following among other divisions[2]—Sikkarahārīya—72, Vāhirihāra—70,

1. Another imaginary story about the origin of the Kāyastha caste occurs in the Rewa stone inscription of Kalachuri Karṇa (dated A. D. 1048-49). See *C I.I.*, Vol. IV. pp. 266 f

2. These localities have kindly been identified for me by Dr. H. G. Shastri of Ahmedabad. Annapālīva is probably identical with Anāval in the Surat District It was the original home of the Anāvala Brāhmaṇas of South Gujarat. Vāhirihāra may be the same as Vihāra in the Olpāḍ *tālukā* of the Surat District, or Vāhara in the Mangrul *tāluka* of the same district. Sikkarahārī may be Siker in the Vālod *Mahāl* of the Surat District. The numbers following the names of these localities indicate the numbers of villages included in them.

and Annapālīya—70. Soḍḍhala mentions his ancestors—Chaṇḍapati, his son Sollapeya, and his son Sūra.[1] To Sūra Soḍḍhala was born from his wife Padmāvatī. This family enjoyed the patronage of the Chaulukya kings of Lāṭa. Soḍḍhala lost his father in his childhood. Then Gaṅgādhara, son of the then reigning king Goggirāja[2] of Lāṭa, brought him up. Goggirāja was succeeded by his son Kīrtirāja. His son Siṁharāja was a fellow-student of Soḍḍhala. They studied under a teacher named Chandra. Soḍḍhala gave evidence of poetic talent even in his student life. Later, as political condition in Lāṭa changed, Soḍḍhala migrated to Sthānaka (modern Ṭhāṇā near Bombay), the capital of the Northern Śilāhāras. He became a court-poet of the Śilāhāra king Chhittarāja. Once upon a time Soḍḍhala composed a beautiful verse containing the word *pradīpa*. Being charmed with it, Chhittarāja gave him the title of *Kavipradīpa*. Similar soubriquets (e.g. *Dīpaśikhā-Kālidāsa*, *Chhatra-Bhāravi*) are known to have been borne by some other Sanskrit poets.[3] Chhittarāja's brothers Nāgārjuna and Mummuṇirāja, who succeeded him one after the other, also treated Soḍḍhala with great respect.

At Sthānaka Soḍḍhala received a cordial invitation to come back to Lāṭa from Vatsarāja, who was a dear friend of the Śilāhāra king.[4] Once upon a time while Vatsarāja was sitting in his *Sabhā* with his courtiers and poets around him, a merchant showed him a collection of pearls. The king then uttered the following significant verse :—

एकैकशः प्रकीर्णैर्मुक्तामणिभिः किमेभिरेभिस्तु ।
यं सृजसि हन्त हारं तस्यान्यः कोऽपि परिभोगः ॥

1. *Udayasundarīkathā*, P. 12.

2. In the printed edition of the *Udayasundarīkathā* this name is given as *Gogirāja* (See Errata at the end), but it occurs in the form *Goggirāja* in inscriptions. See Bhandarkar's *List of Northern Inscriptions*, Nos. 1088 and 1092.

3 Kālidāsa received the soubriquet *Dīpaśikhā-Kālidāsa* on account of the verse *Sañchāriṇī dīpa-śikh-eva* in the *Raghuvaṁśa* (VI. 67), and Bhāravi that of *Chhatra-Bhāravi* on account of his verse *Utphulla-sthala-nalinī* etc. in the *Kirātārjunīya* (V, 39),

4. *Udayasundarīkathā*, p. 12.

(What is the use of these stray pearls ? If you make a necklace of them, it will give us rare pleasure.)

Soḍḍhala at once understood the suggested sense of the verse. When he came home, he said to himself. "The king has indeed rebuked me. He wants to suggest to me that instead of wasting my energy in composing stray verses of the *muktaka* type, I should compose a great *kāvya*. If such a *kāvya* is to be composed, it should rather be of the *champū* type than of the *gadya* or *padya* type." For the composition of such a work, he repaired to one of his villages, where he could get the necessary facilities and tranquility. He completed the composition in a few days. Thereafter, he started for the capital of Lāṭa with the *kāvya* tied in a piece of cloth. On his way through a dense forest he noticed a very white shrine of Goddess Sarasvatī.[1] He entered it and praised the goddess with an *extempore* verse. As it was evening and his fellow-travellers had gone ahead, he sat down in a *mattavāraṇaka* (aisle)[2] of the *maṇḍapa* of the shrine for rest. He then noticed two beautiful statues of door-keepers, one on each side of the *garbha-gṛiha*. At night there arose a bright flame of light, not fed by oil. Immediately thereafter, there issued from the statues two heavenly beings, wearing the sacred thread. They praised the goddess with an *extempore* verse and sat in the opposite *mattavāraṇaka*. They then asked the poet about the book on his bed. The poet also felt curious about the surprising incident and said, "I shall tell you about it. But first tell me who you are." Then one of them replied, "This noble companion of mine is Tilaka and I am Tālaka. Being always with the Goddess Sarasvatī we have attained poetic talent. But tell us what your book is about." The poet then said, "This is my own *kāvya*. It will remain tied like this until I have a good poet willing to listen to its reading." On this they pressed him to read it out to them. Then the poet said, "I have sent my

1. This shrine is described as having been built by Bhārgava. So it may not have been distant from Bhṛigukachchha (Broach).

2. Soḍḍhala has used this word in many places. *Mattavāraṇī*, from which it is apparently derived, denotes a wing in Bharata's *Nāṭyaśāstra* as shown by me elsewhere. *Mattavāraṇaka* is used here to denote 'an aisle' separated from the middle portion of the hall by a row of pillars, Later. *mattavāraṇa* came to denote 'a verandah'.

attendants to fetch some fuel-sticks for lighting a fire; but now it is not necessary. I shall arrange my bed in the attached shrine of the Kshetrapāla and then coming back here, I shall read it out to you." That being done, he came back to the *mattavāraṇaka* and taking the book out of the bundle, he began to read it aloud (*Uchchhvāsa* I).

The Udayasundarīkathā

In the magnificent city of Pratishṭhāna[1] on the bank of the Godāvarī in the country of Kuntala there reigned a great king named Malayavāhana. One day, while he was sitting in his assembly, the door-keeper came and informed him of the return of the gardener Vasantaśīla, who had gone to the town of Nandāvaṭa[2] in the Ābhīra country[3] with the king's permission. When he was ushered in, the king asked him to state if he had noticed any thing noteworthy in his journey.

The Story of the parrot Chitraśikha

Vasantaśīla said, "As I was returning, I noticed a Buddhist *chaitya*. When I had seen it in the morning, it appeared quite white, but then it appeared very green. Just then I heard the followlng verse recited by some one :—

अहो वैचित्र्यमेतस्य संसारस्य किमुच्यते ।
गुणोऽपि क्लेशहेतुः स्याद्विभ्रान्तः क्वापि देहिनि ।।

(Oh ! How wonderful is this worldly condition ! Even a good quality of an embodied being becomes a cause of trouble to him !)

Just then I noticed a parrot of bright lustre issuing out of the *chaitya*, It was by his lustre that the *chaitya* had appear-

1. Modern Paiṭhaṇ, the ancient capital of the Sātavāhanas. It lies on the northern bank of the Godāvarī. Generally, the country to the south of the Godāvarī was known as Kuntalā.

2. Soḍḍhala has given imaginary names of places in some cases, but this name may be true. The modern places corresponding to it seem to be Nāndurkheḍe in the Rāver *tālukā* and Nāndeḍ in the Amaḷner *tālukā* of Khāndesh. Of them, Nāndeḍ is nearer to the Tāpī. From the description in the story it seems to be old Nandāvaṭa.

3. Ābhīra deśa is modern Khāndesh. It still has a large population of the Ābhiras (Ahīrs). See the later mention of the river Tāpī.

ed green. It was he who had uttered the verse. To catch him for being presented to Your Majesty, I ran after him, but he outstripped me. Running after him, I came to the bank of the river Tāpī, where I noticed a hut near a threshing floor. As it was then evening, I sat down to take rest there. Soon there came a farmer with a load of grass on his head and the parrot tied with a rope in his hand. He welcomed me and treated me to his frugal meal. To my question, "How did you catch this parrot," he replied, "I noticed him on an ear of corn as I was going about for grass. I caught him in a snare stealthily. I shall now offer him to my pregnant wife." I entreated him to hand it over to me, but he declined and prepared a cage for him. Just then the parrot uttered the following Āryā—

एकेन ध्रियमाणः पलायितोऽन्यस्य गोचरे पतितः ।
गतोऽन्यस्य मुखे किल यदहमहो बलवती नियतिः ॥

(I escaped from the grasp of one person to fall into the hands of another. Now I am going to fall into the mouth of a third one. How powerful is Fate !)

The farmer was struck with terror when he heard the parrot talking in Sanskrit and fled away. I have come to offer him to Your Majesty."

When the parrot was taken out of the cage, he addressed the king in the following verse :—

वृत्तिः सम्प्रति कार्पण्यो च किमपि त्यागप्रवीरे हठं
विश्रान्ता त्वयि नाथ येन भवता ब्रह्माण्डनामा घटः ।
सद्यः सद्गुणरत्नराशिभिरसौ भृत्वा निधानीकृतः
क्वान्यत्रोपरि विस्फुरत्यनिभृतं ज्योतिःप्रतापस्तव ॥

[Oh King ! You are indeed foremost among donors ! But how miserly now is this attitude of yours ! For, you have filled to the brim this (enormous) jar of Brahmāṇḍa with the jewels of your merits and stowed it away in some secret place. And in order to protect it you have spread everywhere this lustre of (your) valour !]

When the king asked him to narrate his account, the parrot said, "I was born in the hollow of an old banyan tree in the dense jungle of the Sahya mountain. From my very birth I have this *śikhā* (tuft of hair) on my head. At its sight my people deserted me, but the sylvan deity Śāradī brought me up. As this *śikhā* grew, my knowledge of the śāstras, Purāṇas *etc.* also increased. The deity then allowed me to fly away. But as I began to fly, other parrots, noticing this wonderful *śikhā* on my head, began to harass me with their beaks. So I entered the hole of a *chaitya* and uttered the verse अहो वैचित्र्यमेतस्य etc. with reference to this *śikhā*. This gardener attempted to catch me, but I escaped. Later, I was caught by a farmer and now I am in the presence of Your Majesty, who have been blessed by sylvan deities for good government." The king then ordered that the parrot should be kept in a jewelled cage (*Uchchhvāsa* II).

After spending some days in pleasant conversation with the parrot, the king took him with himself when he went ahunting. In the course of hunting he came to a pleasure-garden named Kusumasundara. It had a *maṇḍapa* decorated with jewelled statues of damsels. As the king was engaged in looking at the lovely scenery of the garden, he heard the following verse uttered by some one :—

हे चन्द्रोपलगौरि ! हे मरकतश्यामाभिरामाकृते !
हे चामीकरभिन्नवर्णसुभगे ! हे पद्मरागाम्बरे !
एषा पश्यत हन्त ! वज्रघटिता दूरे फलं वाञ्छितं
दत्ते नोत्तरमात्रमप्यतिशठा चाटूक्तिदीनस्य मे ॥

(O you as fair-complexioned as the moon-stone ! O you of lovely emerald-like dark complexion ! O you of beautiful golden complexion ! O you clad in a ruby-like garment ! See this diamond-fabricated damsel. Exceedingly crafty as she is, she, far from giving me the desired fruit, does not even reply to me though I entreat her in flattering words.)

Vasantaśīla then said to the king, "In the hurry of this morning, I forgot to feed this parrot. Seeing the lotus-like pomegranate in the hand of a Śālabhañjikā, this Chitraśikha is making this complaint to her friends." Just then the parrot issued out of his cage after breaking its coral-made door and began to peck at the pomegranate in the hand of the Śālabhañjikā. He broke his beak in the attempt. And lo ! There issued from his body a handsome youth of eighteen years. At the same time Vasantaśīla picked up what had fallen from the parrot's body. It was a beautiful portrait of the king. Then Siṁhalāgaṇḍa, a General of the king, stepped forward and said, "Pāñchālasiṁha, the Commander of Your Majesty's forces, had taken this portrait with himself when he started for *digvijaya*. He had forgotten it on an island. This is the same portrait." Just then the king noticed another thing on the floor. It turned out to be the portrait of a lovely lady. Struck with wonder at these incidents, the king asked the youth to narrate his account (*Uchchhvāsa* III).

The Story of Kumārakesarī

The youth said, "Your Majesty, there is a well-known city named Mathurā in Uttarāpatha, where king Kandarpaketu is reigning. I am his son Kumārakesarī. Being addicted to gambling, I spent the whole treasure of my father in betting. I then thought of conquering and looting the golden city of Laṅkā in the south for obtaining the wealth necessary for gambling, and effected my escape from the capital, unnoticed by servants and others. After some days I reached a forest on the bank of the Narmadā. At night I took shelter in a dilapidated temple of Kātyāyanī (Chaṇḍikā). There came a Kāpālika carrying a *khaṭvāṅga*, his body being smeared with ashes and his matted hair tied with bones and skulls.[1] I told him my account. He then presented me with a heavenly sword. I lost it, however, to a gambler, but I won his aircraft. I began to fly in it, but it crashed in the sea. I thought that my end had come, but no ! I found myself standing in a temple of Śiva. As I was resting in the *mattavāraṇaka*, there came a large group of young women, including a very lovely unmarried girl. She repaired to the garden attached to the temple to pick up flowers together with her friends. In the meanwhile her attendant left a portrait covered in a piece of heavenly cloth in the tem-

1. Here a considerable portion of the MS. has been lost. (See the note on p. 62). It has been conjecturally restored from the description on pp. 37-38.

ple, and followed the other girls. When I opened it I noticed that it was a beautiful portrait of Your Majesty, Just then I unwittingly stepped on a ruby-shell used in worship and broke it to pieces. The female hermit of the shrine then cursed me as follows :—"As you broke a ruby shell, you will be born as a parrot with a beak of the same colour and this portrait will be turned into a *śikhā* (crest) on your head." Hearing her angry words, the young girl came there and persuaded the hermit to revoke her curse. She then relented and said. "Even in his parrot-life he will be able to lead his life like a human being and when his beak will break in a temple of Śiva, he will be restored to his original form." All that has now come to pass. I have come here as I had heard about the fame of your Kuntala country. Since the lovely maiden has carefully preserved your portrait, she will surely be yours." The king then returned to his capital (*Uchchhvāsa* IV).

The king fell in love with the damsel whose portrait it was. His pangs of love increased as days passed by. One moonlit night he noticed a large mass of darkness coming down from above near him and soon thereafter he heard a piteous cry. He proceeded to investigate it, sword in hand, and soon noticed a terrible demon ready to kill a hermit girl of fourteen years in a lonely temple of Chaṇḍikā. The king fought with him and vanquished him after a terrible struggle. The demon then submitted to the king and presenting his sword to him, he promised to present himself as soon as the king thought of him. When the king asked him about his account, he told him as follows :—

The Story of Māyābala

"There is in the South a prosperous city named Laṅkā, where rules Bibhīshaṇa who owed his throne to the grace of Rāma. I am his maternal cousin. Once, while King Bibhīshaṇa was sitting in his assembly, there appeared before him a spirit named Kaṅkālaka, who reported that a brave prince of Mathurā named Kumārakesarī had started for Laṅkā for obtaining wealth. Then King Bibhīshaṇa ordered me to take Kaṅkālaka with me and with his help to kill the prince. I noticed him in a temple of Chaṇḍikā. He had just then received a magic sword from a Kāpālika who was pleased to hear his account. He had become invincible by that sword. So in order to take it away from him, I turned Kaṅkālaka into an aircraft and assuming myself the form of a Vidyādhara, I went to the temple of Chaṇḍikā and challenged him to gamble. In the game I deceitfully made him lose the sword but win the aircraft. He left for Laṅkā by that aircraft. Kaṅkālaka, who had transformed himself into that aircraft, made it crash into the sea. I then repaired to Laṅkā together with Kaṅkālaka and told King Bibhīshaṇa what had occurred. He presented this sword to me. I noticed this hermit girl roaming about in Laṅkā. I fell in love with her, but she suddenly flew into the air. I pursued her and wanted to kill her here when Your Majesty came to her rescue." The King then allowed him to go away.

In order to hear the account of the hermit girl, the king went to the *maṭha* of Viśvabhūti, a female hermit in the capital (*Uchchhvāsa* V).

The Story of Tārāvalī

The hermit girl gave the following account about herself when the King questioned her—

"Besides the earth and heaven there is a third world called Pātāla where reigns King Bali, who obtained his kingdom by the grace of Vishṇu in his Dwarf incarnation. In that region there is a city named Indīvara where King Śikhaṇḍatilaka holds sway. He has a daughter named Udayasundarī from his queen Vijayarekhā. At her birth, astrologers had foretold that she would marry an incarnation of God Vishṇu. I am her dear friend of the same age, Tārāvalī by name, the daughter of the King's Commander-in-Chief. Once upon a time a Kinnara couple dropped a rolled portrait before her. Udayasundarī felt attracted by the portrait of a Cupid-like young man and began to languish by the pangs of love. Once upon a time an old hermit named Pātālagaṇa told her that he had seen the young man whose portrait it was when he had halted for some time on the earth while fetching celestial flowers from heaven for the worship of God Hāṭakeśvara, but he had not made any further inquiries about him. I then got another portrait—

that of Udayasundarī—painted on another piece of canvas. As directed by her mother, Udayasundarī goes to the temple of Hāṭakeśvara for the *darśana* of the God. Once upon a time as she was picking up flowers for the worship of Hāṭakeśvara with her friends, she heard the angry words of the female hermit. She then rushed inside and prevailed upon her to revoke her curse. But the portraits which had been left there by her attendant got transformed into the *śikhā* of a parrot and disappeared all of a sudden. She felt extremely grieved by this incident and since then has been suffering from pangs of separation.

Once Udayasundarī, sleeping on the terrace of her mansion disappeared all of a sudden. Her father sent his Nāga servants in all directions in search of her. I thought that it might be an act of some Rākshasa. So I went to Laṅkā in search of my friend, but there this Rākshasa began to molest me. You have kindly rescued me from his clutches. On seeing you, I feel convinced that you are the person with whom Udayasundarī has fallen in love. But what country is this ? Who are you having on your person the signs of sovereignty ? Is this your capital ? Shall I even now succeed in tracing the lover of my friend Udayasundarī ?"

The King then arranged for her residence in the monastery of Viśvabhūti and himself repaired to his palace (*Uchchhvāsa* VI).

Next day the King performed his daily duties and worshipped the family deities. Then he repaired to the monastery of Viśvabhūti together with Kumārakesarī. Tārāvalī recognised the latter as soon as she saw him and said, "This is he for whom my friend Udayasundarī interceded and made the female hermit revoke her curse." Tārāvalī could not bear the grief of separation from Udayasundarī and one morning she left the monastery on the pretext of gathering flowers. The King spent several days in search for her.

One day a Chief of the Kirātas brought an excellent mare to the King and said, "As I was roaming on the outskirts of the Vindhya mountain, this mare all of a sudden descended from the sky in front of me. She is of such excellent breed that no ordinary person deserves to ride her. Be pleased to accept her." Kumārakesarī also praised her good signs, and requested the king to ride her. Just then the guardian of the neighbouring garden rushed to the place and reported the destruction that a huge monkey was causing in the garden. The king at once mounted the mare and pursued the monkey. The latter brought him to a dense forest and then disappeared. The king sought him in different parts of the forest and ultimately came to the bank of a large lake. Just then he noticed a jewel thrown up by the mare's hoof. At its touch the mare regained her original form. She was Tārāvalī. She at once began to run in the direction of a mansion behind a wall inside a hill. Udayasundarī emerged from it and, seeing her friend Tārāvalī, gave her a close embrace.

Then they all sat together. Then Udayasundarī said, "That night I was sleeping on the terrace of our mansion; but when I woke up, I found myself brought by a large monkey to the bank of this lake. He pushed aside the wall and kept me in this Ruby Palace." Tārāvalī also told her own account. She said, "I could not bear to see the pangs of Your Majesty after you saw Udayasundarī's portrait. So I left on the pretext of gathering flowers and as I was flying through the sky, I noticed a cistern of water. But as soon as I began to sip its water I was turned into a mare. Further I do not know."

Udayasundarī was so overwhelmed by grief, when she heard about the hardships her friend Tārāvalī had suffered on her account, that she fell into a swoon; but she regained consciousness when the king sprinkled water on her. The king then accepted the hand of Udayasundarī and narrated how he came there from the monastery of Viśvabhūti. (*Uchchhvāsa* VII).

When the monkey found that the king had deprived him of Udayasundarī, he in rage attacked him, but when the king slapped him on his cheek, he was turned into a celestial being. On being asked by the king, he narrated his own account as follows :—

The Story of Tārākirīṭa

He said, "I am a Vidyādhara, Tārākirīṭa by name. Once, when I had gone to the Nāga-loka for the *darśana* of Hāṭakeśvara, I noticed this Udayasundarī sleeping on the terrace of a mansion. I was attracted by her superb beauty and so I placed her in my aircraft and began to fly. My aircraft struck a sage who was practising penance on the bank of the Ākāśa-Gaṅgā. He lost his temper and cursed me that I would be turned into a monkey. But when he noticed her, he relented and asked me to take her to the Ruby Mansion which he was constructing near the lake Kuvalayāmoda in the vicinity of the mountain Raviśṛiṅga. "You should guard her there. This jewel called *kiraṇakośa*, produced from the ocean, will protect her from poison, swoon, transformation *etc.*" Saying so he placed it in her hair." The Vidyādhara then disappeared.

As the king was wondering where they were and how they would reach Pratishṭhāna, there came two birds. They circumabulated the king and assumed their original forms. Then one of them said to the king, "Your Majesty, I am that Rākshasa Māyābala whom you had ordered to search for that lovely damsel. This is a Nāga named Dambholi, who has been commissioned by Udayasundarī's father to search for her. We met at Somanātha in Saurāshṭra. As we both had the same object in view, we assumed the forms of birds and flew in company. We noticed Your Majesty here."

Then Māyābala turned himself into an aeroplane. They all reached Pratishṭhāna by that plane. Then Māyābala left for Laṅkā and Dambholi for the Nāgaloka to acquaint Udayasundarī's father with what had happened.

Soḍḍhala has described the hurried activities of the town-ladies as they gathered to have a look at Malayavāhana and Udayasundarī when they were passing through the city as Kālidāsa has done on a similar occasion in the *Raghuvaṁśa*.

Malayavāhana then offered Tārāvalī to Kumārakesarī. There was a great nuptial festivity in Pratishṭhāna. Malayavāhana thereafter spent his days happily in the company of his queen Udayasundarī, his friend Kumārakesarī and his wife Tārāvalī.

* * * *

After reading out the story of Udayasundarī Soḍḍhala again tied the book in the piece of cloth. Then Tālaka praised it very much. He said, "We have listened to your *prabandha*. It has all the merits which the former rhetoricians expected in a *kāvya*. Its story has an attractive beginning. The *sandhis* of the plot are well connected. Its *rasas* (sentiments) are quite clear. Its composition is charming to the ear. You have very cleverly woven in it practical wisdom. In short, it has a proper combination of all the three styles, *viz.* the Vaidarbhī or the Cuckoo *rīti*, the Gauḍī or the Peacock *rīti* and the Pāñchālī or the Swan *rīti*. He then recited an example of each. Soḍḍhala felt greatly surprised at this, and, with becoming modesty, inquired who they were and how they came to be there in the form of statues. Then Tālaka said, "This is Bāṇa, the *Kavīndra-tilaka* (ornament of great poets), the world-famous author of the *Kādambarī* and the *Harshacharita*, who belongs to the Vātsyāyana *gotra* and is a disciple of Sarasvatī. I am a humble Devarshi (divine sage) named Tālaka, a member of God Brahmā's assembly. Once, when I had gone to that assembly, I recited the following verse in praise of God Brahmā :—

ब्रह्मंस्त्वां स्तौमि तं यस्य पुष्पलिड्भिः प्रलक्षितम् ।
पाण्ड्वाभं वल्गु सुष्ट्वब्जं जन्मधिष्ण्यं च विष्टरम् ।।

(O God Brahman, I praise you who have a beautiful white lotus, surrounded by bees, for your birth-place as also for your seat.)

Being delighted by this composition of mine, I went to the assembly of Sarasvatī, where under the presidentship of poet Bāṇa several great poets such as Kālidāsa, kings like Vikramāditya, Śrī-Harsha, Muñja and Bhoja, and *sāmantas* like Vākpatirāja, Māyurāja and Viśākhadeva were engaged in poetic discussions. There I recited the verse. They all welcomed me and praised my composition. Only Bāṇa pointed out the fault of harsh wording (*aśravyapada*) in it.[1] Then I got

1. See the expressions *Pushpa-liḍbhiḥ*, *pāṇḍv-ābham*, *sushṭvabjam* in the verse.

angry and cursed him as follows, not minding that he was a dear disciple of Goddess Sarasvatī :—"O poetaster, as you remained dumb like a stone-pillar while I recited my verse here, you will have to stay for some time as a stone statue in a temple of Sarasvatī." There was a great commotion there. The poets gathered there entreated me to revoke the curse. Then I said, "This poet Bāṇa will become, by the light in the temple of Sarasvatī, proficient in all *śāstras* and a connoisseur of poetry. At night he will be able to shed off his stony form and become happy. When he will listen to the reading of the *Udayasundarīkathā*, he will be restored to his original form." When the Goddess Sarasvatī saw that her dear disciple Bāṇa was cursed, she gave me a similar curse. She said, "You will remain in Bāṇa's company and will be restored to your original form along with him.[1]" Since then we both have been staying here. At night the sylvan deity here arranges to provide us with a divine light. We know all about you." Saying so, he told Soḍḍhala all particulars about him such as his family, his royal patronage and so forth, and said, "Not only we but all great sages in heaven know about you." Bāṇa also praised his work and said, "Do not read out this work to all, but only to good people. You have attained the position of *Kavindra* (Great Poet)." Then they bowed to Goddess Sarasvatī and repaired to the world of Brahmā.

Then Soḍḍhala spent the night in the *mattavāraṇaka*, using the book as his pillow. In a dream at night he noticed that his name was written in the genealogy of poets, commencing from Vālmīki. In the morning he obtained an instrument of engraving from his attendants and engraved a *kavi-praśasti* (eulogy of poets) on the emerald wall of the temple. The *praśasti* included a *maṅgala-śloka* in praise of Śiva and then verses in eulogy of great poets of the past like Vālmīki, Vyāsa, Guṇāḍhya, Bhartṛimeṇṭha, Kālidāsa, Bāṇa, Bhavabhūti, Vākpatirāja, Abhinanda, Yāyāvara and Kumāradāsa. Thereafter he inscribed the following verses about himself :

तस्मिन्सुवंशे कविमौक्तिकानामुत्पत्तिभूमौ क्वचिदेकदेशे ।
कश्चित्कविः सोड्ढल इत्यजातनिष्पत्तिरासीज्जलबिन्दुरेव ॥

1. Here also some portion of the text is lost.

यो वत्सराजेन वरेण राज्ञां लाटावलीमण्डलनायकेन ।
सूक्ष्माद्दृढस्तोकगुणाश्रितोपि मित्रीकृतो भानुमतेव पद्मः ॥
जडेन तेनोदयसुन्दरीति कथा दुरालोकिनि काव्यमार्गे ।
सारस्वतालोकलवैकदृष्टा सृष्टा कविमन्यमनोरथेन ॥
सा चात्र देवीभवने निवृत्तशापार्तिना बाणकवीश्वरेण ।
कविश्रमोद्भूतकृपेण सम्यक् श्रुता धृता हृद्यमिनन्दिता च ॥

(In that great bamboo-like family, which has produced pearl-like poets, there was born in a certain place a poet named Soḍḍhala, like a drop of water that has not yet attained the shape of a pearl.

Vatsarāja, the best of kings and the lord of the Lāṭa country, regarded him as a friend, notwithstanding his insignificant, infirm and slight merits, even as the sun treats a lotus. That dull-witted Soḍḍhala, with the ambition of becoming a poet, has composed the *Udayasundarīkathā*, which, by its insignificant merit, has obtained a place in the inaccessible realm of poetry. In this temple of Sarasvatī, Bāṇa, the foremost among poets, listened to it out of sympathy for the poet's labour, when he was freed from the anguish of a curse and bestowed his praise on it.)

After praising and worshipping Sarasvatī, Soḍḍhala returned to the capital. There his *prabandha* was read and praised by poets such as the Śvetāmbara Jaina *Mahākavi* Chandanāchārya, the author of the *kathā Aśokavatī*, and *Śīghrakavi* Vijayasiṁhāchārya, the author of the *Khaḍga-kāvya*, who had been honoured with the title of *Khaḍgāchārya* by (the Śilāhāra king) Nāgārjuna, the Digambarāchārya Mahākīrti, who was conversant with three languages, and Indra, the author of the *Champūkathā Ratnamañjarī*.[1] Some days after, King Mummuṇi of Koṅkaṇa sent his poet-friend Madhurasāhāra, who was brave and proficient in three languages, to call Soḍḍhala to his court. He met the poet and told him, "King Mummuṇi has heard that you have composed a *kathā* named *Udayasundarī*, which you read out to Bāṇa in a temple of Sarasvatī in a lonely forest and that it was praised by him.

1. These authors and their works are not known from any other work.

King Mummuṇi's friend Vatsarāja, King of Lāṭa, saw the *praśasti* written by you in the temple of Sarasvatī while on his way from Śūrpāraka.[1] He thought that you had written the *kathā* with reference to the Āryā he had uttered in his court, and called you to meet him and read your work. He told Mummuṇi about it and about the praise bestowed on it by Bāṇa. Having heard that surprising account, King Mummuṇi has sent me to fetch you." When Soḍḍhala accompanied him to the court of Mummuṇi, the latter asked him to read out the work to him. Soḍḍhala took it out from its cloth wrapper and first praised the Goddess Sarasvatī and then the following great predecessors of his :—

वागीश्वरं हन्त ! भजेऽभिनन्द-
मर्थेश्वरं वाक्पतिराजमीडे ।
रसेश्वरं नौमि च कालिदासं
बाणं तु सर्वेश्वरमानतोऽस्मि ॥

(I bow to Abhinanda, who is a master of words, to Vākpatirāja, who is a lord of sense, to Kālidāsa, who is proficient in the delineation of sentiments, and to Bāṇa, who excels in all these.)

All these poets are well known. Abhinanda, a poet of Gauḍa, the author of the *Rāmacharita*, flourished in the second half of the ninth century A. D. Several of his *subhāshitas* have been included in the earliest known anthology, the *Subhāshitaratnakosha* of Vidyākara. Vākpatirāja is the Prakrit poet of that name, the author of the *Gaüḍavaho* and the *Madhumathanavijaya*. Kālidāsa and Bāṇa are too well known to need any note.

King Mummuṇi honoured him with suitable presents. His courtiers congratulated him and his poet-friends embraced him closely. This gave him more joy than the overlordship of the three worlds. Soḍḍhala has ended his work with a verse in praise of Śiva (*Uchchhvāsa* VIII).

1. Śūrpāraka is modern Sopārā in the Ṭhāṇā District. It was the ancient capital of North Koṅkaṇ. Some edicts of Aśoka have been found there.

The date of Soḍḍhala does not present any difficulty, He enjoyed the patronage of the following three kings of North Koṅkaṇ :—

Chhittarāja[1] (known years 1026, 1034)
|
(brother)
Nāgārjuna (known year A.D. 1039)
|
(brother)
Mummuṇirāja[2] (known dates A.D. 1049, 1060)

So Soḍḍhala may have stayed at the court of the Śilāhāras from *circa* A.D. 1030 to 1045. He had also the support of the Chaulukyas of Lāṭa. The following three princes of this family have been named in the *Udayasundarīkathā*.

Goggirāja
|
Kīrtirāja[3] (known date A.D. 1018)
|
Vatsarāja
|
[Trilochanapāla[4] (A.D. 1051)]

Goggirāja's son Gaṅgādhara and Kīrtirāja's son Siṁharāja have been mentioned in the *Udayasundarīkathā*, but they did not come to the throne. No inscriptions of Vatsarāja have been discovered, but from the grants of his father and his son he seems to have flourished in the period *circa* A.D. 1030-1050. As described by Soḍḍhala, he was a contemporary of Mummuṇirāja. His date has thus been corroborated by the date of Soḍḍhala fixed above.

Soḍḍhala's *Udayasundarikathā* is modelled on Bāṇa's *Kādambarī*. Bāṇa's *Harshacharita* and *Kādambarī* are well known. As in the *Harshacharita*, Soḍḍhala has given in the beginning of his work an imaginary story about the origin of his family and furnished information about himself and his patron. But

1. *Ep. Ind.*, Vol. XII, pp, 250 f. ; *Z. D. M. G.*, Vol. XC, pp. 26 f.
2. *J. B. B. R. A. S.* (Old Series), Vol. XII, pp. 329 f.
3. Bhandarkar's *List of Northern Inscriptions* No. 1088.
4. *Ibid* , No. 1092. He is not mentioned in the *Udayasundarīkathā*.

Bāṇa's *Kādambarī* seems to have influenced his work more. Both these works are of the *Kathā* type, *i.e.* their stories are invented. The themes of both are very much complicated. The *Kādambarī* describes incidents which happened on the earth and in heaven, but the *Udayasundarīkathā* narrates some that happened in the *pātāla* (nether world) also. Both describe that some of their characters had, as a result of curses, to go through the lives of the parrot and the horse (or the mare). In both the parrots are learned and proficient in the Purāṇas and the Śāstras, and in both the horse (or the mare) is as swift as wind. Both the works are full of long compounds. Unlike Bāṇa, Soḍḍhala has not, however, used the *Ślesha* and other *alaṅkāras* to any appreciable extent. He relies mainly on *Utprekshās* for effect. His imagination does not take as high flights as Bāṇa's. In many places his description is of the stereotype. His story has more characters and is more complicated than that of the *Kādambarī*. Still, he has unravelled all the threads in the end.

Soḍḍhala had before him Bāṇa's *Kādambarī* as a model. So he has not only praised Bāṇa above all other poets, but has also brought him on the earth and made him praise his *Udayasundarīkathā*.

Soḍḍhala has used three *rītis* (styles), *viz.* Vaidarbhī, Gauḍī and Pāñchālī in his work. He calls them *Kaukilī* (of the cuckoo), *Māyūrī* (of the peacock) and *Mārālī* (of the swan) respectively. He generally uses the *Vaidarbhī* in verses and the *Gauḍī* in prose passages. His compounds in prose sometimes cover several pages at a time, but as he has not generally used *Ślesha* (*double entendre*), his style has not become difficult to understand. He has developed several *rasas* (sentiments) in his work. See *e.g.* the *Vipralambha Śṛiṅgāra* in the description of the pining Malayavāhana and Udayasundarī, *Bhayānaka* in that of the Kāpālika and the Rākshasa, *Bībhatsa* in that of the cemetery, and *Adbhuta* in that of the flying aeroplane. He has shown his love of nature and keen observation in the descriptions of gardens, forests and lakes. As an instance of his style, we may point to the following description of a journey through the air :—

आरूढे मयि झटित्येवोत्पत्य हरगलगरलकज्जलमलीमसं सुदूरमन्तरशिरोभागमारुरोह। ततः परमुपक्रान्तं प्रयातुम्। अनन्तरमारचितगुरुवेगनिर्गमप्रसरं परितो विस्फुरन्तीभिरतिधवलवैजयन्तीभिर्गगनगङ्गाडिण्डीरवल्लरीपटलमिव मरुता नीयमानम्, अनणुमणिकर्मनिर्मलोद्योतडम्बरेण प्रदीपतन्त्रमिव तिमिरविग्रहेणोच्चालितम्, उच्चलत्किंकिणीरणत्कारनिःस्वनैर्वेगोज्झितसमीरमिवारब्धविजयकोलाहलम्, उल्ललद्ध्वजपटफटत्कारितोपकण्ठकनकदण्डिकादारितनमस्तलम्, उल्लोठिताध्वजलधरम्, उत्सारिताग्रतारकं, स्वरूपमविकृत्य त्वरितमन्तरिक्षेण गच्छतस्तस्य तिमिरपटलोन्मूलितालोकवृत्तिरहमन्धेन नीयमानोऽन्ध इव, क इव ककुभो विभागः, कियदतिक्रान्तं पश्चात्, अग्रेऽपि कियद्गन्तव्यम्, कीदृशी चासौ वसुमती, कीदृशा हि गिरिसरित्कान्तारपरिगताः पन्थानः, कीदृशोऽप्यसौ जनपदप्रचार इति न जानामि, केवलं चरणचङ्क्रमणपीडाभिरुज्झितः पदे पदे मृदुसमीरलहरीनिवेशशीतलोचनो यानेन गतिसुखमनुभूतवानस्मि।

(As soon as I boarded the aeroplane at night, it flew up and rose high in the dense darkness resembling the collyrium-like poison in the throat of Śiva. Then it began its flight. As it flew with great speed, it appeared with its very white flags as if a mass of the foam of the Ākāśa-Gaṅgā (milky way) was being wafted by a strong wind. By the bright light of its large jewels it looked as if darkness was lifting up a large number of lights. With the jingling of the small bells attached to it, it seemed as if it was indulging in cries of victory as it surpassed even wind in its speed. With the golden staffs of its fluttering flags, it was, as it were, tearing the sky without altering its form. I could not notice any thing, my sight being clouded by darkness. Like a blind man led by another blind one, I did not know where I was, how much distance I had flown, how much more I had to go, what sort of country I was flying on, what were the paths of the mountains, rivers and forests, and the countries through which I was going. I only enjoyed the pleasure of travelling by the plane without experiencing any fatigue of going on foot, with my eyes feeling the cool touch of gentle breezes.)

Soḍḍhala had not indeed travelled by a plane, but this imaginary description given by him agrees with the experience of modern air passengers. This well exemplifies the flight of his imagination and his power of description.

Soḍḍhala has described or mentioned by name several of his predecessors and contemporaries. As his date is certain, the lower limit of the dates of these authors can be determined. Among his predecessors, Vālmīki, Vyāsa, Guṇāḍhya, Bhartṛimeṇṭha, Kālīdāsa, Bāṇa, Bhavabhūti, Vākpatirāja, Māyurāja[1] and Viśākhadeva are well known. Soḍḍhala, however, gives us the additional information that Vākpatirāja, Māyurāja and Viśākhadeva were *Sāmantas* or feudatories. From a *subhāshita* we know, of course, that Māyurāja was a prince of the Kalachuri family, but the information given here about Vākpatirāja and Viśākhadeva is new. Viśākhadeva is probably identical with Viśākhadatta,[2] the author of the Sanskrit plays, the *Mudrārākshasa* and the *Devi-Chandragupta*.

Soḍḍhala has mentioned some of his Jaina contemporaries, both of the Digambara and the Śvetāmbara sect, and their works, from which it appears that the Lāṭa (South Gujarat) country was then famous for Jaina literature. Unfortunately, none of the works of any of these Jaina authors has come down to us. Soḍḍhala's *Udayasundarīkathā* is a *Champū* work of early times. Some *Champū Kāvyas* of an earlier age such as the *Nalachampū* (or the *Damayantī-kathā*) of Trivikrama and the *Yaśastilaka-champū* of Somadeva are still extant, but they find no mention in Soḍḍhala's work. He has mentioned two *Champūkāvyas*, *viz*. the *Aśokavatī* of Chandanāchārya and the *Ratnamañjarī* of Indrakavi, but both of them have now been lost. Several *Champūs* such as the *Rāmāyaṇa-champū*, the *Bhārata-champū* and the *Bhāgavata-champū* were composed, but they have no intricate themes as in Soḍḍhala's work. In course of time the style of the Champūs became more and more obscure on account of a profuse use of *Ślesha*. The *Udayasundarī-kathā* of Soḍḍhala, being of an early age, has its own importance in the history of Sanskrit literature.

1. See *C. I. I.*, Vol. IV, Introd. p. clxxiii.

2. In the *Mudrārākshasa* he is described as the grandson of *Sāmanta* Vaṭeśvaradatta, and the son of *Mahārāja* Bhāskaradeva. In one MS. his name occurs as *Viśākhadeva*.

IX. MATTAVĀRAṆĪ

The *Nāṭyaśāstra* of Bharata is a work on dramaturgy unique not only in Sanskrit literature but also in the literature of the world. It contains a detailed discussion of various matters relating to dramas such as a rational interpretation of the joy we derive from dramas, the construction of the theatre, the metres used in Sanskrit plays, the acting and speeches of the *dramatis personae*, the varieties of Sanskrit plays, their constituent parts, music, song and dance to be employed in the plays, their object *etc*. In later times several works on dramaturgy such as the *Daśarūpaka*, the *Sāhityadarpaṇa* and the *Nāṭyadarpaṇa* were written, but in none of them we notice such a comprehensive treatment of dramaturgy. In respect of the ancient Indian theatre especially, our only source of information is the *Nāṭyaśāstra* of Bharata. We propose to discuss here one controversial topic in that work.

The date of Bharata's *Nāṭyaśāstra* is not yet certain, but it is generally held to be not later than the third century A.D. So more than fifteen hundred years have passed since its composition. In this long period several commentaries were written on it, but now only one of them, *viz*. the *Abhinavabhāratī* of Abhinavagupta, who flourished in the beginning of the eleventh century A.D., is now extant. Abhinavagupta flourished more than eight hundred years after Bharata. So though he was a learned and appreciative critic, he could not correctly grasp the meaning of Bharata's work; for he has given alternative meanings of some verses of Bharata. Recently a Sanskrit-knowing architect, who has put forward a new interpretation of Bharata's directions for the construction of the theatre says[1]—

1. *Nāṭyaśāstra* (Gaewad's Oriental Series), Vol. I (Second ed.), Appendix VI, p. 454.

अभिनवगुप्तोऽप्यनुभवलुप्तो ह्यनुमितमर्थं वितरति यत्र ।
अभिनवदृष्ट्या समुदितमर्थं प्रमुदितबुद्ध्या विमृशत तत्र ।

He means to say that we have no evidence that any theatres of the types described by Bharata were constructed in later times. We have not come across any in the excavations done so far. Abhinavagupta also may not have noticed them. So he has offered conjectural interpretation of the relevant verses of Bharata. It is wrong in many places. We must, therefore, interpret Bharata's verses independantly in order to understand his conception of the theatres. Prof. Subha Rao has tried to do so. The *Nāṭyaśāstra* contains several technical terms in its description of the theatre. Prof. Subba Rao has given a new interpretation of many of them. It is not intended to discuss all of them here. We propose to discuss only one of them, *viz. mattavāraṇī*, in regard to which there is a sharp difference of opinion among scholars.

The *Nāṭyaśāstra* has used the term *mattavāraṇī* in several places. Bharata has described three types of theatres, *viz. vikṛishṭa* (rectangular), *chaturasra* (square) and *tryasra* (triangular). After describing the *raṅga-pīṭha* (stage), *nepathya-gṛiha* (retiring room) and *preksha-gṛiha* (auditorium), Bharata says[1]—

रङ्गपीठस्य पार्श्वे तु कर्तव्या मत्तवारणी ।
चतुःस्तम्भसमायुक्ता रङ्गपीठप्रमाणतः ॥
अध्यर्धहस्तोत्सेधेन कर्तव्या मत्तवारणी ।
उत्सेधेन तयोस्तुल्यं कर्तव्यं रङ्गमण्डपम् ॥

(२, ६३-६५)

Again, while describing *raṅga-pīṭha* further, he says—

अष्टहस्तं तु कर्तव्यं रङ्गपीठप्रमाणतः ।
चतुरस्रं समतलं वेदिकासमलङ्कृतम् ॥
पूर्वप्रमाणनिर्दिष्टा कर्तव्या मत्तवारणी ।
चतुःस्तम्भसमायुक्ता वेदिकायास्तु पार्श्वतः ॥

(२, ९७-९९)

God Brahmā composed the Nāṭya-veda for the diversion of the people of all castes and asked Bharata to teach it to actors. He also created the Apsarās necessary for the perfor-

1. The references are to the Critical Edition in G. O.S.

mance of plays. After all the necessary arrangements for the performance had been made, the play commenced in a *Nāṭya-maṇḍapa*. But the demons caused obstacles in it. Then Indra subdued them with his flag-staff, which since then came to be known as *jarjara*. Still the demons continued to obstruct. So Brahmā asked the divine architect Viśvakarmā to construct a theatre and when it was completed, he installed various deities to protect it. In that connection occur the following verses :—

पार्श्वे च रङ्गपीठस्य महेन्द्रः स्थितवान् स्वयम् ।
स्थापिता मत्तवारण्यां विद्युद्दैत्यनिषूदिनी ॥
स्तम्भेषु मत्तवारण्याः स्थापिताः परिपालने ।
भूतयक्षपिशाचाश्च गुह्यकाश्च महाबलाः ॥

(१, ८०-८१)

These verses state that Brahmā appointed *Vidyut* for the protection of the *mattavāraṇī* and the *yakshas* and others for that of its pillars. Later, in the third *adhyāya* it is laid down that these deities should be worshipped with flowers, honey and milk-offerings. In this connection it is stated—

अनेनैव विधानेन सम्पूज्या मत्तवारणी ।
पक्वामेन तु मांसेन संपूज्या रक्षसां गणाः ॥

All these statements show the importance of the *mattavā-raṇī*. But scholars are not agreed about the meaning of the *mattavāraṇī*. Many have assumed it to be a part of the *Raṅga-pīṭha* as shown in the following sketch of the Rectangular Theatre[1] :—

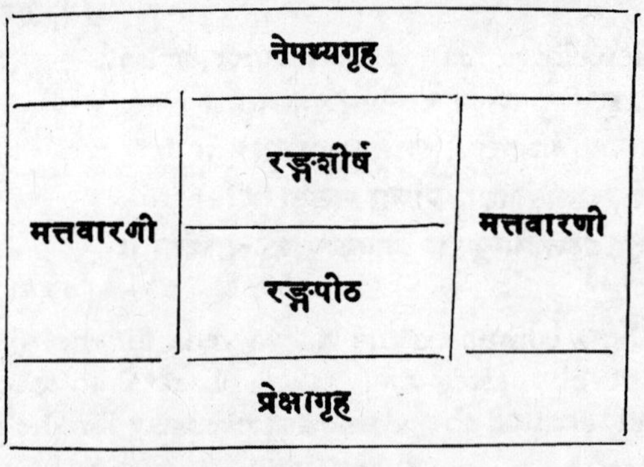

1. *Ind. Hist. Quart.*, Vol. VIII, p. 481.

Many scholars have accepted this position of the *mattavāraṇis*. But they are not agreed about the derivation of the term. Some have offered no explanation of it, while others have connected it with elephants. The word *matta* (intoxicated) in the term may have suggested this explanation ; for elephants, when in rut, are 'intoxicated'. Some others say that the part of the stage may have been so called because the pillars there had large figures of elephants.[1]

Dr. H.R. Divekar has suggested another explanation.[2] He connects the term with the elephant-fights that were in vogue in ancient times for diversion of princes. In this sport there were erected two *maṇḍapas* for elephants on the two sides of a *vedī* or raised platform. Before the sport began, there used to be a curtain hung between the two *maṇḍapas* in order that the two elephants should not see each other. At the commencement of the sport the curtain was removed and the elephants were made to fight with each other. The elephant which routed its competitor and made it turn back to its *maṇḍapa* was declared victorious. Dr. Divekar has shown that Kālidāsa has referred to this royal sport in the *Raghuvaṁśa* (XII, 93). The *maṇḍapa* erected for this sport had the name *mattavāraṇi*, which was also applied to the two small enclosures on the two sides of the stage.

Prof. Subba Rao does not agree with this explanation. He takes the word *mattavāraṇi* as an adjective, not of *kakshyā* (apartment) but of *śreṇī* (a row) understood. He takes the term to mean a row of intoxicated elephants. The hemistich रङ्गपीठस्य पार्श्वे तु कर्तव्या मत्तवारणी means that a frieze of such elephants was carved in front on the plinth of the stage (*raṅgapīṭha*). He takes the expression *adhy-ardha-hasta* in the passage to mean that the height of the carved elephants was to be more than half a cubit (*adhy-ardha-hasta*), *i.e.* more than nine inches.[3] This *mattavāraṇī* had four pillars carved on the frieze as they were necessary to be shown to curb the elephants which were intoxicated.

1 *Dr Mirashi Felicitation Volume*, p. 134.

2. *Journal of Oriental Institute*, Vol. X, pp. 435 f

3. *Nāṭyaśāstra* (Second Ed), p. 440.

Prof. Subba Rao is a renowned architect with a good knowledge of Sanskrit. He has offered better explanations of some statements in Bharata's *Nāṭyaśāstra*,[1] but we cannot accept his interpretation of the aforementioned hemistich. The expression *raṅga-pīṭhasya pārśve* means 'on a side of the stage', not 'on the plinth of the stage'. Besides, Bharata refers to not one but two *mattavāraṇis* as *e.g.* in the following verse :—

अध्यर्धहस्तोत्सेधेन कर्तव्या मत्तवारणी ।
उत्सेधेन तयोस्तुल्यं कर्तव्यं रङ्गमण्डपम् ॥

The word *tayoḥ* in this verse indicates that there were two *mattavāraṇīs* on the two sides of the stage which were one and a half cubit in height and that the stage also was of the same height. *Adhy-ardha* means one and a half, not 'more than a half' as Subha Rao supposes. As stated before, the *Nāṭyaśāstra* provides for the protection of these *mattavāraṇīs* and their pillars and also lays down their worship with flowers, honey and milk-offerings. There is no purpose served by the worship of the frieze of elephants carved in front of the plinth of the stage.[2]

Besides, the expression *mattavāraṇi* cannot denote a mad or intoxicated elephant. All scholars who have attempted to explain the expression take it as a Bahuvrīhi compound, which they dissolve as मत्ता वारणा यस्यां सा मत्तवारणी कक्ष्या श्रेणिर्वा । But if that had been the intended meaning of it, the feminine form of the compound would have been *mattavāraṇā*, not *mattavāraṇi*, according to the Paṇinian sūtra अजाद्यतष्टाप् ।[3] So *vāraṇa* in that compound cannot mean 'an elephant'.

What is then the meaning of the expression *mattavāraṇi* ? It is a Tatpurusha compound and should be understood as मत्तानां राक्षसादीनां वारणी मत्तवारणी. As the affix is *lyuṭ*, the feminine form of the compound would be formed with the affix ङीप्. So the form is *mattavāraṇi*.

The *Nāṭyaśāstra* shows great anxiety for the protection of the stage and the auditorium. It recommends the installation

1. See e. g. his explanation of the terms *Raṅga-pīṭha*, *Shaḍ-dāruka* etc.

2. See Dr. Divekar's criticism of his explanations. *Journ. Or. Inst.*, Vol. X, pp. 431 f.

3. *Vāraṇa* is formed with the affix *lyu*. See वारण: वारयति शत्रुबलम् ल्यु: । in Bhānujī Dīkshit's com. on *Amarakosha*, II, 34.

of gods for the protection of their various parts and the worship of the latter with flowers and offerings. The theatre has the *prekshāgṛiha* in front and the *nepathyagṛiha* (tiring room) at the back. So there was not much need for protection on these two sides. But there was danger of attack from demons on the other two sides. So two small apartments were constructed for the protection of the stage on its two sides. They were appropriately named *mattavāraṇī* 'Warders of the intoxicated (demons).'

Bharata does not state what purpose was served by these *mattavāraṇīs*. He, however, mentions two doors for the entry on the *raṅgapīṭha* (Stage) from the *nepathya-gṛiha*(tiring room).[1] They were evidently used by the actors for approach to the two *mattavāraṇīs* which were like the wings of the modern theatre. Otherwise, even one door would have been sufficient for access to the *raṅga-pīṭha* from the *nepathya-gṛiha*. Besides, there was a curtain at the back of the Stage.

The *Nāṭyaśāstra* mentions the *raṅga-pīṭha* and *raṅga-śīrsha* separately. Abhinavagupta takes them as denoting two different parts of the Stage. He says that actors after they were properly equipped, used to enter the *raṅga-śīrsha* and wait there till their time of appearance on the Stage.[2] In another place he says that the actors use the *raṅga-śīrsha* for taking rest. Others, however, hold the view that the two terms denoted only the Stage. In that case, the two *mattavāraṇīs* must have served the same purpose as the *raṅga-śīrsha* in Abhinavagupta's interpretation.

As stated before, we have no description of the ancient stage in any later work on dramaturgy. But the expression *mattavāraṇī* is noticed in a few works of Sanskrit literature in the sense of an aisle, *i.e.* space on each side of a hall separated from its nave by a row of pillars. We shall turn to it now.

1. *Nāṭyaśāstra*, II, p. 39.

2. See Abhinavagupta's com., p. 56—अष्टहस्तं रङ्गशिरः। प्रविशतां पात्राणां चान्तःस्थानम्। तत्पात्राणां विश्रान्त्यै अगच्छतां च गुप्त्यै रङ्गस्य शोभायै रङ्गशिरः कार्यम्।

The expression occurs in the Sanskrit play *Bālarāmāyaṇa* of Rājaśekhara, who flourished in the tenth century A.D. The fourth Act of the play shows Paraśurāma as defeated by Rāma.

In that Act there is a scene in which Daśaratha is shown as returning to the earth in Indra's chariot from heaven in view of the impending conflict of Rāma and Paraśurāma. On the way, Daśaratha asks the charioteer Mātali if Indra has great regard for Paraśurāma. To this the charioteer replies in the affirmative and tells him in the following verse that Indra has got the exploits of Paraśurāma painted in pictures which he (Indra) has got hung up in his assembly hall, pleasure-house, aerial car and victorious chariot, and keeps on looking at them curiously.

आस्थानसद्मनि विलासगृहे विमाने
जैत्रे रथे च सततं सुरचक्रवर्ती ।
रामस्य चित्रलिखितानि कुतूहलेन
वीरो विलोकयति पूर्वविचेष्टितानि ॥

Then, pointing to the picture-galleries in that very chariot he says,

यदस्यैव पुरन्दरस्यन्दनस्य चतुर्दिशं मत्तवारणीफलकेषु रामचित्रं लिखितम् । (अङ्गुल्या निर्दिशन्) तत्तावदितो दीयतां दृष्टिः । इयं प्ररोचना भृगुपतिपराक्रममहानाटकस्य यदुत भगवतस्त्र्यम्बकात् कार्मुकोपनिषल्लाभः ।

(See the pictures of Paraśurāma's exploits on the boards hung up in the *mattavāraṇis* of this very chariot. (*Pointing by his finger*) Look at this here first of all. Here is as it were the prologue of the great play of Paraśurāma's valour, *viz.* his obtaining the secret of archery from the divine Śiva).

He then describes other pictures of Paraśurāma's exploits such as his fight with Kārttikeya, Pārvatī's intervention, Śiva's presentation to him of a piece of his *paraśu* (axe), his beheading his mother Reṇukā and her revival, his extermination, first, of Sahasrārjuna and, later, of all Kshatriyas twenty-one times etc.

These pictures are described as hung up in the *mattavāraṇīs* of the chariot. The latter appear to be the galleries on the three sides of the chariot. Rājaśekhara has evidently taken the word *mattavāraṇī* from Bharata's *Nāṭyaśāstra*. These galleries correspond to the wings of the theatre.

Another use of the word in the slightly altered form *mattavāraṇaka* occurs in the *Udayasundarīkathā* of Soḍḍhala, who flourished about the middle of the eleventh century A.D. at the court of the Śilāhāra kings of North Koṅkaṇ. See the following passages :—

P. 15—स्वयं पुनः प्रविश्य...तवेव पटतल्पाच्छादितमुपरिविन्यस्तपुस्तकं मत्तवारणमध्यासितः प्रदीपचिन्तया तस्थौ ।

p. 16—द्वावपि तौ...देवीं... स्तुत्वा च पुनः पुनर्भालफलकाहतमहितलं प्रणम्य निराकुलीभूतावागत्य द्वितीयमत्तवारणकमध्यास्योपविष्टौ ।

p. 17—ततश्चासौ तवेव मत्तवारणकमनुसृत्योपविष्टः ।

p. 18—छायार्थी सौगतमवाप्य हृद्यमायतनं तस्मिन्बहिरेव द्वारमत्तवारणके समुपाविशत् ।

p. 153—तस्मिन्नेव मत्तवारणके पुस्तकमुच्छीर्षकीकृत्य सुप्तवान् ।

In these passages the word *mattavāraṇaka* is used in the sense of an aisle, which, as shown above, is similar to that of the wing of a theatre in Bharata's *Nāṭyaśāstra*.

In some passages, however, *mattavāraṇa* seems to have been used in the sense of a verandah. See, *e.g.*, the following verse from the *Kuṭṭanīmata* descriptive of Vārāṇasī[1] :

विन्ध्यधराधरभूरिव सा राजति मत्तवारणोपेता ।
बहुलनिशीथवतीव प्रोज्ज्वलधिष्ण्योपशोभिता या च ॥

This description of Vārāṇasī is full of *double entendre*. Vārāṇasī, which has *mattavāraṇas* (verandahs or courtyards) appeared like the outskirts of the Vindhya mountain which has elephants in rut; the city, which has magnificent mansions, resembled a night of the dark fortnight of a month with its brilliant *nakshatras*.)

This word *mattavāraṇa* in the sense of a verandah has no connection with the *mattavāraṇī* of Bharata. The earlier mean-

1. I owe this reference to Dr. G. T. Deshpande.

ing seems to have been forgotten; for the lexicon *Viśvaprakāśa* gives only the following meanings of mattavāraṇa :

मत्तवारणमिच्छन्ति दानक्लिन्नकरे द्विपे ।
महाप्रासादवीथीनां वरण्डे चाप्यपाश्रये ॥

Mattavāraṇa became current in the sense of a courtyard or a verandah because palaces of kings had elephants in rut tied in their courtyards. In this sense *vāraṇa*, a part of the word, means an elephent.

Dr. Sandesara and Dr. Shah have pointed out a third meaning of the word *mattavāraṇa*, *viz.* the balcony of a mansion from where ladies could have a view of what goes on in the streets below.[1] In this sense, of course, there cannot be any connection with the elephant. It has therefore to be explained as follows :

मत्ताः प्रमादेन पतन्तो वार्यन्तेऽनेनेति मत्तवारणः ।

This derivation has resemblance to tho meaning of 'a wing' which occurs in the *Nāṭyaśāstra*.

Sten Konow[2] and Keith[3] have taken the *mattavāraṇī* of the *Nāṭyaśāstra* in the sense of a verandah, where, according to both of them, the spectators of the plays used to sit. But this is incorrect. As shown above, the word has not that sense in the *Nāṭyaśāstra* of Bharata.

1. *Journ. Or. Inst.*, Vol. X. pp. 438 f.
2. Sten Konow, *Das Sanskrit Drama*, p. 4.
3. Keith, *Sanskrit Drama*, p. 359.

SECTION II

ANCIENT INDIAN HISTORY AND CULTURE

X. IS VIJAYA MENTIONED IN NĀGĀRJUNĪKOṆḌA INSCRIPTIONS THE NAME OF A CYCLIC YEAR ?

Dr. Sircar read the word *Vijaya* in the following two Nāgārjunīkoṇḍa inscriptions and took it to mean the year of that name in the sixty-year cycle of Jupiter :—

(1) Inscription of Vīrapurushadatta (*Ep. Ind.*, Vol. xxxv, pp. 3 f.)—(Line 2) siri Chāṁtamūlasa putasa raṁño Māḍhari-putasa Ikhākuna siri-Virapurisadatasa.

(Line 3) vasa-satāya savacharaṁ Vijayaṁ vāsa-pakhaṁ paṭhamaṁ 1 divasa bitiyaṁ saga-gatasa.

(2) Inscription of Ehavula Chāntamūla (*Ibid.*, Vol. xxxv, pp. 6 f.)–

(Line 2) Siri-Virapurisadatasa putasa raṁño Vasiṭhi-putasa Ikhākuna siri-Ehavala-Chatamulasa savaccharaṁ Vija . . [mha]-pakha [2] diva 1.

In a note published in the *Epigraphia Indica*, Vol. xxxvii, pp. 70 f. I pointed out that the word *vijaya* in the two epigraphs could not have meant a cyclic year as such years were not cited in that period and that the expression *savachharaṁ vijayaṁ* in both the passages probably meant 'a victorious year'. Mr. I. Karthikeya Sarma has examined this question in a lengthy article published in the *Journal of the Oriental Institute*, (Vol. xviii, pp. 126-144) and has supported the view of Dr. Sircar with some modifications. It is proposed to examine his explanation critically in this article.

Dr. Sircar had taken *vijaya* as a year of the sixty-year cycle of Jupiter according to the Southern System and as corresponding to A.D. 273-74 in the first epigraph. I pointed out that the southern reckoning was not current at the time in South India. Mr. Sarma concedes that point and takes the year as corresponding to A.D. 279-80[1] according to the Northern System. But in other respects he supports Dr. Sircar's view. He puts a novel interpretation on *vasasatāya* in the first epigraph. He takes it to mean *varṣaḥ saptamaḥ* (the seventh year) by the following reasoning[2] :—

'*Satāya-sattāya*-Sanskrit *saptāya*, which is incorrect. Hence taken as *saptamaḥ*'. This is curious reasoning. This interpretation can be easily shown to be incorrect for the following reasons :—

(1) Sanskrit *saptama* does not become *satāya* in Prakrit. It is true that some consonants are elided when Sanskrit words are changed into Prakrit, but the elision is not noticed in the Nāgārjunikoṇḍa inscriptions. *M* in particular is not at all elided in Prakrit. See the following Prakrit words occurring in the Nāgārjunikoṇḍa inscriptions—*vipamuta*, *agiṭhoma*, *navakama*[3] etc. See also the following ordinals—*paṁcamaṁ*, *dasamaṁ* etc. Sarma has himself cited *satame* (for Sanskrit *saptame*). So *vasa-satāya* cannot be taken as equivalent to *varshaḥ saptamaḥ*.

Mr. Sarma has hit on this explanation because that epigraph mentions no regnal year. But it may be noted that the second epigraph also does not mention any regnal year either before or after *saṁvacharaṁ vijayaṁ*.

(2) *Vasa-satāya* probably means *varsha-śatāya* as Dr. Sircar has shown. It refers to no regnal year.[4]

(3) *Varsha* has nowhere been used in the Nāgārjunikoṇḍa inscriptions in the sense of 'a regnal year'. The word used everywhere for the purpose is *saṁvachhara* or *savachhara*. The same word is used in the Pallava or Sātavāhana records of the age. So the meaning *varshaḥ saptamaḥ* could not have been intended here.

1. *Journal of the Oriental Institute*, Vol. XVIII, p. 135.
2. *Loc. cit.*
3. *Ep. Ind.*, Vol. XX, pp. 16, 19 etc.
4. *Vasa-satāya* was explained by Bühler as meaning *viśvasattāyāḥ* 'of universal sovereignty'. It can also be taken to mean *vaṁśa-sattāyāḥ* 'of the government of the royal family'. But Sircar's explanation seems to be better. The expression *vasa-satāya* seems to have become conventional.

This shows that *vasa-satāya* cannot mean 'the seventh year'. This knocks the bottom out of Mr. Sarma's theory.

In support of the view that *vijaya* in the passages cited above means the cyclic year of that name, Mr. Sarma has advanced some curious arguments :—

(1) The only cyclic year cited in the Nāgārjunikoṇḍa inscriptions is *Vijaya* because of its importance as the first year of Kaliyuga.

(2) The observance of the ancient sixty-year calender of Jupiter, at least the beginning year *Vijaya*, was restricted to the royal house and to the nobles, and for certain auspicious occasions whereas the public at large counted the king's regnal year, the specific fortnight of the season and the day in their day to day affairs.

These are strange arguments. One may ask, "How is it that all other royal families of the south were oblivious of the sixty-year cycle of Jupiter and of the importance of the cyclic year *Vijaya* for several centuries ; for we do not find any other citation not only of *Vijaya* but also of any other year of the sixty-year cycle till the seventh century A.D. *i.e.* for about three hundred years after the Ikshvākus ?" It has been shown that the first citation of a year of that cycle occurs in the Mahākūṭa inscription of Maṅgaleśa (A.D. 601)[1]. As for the second argument, we do not find any such restriction imposed on the use of the cyclic years by any other royal family in ancient India.

So *vijaya* cannot be taken to mean the cyclic year of that name whether according to the northern or the southern system. It means 'victorious', *savachharaṁ vijayaṁ* means 'the victorious year'. I have shown that in Prakrit the adjectival word or the word in apposition is often placed after the word it qualifies. Mr. Sarma says, "It may be so with regard to the inscriptions of some other dynasty, but not with those of the Ikshvāku kings". His attention is drawn to the following expressions which occur in the records of Ikshvākus at Nāgārjunikoṇḍa :—

1. *Ind. Ant.*, Vol. XIX, p. 16.

(1) Nāgārjunīkoṇḍa Inscription of Vīrapurușadatta, Year 6, No. 1—(Line 3) Saṁma-saṁbudhasa dhātu-vara-parigahitasa.[1]

(2) No. 3—
(Nine 8) Achariyānaṁ Aparamahāvinaseliyānaṁ.[2]

In both these cases the adjective follows the word it qualifies. Since I wrote my article on the subject, the Rentala pillar inscription of Chāntamūla has been published in the *Epigraphia Indica* (Vol. xxxvii, p. 31). It has in lines 2-3 the expression *siri-Chaṁtamulasa vijaya-saṁvacharaṁ*. This corresponds exactly to *saṁvachharaṁ vijayaṁ* in the two epigraphs cited above. The only difference is in regard to the position of the two words. The regnal year is omitted inadvertently in both the cases. In this third passage *vijaya* cannot, by any stretch of imagination, be taken to mean the cyclic year of the name.

Kielhorn has shown that cyclic years are cited according to the southern system in southern inscriptions from Śaka 855 onwards.[3] I have also found this to be true. In a grant of Govinda IV recently discovered in Vidarbha dated Śaka 851,[4] the cyclic year is cited according to the northern system, but in that of the same king dated Śaka 855[5] the cyclic year cited is according to the southern system. Mr. Sarma has objected to Kielhorn's statement and has drawn attention to the following records in which, according to him, the southern system has been used in citing cyclic years :—

(1) Paiṭhaṇ plates of Govinda III, Śaka 716[6] :
(2) Anjanavati plates of Govinda III, Śaka 722[7] ;
(3) Rādhapur plates of Govinda III, Śaka 730[8] ;

1. *Ep. Ind.*, Vol XX, p. 16.
2. *Ibid.*, Vol XX, p. 17.
3. *Ind. Ant.*, Vol XXV, p. 269.
4. *Ep. Ind.*, Vol. XXXVI, p. 259.
5. *Ind. Ant.*, Vol. XII, p. 251.
6. *Ep. Ind.*, Vol. III, p. 105.
7. *Ibid.*, Vol. XXIII, pp. 13 f.
8. *Ibid.*, p. 242. See Kielhorn's remark, "Here also the year *Sarvajit*, by the southern luni-solar system, cannot be connected with Ś. 730 expired." *Ind. Ant.*, Vol. XXV, p. 269.

(4) Sirur stone inscription of the reign of Amoghavarsha I, Śaka 788.[1]

These records do not prove Mr. Sarma's contention at all.

The first two of the above records do not cite any cyclic year. The cyclic year in the other two is according to the northern system.[2] See S.K. Pillai's *Indian Ephemeris*, Vol. I, Table I (ii), p. 196. As regards the Hatti-Mattur inscription[3] of the time of Indra III, dated Śaka 838, Kielhorn himself has shown that it is an exception.[4] That the reckoning in that inscription is according to the southern system is explicitly stated in that record itself; for it states the date in following words :—*Śaka-bhūpāl-ākrāṁta-saṁvatsara-Prabhav-ādināmadheyaṁ ...Dhātu-saṁvatsar-āntargata*. The expression *Prabhav-ādi-nāmadheyaṁ* is inserted here to show that the system of reckoning is southern; for the southern cycle begins with *Prabhava* as the northern does with *Vijaya*. In other records of Indra III's reign, where the northern system is used, such an expression does not occur. See e.g. the Jambgaon plates of Indra III, dated Śaka 836, edited by me in *Epigraphia Indica*, Vol. xxxvi, pp. 223 f. So this exception only proves the statement of Kielhorn that the southern system became current in South India from Śaka 855.

There are several other wrong statements in Mr. Sarma's article, but I would here refer to only one. He says, "We have Kapadvanj (Kaira District) plates[5] of Akālavarsha Śubhatuṅga Kṛishṇarāja II, in which both the Śaka year and the 12-year cyclic year of the north *Mahā-Vaiśākhyāḥ* were together mentioned." Mr. Sarma is misled by the name *Mahā-Vaiśākhī*. As the years of the twelve-year cycle in the records of the Gupta age have *mahā* prefixed to them (e.g. Mahā-Caitra, Mahā-Vaiśākha etc.) he thinks that here also the same cycle is intended. In this he is mistaken. The full-moon day of Vaiśākha is called *Mahā-Vaiśākhī* when it falls on Sunday and

1. *Ind. Ant.*, Vol. XII, p. 218. See also Kielhorn's remarks *loc. cit.*
2. *Ind. Ant.*, Vol. XXV, p. 269.
3. *Ibid.*, Vol. XII, p. 224.
4. *Ibid.*, Vol. XXI, p. 289 and n. 14.
5. *Ep. Ind.* Vol. I, p. 53.

the sun is in Mesha, Jupiter in Dhanus, Mars in Makara, Saturn in Tulā with the nakshatra Viśākhā and the yoga Varīya. See *Indian Ephemeris*, Vol. I, p. 60. Compare a similar full-moon day *Mahā-Kārttikī* cited in some records. *Mahā-Vaiśākhi* has no reference to the cyclic year Mahā-Vaiśākha.[1]

The foregoing discussion will have shown that Sarma's view that the word *vijaya* in the aforementioned Nāgārjunī-koṇḍa records denotes the cyclic year of that name and that it was the seventh regnal year of Vīrapurushadatta, corresponding to A.D. 279-80 is not borne out by the available evidence.[1] *Vijaya* in the two epigraphs means 'victorious'.

1. Mr. Sarma seems to have thought that if *savachharaṁ vijayaṁ* in the inscription of Vīrapuruṣadatta is taken in the sense of the cyclic year *Vijaya*, there must be a mention of the regnal year and so he has proposed the novel interpretation of *vasa-satāya*; but there is no such mention in the aforecited inscription of Ehavala Chāntamūla either before or after *savachharaṁ vijayaṁ*. The regnal year seems to have been omitted in both the cases.

XI. SOME ASPECTS OF THE RĀMAGUPTA PROBLEM[1]

In the *Journal of the Oriental Institute* (Vol. XVIII, No. 3), Dr. G.S. Gai has published three important inscriptions of *Mahārājādhirāja* Rāmagupta. They have unquestionably proved the historicity of that king which had long been in doubt. Still, there are some problems about that king which remain to be solved. It is proposed to deal with them in this article.

(I) The first of these is about the bearing of the available evidence on the characters of Rāmagupta and Chandragupta. The Rāmagupta episode is generally interpreted as follows[2] :—

Rāmagupta's dominions were invaded by a powerful Śaka king and the Gupta king was reduced to such straits that he had to accept the humiliating condition that he should send his crowned queen Dhruvadevī (or Dhruvasvāminī) to the Śaka king. His younger brother Chandragupta was a brave and adventurous youth. He volunteered to save the honour of the family by going himself to the Śaka king in the disguise of Dhruvadevī. He was accompanied by a few soldiers who also were disguised as female attendants of the queen. Chandrgupta, finding a suitable opportunity, killed the lascivious Śaka king and escaped unhurt with his companions. Thereafter, Chandragupta became the darling of the people for having saved them from a great calamity. Dhruvadevī also seems to have begun to hate her husband for his pussillanimity, and to love Chandragupta for his adventurous spirit which had rescued her honour from ignominy. Rāmagupta and Chandragupta were previously attached to each other, but

1. *Journal of the Oriental Institute*, Vol. XIX, pp. 138 f.
2. See *J.B.O.R.S.*, Vol. XIV, pp. 223 f.

after this incident their relations became strained. Chandragupta suspected that his brother wanted to put him out of the way. So he feigned madness in order to save himself and to find an opportunity to get rid of his brother. Rāmagupta was soon killed and then Chandragupta ascended the throne and married Dhruvadevī.

This story was regarded by some as too romantic to be believed. Several objections were raised against it. They may be stated and critically examined as follows[1] :—

(1) "There is no mention of Rāmagupta in any Gupta record."

This objection can be easily answered. As Dr. Altekar pointed out long ago, epigraphical lists are usually genealogical, not dynastic. They generally omit the names of collaterals. Besides, Rāmagupta was a disgrace to the fair name of the Gupta family. It is no wonder, therefore, that his name is omitted from all subsequent Gupta records. We have now as many as three inscriptions describing him as *Mahārājādhirāja* and on the evidence of paleography there is no doubt that they belong to the Gupta age. It is true that we have as yet no inscription mentioning Dhruvadevī as his crowned queen. It will be admitted that in the circumstances of the case such an inscription is extremely unlikely to be discovered. The names of Gupta queens are generally found mentioned in connection with the description of their sons who had come to the throne. As Rāmagupta's son, if he had any, did not reign, no inscription mentioning Dhruvasvāminī as his queen is likely to be discovered. We have no contemporary record mentioning the name of Samudragupta's queen Dattadevī. She is named only in the records of her descendants. So we must be satisfied with the evidence that has fortunately come to light and not insist on such as may never be discovered.

(2) "Rāmagupta's gold coins have not been discovered in any hoard—not even in the Bayana hoard, which contained several gold coins of his predecessors and successors."

This is true. But we have now his copper coins discover-

1. See *H.C.I.P.*, Vol. III, pp. 17 f.

ed at Eraṇ[1] and Vidiśā[2], and some of them have the symbol of Garuḍa, characteristic of the Gupta family.[3] All doubts about their being coins of Rāmagupta should now cease since as many as three inscriptions of that king have now been discovered in the same region, *viz.* Vidiśā. It is no doubt true that no gold coins of Rāmagupta have yet come to light, but that may be because his reign was very short and he had not sufficient time to issue gold coins.

(3) "It is difficult to believe that the inheritor of the mighty empire left by Samudragupta could be so decisively defeated by a Śaka king that he had no means of saving his army or kingdom."

This is not unlikely. As shown below, the encounter of Rāmagupta and the Śaka king did not occur in the former's capital or even elsewhere in his kingdom. It took place in the course of a thoughtless invasion of the Śaka dominion by Rāmagupta in the distant Himālayas where he had no hope of succour from any ally.

(4) "The marriage of the brother's widowed queen by the regicide certainly clashes with our cherished notions of morality and social decorum."

This is true; but it may have been tolerated by the people of the age in the special circumstances of the case. They must have felt that there was none so able in the royal family as Chandragupta who could save the great empire built by Samudragupta and they must have connived at the blemish in view of Chandragupta's sterling qualities such as undaunted courage, learning and liberality. Has not Kālidāsa said[4]—

एको हि दोषो गुणसंनिपाते निमज्जतीन्दोः किरणेष्विवाङ्कः । ?

"One blemish in the midst of several virtues is not noticed even as the black spot on the moon's disc is not seen in the midst of its bright rays."

But future generations did not connive at this objectionable feature of the incident. We have as many as three passa-

1. *J.N.S.I.*, Vol. XXIII, p. 340.
2. *Ibid.*, Vol. XII, pp. 103 f.; Vol. XIII, pp. 128 f. etc.
3. *Ibid.*, Vol. XXIII, p. 341 f.
4. *Kumārasambhava*, I, 3.

ges—two of them occurring in inscriptions[1]—condemning Rāmagupta for surrendering his queen to the enemy and Chandragupta for slaying his own brother, marrying his wife and usurping the throne, though they praise the latter's adventurous spirit and great liberality. The Vikrama saga developed in course of time to such an extent that the objectionable features of the incident were forgotten and Vikramāditya became the beloved hero of all times on account of his adventurous spirit, charity and unique achievements.[2]

Dr. U.P. Shah has, however, attempted to answer this objection in a different manner. He had previously published a lengthy article in the *Journal of the Oriental Institute* (Vol. IV, pp. 218 f.) in which he had attempted to put a new interpretation on the passages of the *Devī-Chandragupta*, on which the story of Rāmagupta is based. In a recent article of the same Journal (Vol. XVIII, pp. 254 f.) he has reiterated his view and has requested scholars to consider his interpretation of the characters of Rāmagupta and Chandragupta. Before we take leave of this aspect of the Rāmagupta problem, we must critically examine his interpretation. His view may be stated as follows :—

"Rāmagupta bore great love for Chandragupta. The latter was dearer to him than even his queen Dhruvadevī. See the following passages from the *Devī-Chandragupta*—

(१) त्यजामि देवीं तृणवत्त्वदन्तरे ।

(२) त्वय्युपारोपितप्रेम्णा त्वदर्थे यशसा सह ।
परित्यक्ता मया देवी जनोऽयं जन एव मे ।।

He tried to dissuade Chandragupta from going to the Śaka king and exposing himsclf to great risk. He would rather surrender his queen and incur infamy. Rāmagupta was thus a cultured man who was prepared to sacrifice his all—his good name, his dear wife *etç.*—for the safety of his people and his younger

1. See the Sanjān plates of Amoghavarṣa I, *Ep. Ind.*, XVIII, p. 248; the Cambay plates of Govinda IV, *ibid.*, Vol. VII, p. 36 and the Sangli plates of the same, *Ind. Ant.*, Vol. XII, p. 249.

2. See the following *subhāshita*—

तत्कृतं यन्न केनापि तद्दत्तं यन्न केनचित् ।
तत्साधितमसाध्यं यद्विक्रमार्केण भूभुजा ।।

brother. His ministers would not have allowed him to go himself in that critical stage of Gupta history.

After Chandragupta killed the Śaka king, Rāmagupta fell in Dhruvadevī's esteem mainly on account of her misunderstanding of her husband's character. He was a coward (as a husband) in her eyes, though not a real coward.

Chandragupta did not murder his brother though the Sanjān plates say so. The composer of the text of that inscription, who was far removed in time and place from that incident, wanted to emphasise the greatness of his patron (Amoghavarsha I) and to show that he was superior in character and ability even to the great Vikrama, who had by that time become the ideal of Indian kings. So he has stated, wrongly of course, that Chandragupta killed his brother, married his wife, and usurped his kingdom. If this had been true, the Sanskrit dramatist Viśākhadatta would not have named his play *Devī-Chandragupta* and made Chandragupta the hero of it. Viśākhadatta was probably a poet of the Gupta age. Can we expect that such a playwright would introduce the scene of the murder of Rāmagupta by the hero of his play ? Chandragupta would, in that case, never have become the national hero.

Rāmagupta was a man of spiritual temperament. To him woman, worldly pleasures or pride of an emperor had not so much attraction as they had to Chandragupta. He perceived that love had grown between Chandragupta and his queen. He wanted to make his brother happy and so he decided to go out of the world. In doing so he must have thought of the safety of the people and of the Gupta empire. So he willingly renounced.

Rāmagupta is identical with Bhartṛihari of Indian legend. The latter is now shown to have lived in the fourth century A.D. Besides, the following floating verse tells us that he was a brother of Vikramāditya (*i.e.* of Chandragupta)—

ब्राह्मण्यामभवद्वराहमिहिरो ज्योतिर्विदामग्रणी
राजा भर्तृहरिश्च विक्रमनृपः क्षत्रात्मजायामभूत् ।
वैश्यायां हरिचन्द्रवंशतिलको जातश्च शङ्कुः कृती
शूद्रायाममरः षडेव शबरस्वामिद्विजस्यात्मजाः ॥

This verse tells us that Bhartṛhari and Vikramāditya were sons of Śabarasvāmin. The latter flourished in A.D. 350. The word *ātmaja* in the above verse is to be taken in the sense of 'a disciple.' They were not actually sons but disciples of the great Mīmāṁsaka Śabarasvāmin.

In his other play *Mudrārākshasa* Viśākhadatta describes Chandragupta as *bundhu-bhṛitya* (one who was loyal to his brother). He wants to say that in his relation with Rāmagupta Chandragupta had not committed any act of ignominy towards or betrayal of the elder brother.

Some extracts from the *Devī-Chandragupta* show that Chandragupta was spending his time in the home of courtesan. Rāmagugupta did not like it. He was in a dilemma. On one side was his dissatisfied wife and on the other, separation from a brother whom he dearly loved. He decided to renounce the world. He was a man endowed with a spiritual turn of mind for whom a sacrifice of such a type would rather be more pleasant and would end all mental torture. He knew the ideal of the house of Raghu. So he renounced.

In one passage of the *Devī-Chandragupta*, Chandragupta is represented as going to the *rāja-kula*, pretending madness and slightly afraid of the enemy. Possibly there was a section of the people which was against him and he wanted to show that he had no hand in whatever had taken place or was about to take place in the palace. So he appeared as a lunatic before Rāmagupta in order to dissuade him from giving up the throne. Possibly Chandragupta's going to the *rāja-kula* was followed by a highly dramatic scene, namely, the renunciation. The dramatic effect of this scene of retirement was possibly enhanced by Viśākhadatta by making Rāmagupta repeat the verse—

त्वय्युपारोपितप्रेम्णा त्वदर्थे यशसा सह ।
परित्यक्ता मया देवी जनोऽयं जन एव मे ।।

while offering the throne to Chandragupta and declaring his decision to retire from worldly life. Chandragupta later married Dhruvadevī because her husband had become a recluse. This is sanctioned by Dharmaśāstra.

The Rāmagupta episode was a golden chapter of Gupta history for Chandragupta as well as for Rāmagupta, both of whom rose bravely to the occasions that arose in their lives, and who, caught in a very delicate crisis, solved it in a way which immortalised them in the hearts of the Indian people for over a millenium and a half down to our days."

We have summarised the argument of Dr. Shah as far as possible in his own words. We shall now proceed to examine it critically.

Our main source for the history of Rāmagupta is the Sanskrit play *Devī-Chandragupta*, which, unfortunately, has not been recovered in full. Only a few extracts from it cited in the *Śṛingāraprakāśa* of Bhoja (11th cent. A.D.) and the *Nāṭyadarpaṇa*[1] of Rāmachandra and Guṇachandra (12th cent. A.D.) have been published. The earliest author who refers to this incident is Bāṇa, who flourished in the first half of the seventh century A.D. He was separated from Rāmagupta by about two hundred and fifty years. It is not known if he had any independent source of information about the history of Rāmagupta or he relied on the version in the *Devī-Chandragupta*. The latter supposition is more likely in view of the general absence of historical works in Sanskrit literature. All other authors who refer to that incident have plainly drawn their information from the *Devī-Chandragupta*. Did Viśākhadatta, its author, have correct information about it ? When did he flourish ? Several views have been expressed about his date, *viz.*, 5th cent. (Jayaswal), 6th cent. (Winternitz), and 9th cent. (Keith and Jacobi). The *Bharatavākya* of the *Mudrārākshasa* composed by him refers to his patron, but the reading there is uncertain. Those who read—

म्लेच्छैरुद्वेज्यमाना भुजयुगमधुना संश्रिता राजमूर्तेः
स श्रीमद्बन्धुभृत्यश्चिरमवतु महीं पार्थिवश्चन्द्रगुप्तः ॥

take him as a court-poet of Chandragupta; but in view of the reference to the invasion of the Mlechchhas (who are probably the Hūṇas) in that *Bharatavākya* and the anachronic mention of the Hūṇas in the *Mudrārākshasa*, it appears more likely that he flourished in a later age, probably in the time of the Maukhari king Avantivarman; for another reading of the

1. For the extracts from the *Nāṭyadarpaṇa*, see the edition of the work published in the G.O. Series (Second ed., 1959).

Bharatavākya is स श्रीमद्बन्धुभृत्यश्चिरमवतु महीं पार्थिवोऽवन्तिवर्मा ॥ and we know that the Maukharis had successfully routed the invading armies of the Hūṇas.[1] Besides, the *Devī-Chandragupta*, as shown below, probably represented that Chandragupta killed his brother and married his wife. Such a play is not likely to have been staged in the time of Chandragupta or his descendants. So Viśākhadatta seems to have flourished in an age when the Guptas had been overthrown, but their history had not been forgotten. We must, therefore, suppose that he had fairly reliable sources of information for the periods of Rāmagupta and Chandragupta. Some scholars point to the anachronisms in the *Mudrārākshasa* to discredit his account of the Maurya period, but we must remember that he was separated by more than nine centuries from the Maurya age and so he may have drawn upon his imagination in describing the incidents at the time of the accession of Chandragupta Maurya. His account of the Rāmagupta incident is, however, more likely to be correct.

All subsequent writers who have referred to the Rāmagupta incident have evidently drawn their material from the *Devī-Chandragupta*. Dr. Shah also has utilised the same source, but he depends mainly on the interpretation of the extant passages from that play in reconstructing the history of the period.

From the summary of his argument given above, it must have been noticed that Dr. Shah relies mainly on conjectures in interpreting the passages from the *Devī-Chandragupta*. He blames the author of the Sanjān inscription for distorting the incident in question with a view to exaggerate the greatness of his own patron by maligning the Gupta Emperor (Vikramāditya). But this is not the only inscriptional passage that states that Chandragupta (called *Sāhasāṅka*) killed his brother, usurped his throne and married his wife. More than

1. See the following passage in the Aphsaḍ stone inscription of Ādityasena—

यो मौखरेः समितिषूद्धतहूणसैन्या
वल्गद्घटा विघटयन्नुरुवारणानाम् ।

Fleet, *Gupta Inscriptions*, p. 203.

thirty-five years ago we drew the attentian of scholars to the following verse in the Cambay[1] and Sangli[2] plates of the Rāshṭrakūṭa king Govinda IV, which refers to this incident—

सामर्थ्ये सति निन्दिता प्रविहिता नैवाग्रजे क्रूरता
बन्धुस्त्रीगमनादिभिः कुचरितैरावर्जितं नायशः ।
शौचाशौचपराङ्मुखं न च भिया पैशाच्यमङ्गीकृतं
त्यागेनासमसाहसैश्च भुवने यः साहसाङ्कोऽभवत् ॥

This verse tells us that Govinda IV did not practise ignominious cruelty towards his elder brother though he had the power to do so; that he did not incur infamy by evil actions such as having illicit intercourse with his brother's wife; that he did not, through fear, resort to the actions of a goblin which are indifferent to purity and impurity; but by his munificence and unparalleled heroic deeds he became known in the world as *Sāhasāṅka* (*i.e.* Vikramāditya). As I have shown elsewhere,[3] the insinuation in the third *pāda* of this verse is corroborated by the reference to the *Vetāla-sādhana* by Chandragupta in an extract from the *Śṛiṅgāraprakāśa,* brought to notice by D.R. Bhandarkar. So there is no doubt that the authors of the two inscriptions, *viz.* the Sanjān plates of Amoghavarsha I, and the Cambay-Sangli plates of Govinda IV, have drawn their material for the description in the verses in question from the *Devī-Chandragupta.* Is it likely that they have twisted the story in that play to the extent of representing that Rāmagupta was killed by Chandragupta when he had actually renounced the throne in favour of his younger brother ? Bāṇa[4] and the poet of the *muktaka* verse दत्त्वा रुद्धगतिः शकाधिपतये *etc.* cited by Rājaśekhara[5] also probably drew on the same play, but since they do not refer to Chandragupta's murder of his brother and marriage with his wife, we do not cite their evidence in this respect.

1. *Ep. Ind.*, Vol. VII, p. 36.
2. *Ind. Ant.*, Vol. XII, p. 249. For a full discussion of this matter, see our *Studies in Indology*, Vol. I (second ed.), pp. 175 f.
3. *Studies in Indology*, Vol. I (Second ed., 1968), pp. 175 f.
4. See

अरिपुरे च परकलत्रकामुकं कामिनीवेषगुप्तश्चन्द्रगुप्तः शकपतिमशातयत् ।
Kāvyamīmāṁsā (Third ed. 1934), G.O.S., p. 47.

Now, instead of relying on conjectures for ascertaining the turn of events described in the lost part of the *Devī-Chandragupta*, is it not better to see how it is reported by subsequent authors of inscriptions ? The *Devī-Chandragupta* was well-known till the time of Hemachandra (12th cent. A.D.). The authors of the two afore-mentioned inscriptions who flourished earlier have evidently drawn upon the play for their statements about Chandragupta. Their evidence is far more reliable than mere conjectures about the lost portion of the *Devī-Chandrugupta*.

And what is the evidence for Dr. Shah's interpretation of the characters of Rāmagupta and Chandragupta ? He cites the following verse to show not only that Rāmagupta loved Chandragupta but also that he renounced the throne in his favour :—

स्वय्युपारोपितप्रेम्णा त्वदर्थे यशसा सह ।
परित्यक्ता मया देवी जनोऽयं जन एव मे ॥

But as Dr. Altekar has shown, this verse occurs in the scene when Chandragupta, disguised as Dhruvadevī, is about to start for the Śaka king's camp (or place)[1] :—

यथा देवीचन्द्रगुप्ते द्वितीयेऽङ्के प्रकृतीनामाश्वासनाय शकस्य ध्रुवदेवी-सम्प्रदाने अभ्युपगते राज्ञा रामगुप्तेनारिवधार्थं यियासुः प्रतिपन्नध्रुवदेवीनेपथ्यः कुमारचन्द्रगुप्तो विज्ञापयन्नुच्यते ।

In this scene Viśākhadatta has very cleverly used words with *double entendre* so that, though they are addressed to Chandragupta, Dhruvadevī, who overhears them, thinks that they are addressed to another woman with whom Rāmagupta is in love. There is, however, no evidence to show that Rāmagupta used the same words at the time of his supposed abdication of the throne and departure out of the capital. If he had done so, he would rather have referred to his renouncement of the kingdom than to that of his queen. Then, again, why should he say that in abdicating the throne he was renouncing his fame also ? Such a noble act should have brought him great renown, not disgrace.

1. *Nāṭyadarpaṇa*, (1959), p. 124.

Again, is there the slightest evidence for supposing that Rāmagupta was identical with Bhartṛihari? The verse cited in support of this supposition is absolutely unreliable. It is one of those verses that have caused confusion in research. It mentions Varāhamihira as a contemporary of Bhartṛihari (*i.e.* Rāmagupta according to Dr. Shah), but he flourished more than a century and a quarter after the latter.[1] The evidence of this verse on the identification of Rāmagupta and Bhartṛihari is thoroughly unreliable. The interpretation of other incidents mentioned in the known extracts from the *Devī-Chandragupta viz.*, that Chandragupta was feigning madness while going to the palace of Rāmagupta, because some people were against his accession and would have done harm to him is merely conjectural. There is not an iota of evidence to support it.

In view of the version of the Rāmagupta episode in the literature and inscriptions from the seventh to the tenth century A.D., it appears very likely that Viśākhadatta dramatised the incidents as described in the beginning of this article. And that play is our only source of information for the history of Rāmagupta's reign. As the recently discovered inscriptions have proved the historicity of Rāmagupta who was known for the first time from that play, it should not be unreasonable to suppose that other events of that Gupta king's reign happened as described in it.

There remains now the question—If Chandragupta really killed his brother and married his wife, how did he come to be recognised as an ideal king? The passages from the Sanjān and Cambay-Sāngli plates show that down to the tenth century A.D. Chandragupta-Vikramāditya had become famous for his daring and liberality, but his questionable deeds, *viz.* the murder of his own brother and the marriage with his wife, were not forgotten. Till then, he had not become an ideal hero. As stated before, his contemporaries may have connived at these incidents in view of his daring, liberality, learning, patronage to art and literature and other noble qualities. That such a supposition is possible is also shown by the aforecited verse of Kālidāsa.

1. His *Pañchasiddhāntikā* was probably composed in A.D. 505.

Perhaps, there were extenuating circumstances for the action of Chandragupta. Some passages from the *Devī-Chandragupta* show that there were some enemies that wanted to put him out of the way. See the following extract from the fifth Act of that play :—[1]

> यथा वा देवीचन्द्रगुप्ते **पञ्चमेऽङ्के**
>
> **"एसो सियकरवित्थरपणासियासेसवेरितिमिरोहो ।**
> **नियविहिवसेण चंदो गयणंगणं लंघिउं विसइ ॥**
> **(एष सितकरविस्तरप्रणाशिताशेषवैरितिमिरौघः ।**
> **निजविधिवशेन चन्द्रो गगनाङ्गणं लङ्घितुं विशति ॥)**

इयं स्वापायशङ्किनः कृतकोन्मत्तस्य कुमारचन्द्रगुप्तस्य चन्द्रोदयवर्णनेन प्रवेशप्रतिपादिका ।

This passage shows that Chandragupta had destroyed all his enemies. This does not refer to his slaying of the Śaka king. That incident must have been reported earlier, *viz.* in the third Act; for we find that Chandragupta is shown as going to the Śaka king's camp in the second Act. The afore-cited passage occurs in the fifth Act. The enemies that were destroyed by Chandragupta must evidently be some persons probably instigated, if not employed, by Rāmagupta to put Chandragupta out of the way. Chandragupta had triumphed over them by his good fortune (*nija-vidhi-vaśena*). We have no information about what was shown in the fifth Act, but at the end of that Act there is the following *dhruvā*[2]—

> यथा देवीचन्द्रगुप्ते **पञ्चमाङ्कान्ते**
>
> **"बहुविहकज्जविसेसं अइगूढं णण्हवेइ मयणादो ।**
> **निक्खलइ लुद्धचित्तउ रत्ताहुत्तं मणो रिउणो ॥**
> **बहुविधकार्यविशेषमतिगूढं निह्नुते मदनात् ।**
> **[नस्सरति क्षुब्धचित्तो रक्ताक्षिप्तं मनो रिपोः ॥**

इयमुन्मत्तस्य चन्द्रगुप्तस्य मदनविकारगोपनपरस्य मनाक् शत्रुभीतस्य राजकुलगमनार्थे निष्क्रमसूचिकेति ।

The last three words of this *gāthā* are corrupt, but the said *gāthā* tells us that Chandragupta was going to the *rājakula*

1. *Nāṭyadarpaṇa* (1959), p. 172.
2. *Ibid.*, p. 173.

(palace) in an agitated mood and with various objects in view. He suspected some foul play there and so he had feigned madness. Perhaps, he suspected his brother in regard to the attempts on his life and was going to the palace to expostulate with him. Subsequently, there may have occurred some altercation between them and in the heat of it Chandragupta may have put his brother to death. As this was done in self-defence it may have been considered defensible and no blame was attached to it.

Dr. Altekar put forward another explanation.[1] "Rāmagupta's end may have been hastened by the sheer sense of shame and disgraee. Or, he may have been killed by a clique in the army, Chandragupta being believed to have connived at it." There is, however, no basis for these conjectures in the known extracts from the *Devi-Chandragupta*.

(II) Another aspect of the Rāmagupta problem is the identification of the place where the incident occurred, and of enemy who had reduced Rāmagupta to the helpless condition. Dr. Altekar at first thought that the incident occurred in Rāmagupta's capital Pāṭaliputra and his enemy was a Western Kshatrapa.[2] R.D. Banerji thought that it occurred at Mathurā[3] and Rāmagupta's enemy was a Kushāṇa king. Recently, some scholars have suggested that it occurred at Eraṇ or Vidiśā.[4] All these conjectures are baseless. The place where the incident occurred is called *Aripura* in the *Harshacharita* and Alipura in the *Śṛiṅgāraprakūśa*, As I have shown elsewhere, the former reading is unlikely, since, if it is accepted, it would involve tautology ; for the passage in the *Śṛiṅgāraprakāśa* mentions शत्रोः स्कन्धावारं in the same sentence. So the reading *Alipura* is preferable. But where was that Alipura ? The *muktaka* verse cited by Rājaśekhara,[5] describing the incident, gives the valuable information that it was situated in the Himālayas :—

दत्त्वा रुद्धगतिः शकाधिपतये देवीं ध्रुवस्वामिनीं
यस्मात्खण्डितसाहसो निववृते श्रीरामगुप्तो नृपः ।

1. *Catalogue of the Gupta Gold Coins of the Bayānā Hoard*, p. xxvi.
2. *J.B.O.R.S.*, Vol. XIV, pp. 231; 240 f.
3. *The Age of the Imperial Guptas*, p. 30.
4. *J.N.S.I.*, Vol. XXIII, p. 344.
5. *Kāvyamīmāṁsā* (G.O.S., Third ed.), p. 47

तस्मिन्नेव हिमालये गिरिगुहाकोणक्वणत्किन्नरे
गीयन्ते तव कार्त्तिकेय ! नगरस्त्रीणां गणैः कीर्त्तयः ॥

This verse states that Rāmagupta made an adventurous raid into the Himālayan territory and that he suffered an ignominious defeat and effected his escape by surrendering (or promising to surrender) his queen Dhruvasvāminī. So the incident did not occur in Pāṭaliputra, Mathurā, Eraṇ or Vidiśā, but in the distant Himālayas. The poet who composed that verse tells us further that at the same place his contemporary king Kārttikeya obtained a memorable victory and so his praises are being sung by the *Kinnaras* in that city.[1] If we could identify this Kārttikeya, we may get a clue to the location of the place where the incident occurred. Altekar at first suggested that Kārttikeya was Kumāragupta I, but this is extremely unlikely. No poet at the court of a Gupta king is likely to have referred to the Rāmagupta episode, which was a blot on the fair name of the Gupta family. More than thirty-five years ago we showed that Kārttikeya was another name of the Pratīhāra king Mahīpāla.[2] Āryakshemīśvara, who was his court-poet, refers to him as Mahīpāla in the *prastāvanā* of his play *Chaṇḍakauśika* and as Kārttikeya in its *Bharatavākya*.[3] So there should be no doubt about this identification. But did this Mahīpāla undertake any expedition in the Himālayan region? The following verse from the *Prachaṇḍa-Pāṇḍava* of Rājaśekhara, who also flourished at his court, describes his conquests as follows :[4]

1. D. R. Bhandarkar took *Kārttikeya-nagara* as a compound word and located the place near the village Baijanāth in the Almorā District of U.P. But it is more likely that the name of the king addressed is mentioned in the verse. For further discussion, see our *Studies in Indology*, Vol. I (second ed.), pp. 168 f.

2. *Loc. cit.*

3. See the *prastāvanā*—

आदिष्टोऽस्मि......श्रीमहीपालदेवेन ।

and see the *Bharatavākya*—

येनादिश्य प्रयोगं घनपुलकभृता नाटकस्यास्य हर्षाद्
वस्त्रालङ्कारहेम्नां प्रतिदिनमकृशा राशयः सम्प्रदत्ताः ।
तस्य क्षत्रप्रसूतेर्भ्रमतु जगदिदं कार्त्तिकेयस्य कीर्तिः
पारे क्षीरारुयसिन्धोरपि कवियशसा सार्धमग्रेसरेण ॥

See *Pracaṇḍapāṇḍava* (or *Bālabhārata*), Act I.

नमितमुरलमौलिः पाकलो मेकलानां
रणकलितकलिङ्गः केलिदः केरलेन्दोः ।
अजनि जितकुलूतः कुन्तलानां कुठारो
हठहृतरमठश्रीः श्रीमहीपालदेवः ॥

One of these conquests was in the Kulūta country, which comprised the *doab* of the Beas and the Sutlaj.[1] It was probably in this region that the battle of Rāmagupta and the Śaka king took place. The city (*nagara*) where it occurred may be identical with Jālandhar. Hiuen Tsang tells us that in his time the country was ruled by a king called 'the king of North India', who had his capital at this city.[2] This was perhaps the scene of the battle.

But who was the Śaka king who worsted Rāmagupta in the battle ? Altekar at first identified him with the contemporary Western Kshatrapa, but the kingdom of these Kshatrapas did not include the Himālayan territory. The king ruling over the Kulūta region may be a scion of the Kushāṇa family. The Allahabad *praśasti* mentions a Devaputra Śāhī Śāhānuśāhī as having submitted to Samudragupta, but he was not completely subdued. When after the death of Samudragupta Rāmagupta undertook the adventurous expedition against the contemporary Kushāṇa king of the north-west, the latter seems to have entrapped him in the Kulūta territory and reduced him to such straits that he had to agree to the humiliating condition of surrendering the queen for the safety of himself and his people (*prakṛtīnām-āśvāsanāya*). It seems that Rāmgupta was so sure of success in this campaign that he had taken his queen also with himself just as the Rāshṭrakūṭa king Govinda III seems to have done in his northern conquests[3] and as Bhāusāheb, the Commander of the Marāṭhā forces, did when he opposed Ahmedshah Abdāli. This was indeed a great *sāhasa* as stated in the verse cited by Rājaśekhara, and Rāmagupta had to pay for it dearly.

1. *A.S.W.I*, Vol. IV, pp. 126 f; *Ind. Ant.*, Vol. XXII, p. 18?; *On Yuan Chwang*, Vol. I, p. 298

2. *On Yuan Chwang*, Vol. I, p. 297.

3. His son Amoghavarsha I was born at Śrībhavana (modern Sārbhoṇ in Gujarat) where he was halting in the course of his northern campaigns.

But, it may be objected, all authorities who refer to this episode mention the enemy as a Śaka king, They do not call him a Kushāṇa. The objection can be easily answered. In ancient Sanskrit literature, the Kushāṇas are referred to as the Śakas. The racial name Kushāṇa occurs nowhere. The era started by the Kushāṇa king Kanishka is called the era of a Śaka king. So it is not unlikely that the enemy of Rāmagupta was a Kushāṇa king of North-west India.[1]

It is noteworthy that Chandragupta, soon after his accession, took measures to punish the contemporary Kushāṇa king for his temerity to ask for the surrender of a Gupta queen. The Meherauli pillar inscription, which is generally believed to record the achievements of Chandragupta II, mentions his victory over the Bālhikas after crossing the seven tributaries of the Indus.[2] This campaigu was evidently directed against the contemporary Kushāṇa king.

We have thus tried to show that the generally accepted view that Chandragupta II—Vikramāditya killed or caused to be killed his brother Rāmagupta and then married his queen Dhruvasvāminī is the only possible view in the light of the available evidence. As shown above, there may have been extenuating circumstances which justified his actions. Further, the enemy who had entrapped Rāmagupta was probably a king of the Kushāṇa dynasty and the encounter took place in the Jālandhar region.

1. Dr. Altekar also ultimately came to this view. See his *Catalogue of the Bayānā Hoard*, p. xxv. He identified the enemy with Piro, the Kidāra Kushāṇa king of the Western Panjab.

2. Fleet, *Gupta Inscriptions*, p. 141.

XII. THE RIDDLE OF THE MĀṬVAṆ PLATES OF THE TRAIKŪṬAKA KING VIKRMASENA : ĀBHĪRA YEAR 284

In my *Inscriptions of the Kalachuri-Chedi Era* (*C.I.I.*, Vol. IV), pp, 22. f. I published three copper-plate inscriptions of the Traikūṭakas, ranging in dates from the year 207 to the year 245, which were known till then (1955). Since then, Mrs. Shobhana Gokhale has published the Māṭvaṇ plates of two Traikūṭaka kings—Madhyamasena (Year 256)[1] and Vikramasena (Year 284).[2] These kings do not mention their father's name in their grants; still, it is not unlikely that Madhyamasena was the son of Vyāghrasena (Year 242) and Vikramasena (year 284) that of Madhyamasena. Though these grants have not yet been published in any English journal, they are important for the history of the Traikūṭakas. It is, therefore, proposed to discuss a riddle presented by the Māṭvaṇ plates of Vikramasena. Their text is given at the end for ready reference.

Like the plates of Madhyamasena, those of Vikramasena also were issued from the victorious Aniruddhapura, which was evidently the capital of the Traikūṭakas. It has not yet been identified, but was evidently situated somewhere in South Gujarat.

The Māṭvaṇ plates record the grant, by Vikramasena, of the village Pañchāmalaka to a Brāhmaṇa of Kallivana (modern Kalvaṇ in the Nāsik district). They are dated on the second *tithi* in the dark fortnight of Chaitra in the (Ābhīra) year 284.

1. *Itihāsa āṇi Saṁskṛiti* (Marathi), No. 32.
2. *Ibid.*, No, 35.

The initial portion of the grant describing the reigning king is exactly as in the Māṭvaṇ plates of Madhyamasena, the predecessor and probably father of Vikramasena, except for the work *Kaṭachchurīṇām* which is substituted here in place of the word *Traikūṭakānām* which usually occurs in the grants of the Traikūṭakas. Mrs. Gokhale takes this word to mean that the Kaṭachchuris were the emperors to whom the Traikūṭaka Vikramasena owed allegiance. But this is not the usual way of naming one's supreme lord.[1] Such words as *Maiṭrakāṇām* which occur in the beginning of the royal genealogies are to be understood in the sense that the ruling king belonged to that royal family.[2] Did Vikramasena then belong to the Kaṭachchuri family ? His description in the present grant is exactly as in the Māṭvaṇ plates of the Traikūṭaka King Madhyamasena. So there is no doubt that he belonged to the Traikūṭaka family. His name is like those of other Traikūṭaka kings, *viz.* Indrasena, Dahrasena, Vyāghrasena and Madhyamasena. How is it then that the word *Kaṭachchurīṇām*, signifying his descent in the Kaṭachchuri family, occurs in the beginning of the present grant ? Once the idea occurred to me that perhaps the word *Kaṭachchurīnṇām* was inscribed later over the original *Traikūṭakānām* in the first plate. So I obtained the photographs of the plates from Mrs. Gokhale, but they did not show tampering of the first plate in this place. How should we then resolve this riddle ?

I would suggest the following solution of this riddle. It seems that there was a political revolution in Mahārāshṭra, Koṅkaṇ and Gujarāt in *circa* Ābhīra year 284 (A.D. 533-34). The Kaṭachchuris of Māhishmatī appear to have invaded and conquered these countries from the Traikūṭakas[3] and the

1. In such cases the name of the suzerain is mentioned with imperial titles and then the feudatory prince is described as meditating on his feet.

2. See e.g. प्रसभप्रणतामित्राणां मैत्रकाणां...श्रीसेनापतिभटार्कः: in the grant of Dhruvesena I, Year 206 (*Ep. Ind.*, XXXI, p. 300).

3. The grants of the Traikūṭakas have been found at Pārḍī and Surat. See *C.I.I.*, Vol. IV, pp. 22 f.

Vishṇukuṇḍins[1] who were then ruling over them. It seems that the Brāhmaṇa grantee who had obtained the present grant from Traikūṭaka Vikramasena could not get a copper plate confirming it issued from the royal office before the revolution. He had perhaps a *bhūrja-patra* or a *tāḍa-patra* with him recording the grant. Seeing no chance of getting the grant confirmed by the new ruler in those troublous times, he seems to have got his grant inscribed on a set of copper plates on the model of some other Traikūṭaka grant like that recorded on the Māṭvaṇ plates of Traikūṭaka Madhyamasena. As the Kaṭachchuris had by then established themselves in Koṅkaṇ, he seems to have asked the engraver to engrave *Kaṭachchūrīṇām* in place of *Traikūṭakānām* in the beginning of the first plate. He may have thought that by getting the name of the royal family then in power recorded in the beginning of the charter, his grant was secure.

Instances of copper-plate charters having been issued long after the respective grants were made are known. If in the meanwhile the ruler who made the grant is dead, his successor issues the charter recording it. For instance, the recently published Panhāḷe plates[2] of the Śilāhāra prince Vikramāditya, dated Śaka 1061, first state that the grant recorded in them was made by his father Aparāditya I for the spiritual well-being of his son (Vikramāditya), but later the same plates record that it was made by Vikramāditya for the religious merit of his parents and of himself. His father had evidently died before the copper-plate charter recording the grant was issued. In the case of the present Māṭvaṇ plates the political revolution seems to have occurred before Vikramasenas (or his successor if there was any) could issue them recording the grant made. So the grantee seems to have got the copper-plate charter enagraved, taking care to get the succeeding regime mentioned in the beginning.

1. A grant of Vishṇukuṇḍin Mādhavavarman I was found at Khānāpur, *Ep. Ind.*, Vol. XXVII, pp. 312 f. The coins of the Vishṇukuṇḍins have been found at several places in Western Mahārāshṭra and Vidarbha.

2. *Itihāsa āṇi Saṁskṛiti*, No. 29, pp. 5 f.

If the solution of the present riddle suggested above is accepted, it would give us a date for this political revolution in Gujarāt, Mahārāshṭra and Koṅkaṇ. It must have occurred in *circa* the Ābhira year 284 (A.D. 533-34). The name of the Kaṭachchuri king flourishing at the time is not known. He was the predecessor, probably the father of Kṛishṇarāja (*circa* A.D. 550-575), the first known Kaṭachchuri king of Māhishmatī. Kṛishṇarāja issued several silver coins in his name, but he describes himself in them only as meditating on the feet of his father and mother, but does not name his father. He is also not named in the grants of his successors.

After conquering Gujarāt and Koṅkaṇ, this unnamed Kaṭachchuri king seems to have appointed feudatories to govern the countries. The Sunao Kalā plates[1] dated only eight years after the present grant (Ābhīra year 292) show that Southern Gujarāt was then ruled by Saṅgamasiṁha, who describes himself only as a *Mahāsāmanta*, though he does not name his suzerain.[1] Koṅkaṇ was given in charge of a Maurya family. A grant of the Maurya prince Suketuvarman, who ruled in this period, has been discovered in the Ṭhāṇā district of North Koṅkaṇ.[2] Western Mahārāshṭra seems to have been under the direct rule of the Kaṭachchuris as their grants have been found in the Nāsik district.[3] Vidarbha was ruled by a feudatory family.[4]

Before closing this note, we would suggest a correction in Mrs. Gokhale's interpretation of a passage in the present grant. Lines 10-11 have अस्माभिर्नरेन्द्रनारायणयोर्मातापित्रोरात्मनश्च पुण्याभिवृद्धये, stating the persons for whose religious merit the grant was made.

Mrs. Gokhale has taken this to mean that Vikramasena made the grant for the spiritual merit of the sons Narendra and Nārāyaṇa (of Vikramasena), his own parents and himself. This does not seem to be correct. If Narendra and Nārāyaṇa had been sons of Vikramasena, they would not have been named before his parents. The expression नरेन्द्रनारायणयोः qualifies

1. *C.I.I.*, Vol. IV, pp. 33 f.
2. *Bomb. Gaz.* (old ed.), Vol. XIV (Ṭhāṇā District), pp. 372-378.
3. *C.I.I.*, Vol. IV, 38 f.; 47 f.
4. *C.I.I.*, Vol. IV, pp. 611 f.

मातापित्रो: and describes the father and mother of Vikramasena as royal personages resembling Nārāyaṇa (Vishṇu) and Nārāyaṇī (Lashmī).[1]

TEXT* OF THE MĀṬVAṆ PLATES OF VIKRAMASENA:
[ĀBHĪRA] YEAR 284.

First Plate

Line

१. स्वस्ति विजयानिरुद्धपुरात्कटच्चुरीणां मातापितृपादानुध्यातो भगवत्पा-

२. दकर्म्मंकर⌒करगतक्रमागतस्फीतापरान्तादिदेशपतिरपरिमितनृपति-

३. नतचरणकमल[:*] स्वभुजपरिपालनप्रतापाधिगतप्रचुरद्रविणविश्रा-णना-

४. वाप्तसर्व्वदिग्व्यापिशुक्लयशा[:*] शारदरजनिकररुचिरवपुरनद्य-कालीनपुरुष-

५. विशेषसदृशोदारचरितस्सुचरितनिदर्शनार्त्थमिव निर्म्मित⌒प्रतिहत-सामन्ता-

५. रातिरन्यनरपतिप्रतिविशिष्टवङ्शालङ्कारभूत⌒प्रभूतप्रवीरसाधनाधि-

७. ष्ठितदुर्ग्गनगरसागरस्सागरगम्भीरगिरिगुरुस्थिरप्रकृति[:*] प्रकृति-जनमनो-

८. हर⌒प्राज्ञसंश्रितगुरुस्वजनसाधुसाधारणधनोभिजनसदृशयन्त्रणोप-

९. गृहीतस्पृहणीयश्रीश्श्रीमहाराजविक्रमसेन[:*] महाकटाहारफरत-टिका-

१०. न्तर्ग्गतपञ्चामलकग्रामनिवासिनस्समाज्ञापयति [।*] विदितमस्तु वो यथास्माभिर्न्न-

११. रेन्द्रनारायणयोर्म्मातापित्रोरात्मनश्च पुण्याभिवृद्धये बलिचरुवै-

१२. श्वदेवाग्निहोत्रक्रियोत्सर्पणार्थमाचन्द्रार्कार्णवक्षितिस्थितिसमकालीन-

1. The compound is to be dissolved as follows—

नारायणश्च नारायणी च नारायणौ । नरेन्द्रौ नारायणाविव ।

* This text has been copied from Mrs. Shobhana Gokhale's article on the plates in the Marathi Journal *Itihāsa āṇi Saṁskṛiti*, No. 35 (October 1972).

Second Plate

१३. ⌒पुत्रपौत्रान्वयभोग्यश्चोरराजापथ्यकारिवर्ज्जमचाटभटप्रावेश्य [:*] सर्व्वादित्यवि-

१४. ष्टिपरिहीणो भूमिच्छिद्रन्यायेन कौण्डिन्यसगोत्रतैत्तिरीयककल्लिवन- वास्तव्य-

१५. ब्राह्मणशिवस्वामिनेयं ग्रामोतिसृष्टो यतोस्मद्वङ्श्यराजभिरन्यैश्च विभवानभावानुबन्धा-

१६. नायुर्व्वियोगानुगतं गुणांश्च दीर्घकालानुगुणान्विगणय्य दानञ्च गुणवतामवदात-

१७. मवदानमिति प्रमाणीकृत्य शशिकररुचिरं चिराय यशश्चिचीषुभिरयं भूमिदा-

१८. योनुमन्तव्यः पालयितव्यश्च ॥ यस्मादुक्तं भगवता वेदव्यासेन व्यासेन [।*]

१९. षष्टिवर्षसहस्राणि स्वर्ग्गे मोदति भूमिदः [।] आच्छेत्ता चानुमन्ता च तान्येव नरके वसेत् [॥१॥*]

२०. बहुभिर्व्वसुधा भुक्ता राजभिस्सगरादिभिः [।*] यस्य यस्य यदा भूमिस्तस्य तस्य तदा फलम् [॥२॥*]

२१. पूर्व्वदत्तां द्विजातिभ्यो यत्नाद्रक्ष युधिष्ठिर [।*] महीं महीमतां श्रेष्ठ दानाच्छ्रेयोनुपालनम् [॥३॥]

२२. विन्ध्याटवीषु घोरासु शुष्ककोटरवासिनः [।*] कृष्णाहयो हि जायन्ते भूमिदायं ह-

२३. रन्ति ये [॥४॥*] दूतकश्चात्रानिरुद्धः [।*] लिखितञ्चैतत्सान्धि- विग्रहिकस्वामिकेनेति [॥*]

२४. सं २०० ८० ४ चैत्र व २ [।*]

XIII. FRESH LIGHT ON TWO NEW GRANTS OF THE VISHṆUKUṆḌINS*

These grants were discovered in the village Tummalagūḍem in the Rāmannapeṭa tāluk of the Nalgoṇḍā district in Andhra Pradesh. They were first brought to the notice of scholars by Mr. B. N. Sastri in the Telugu journal *Bhāratī* (Madras) in the June and July numbers of 1955. I understand that the facsimiles of the grants were also published in the Journal. Later, Dr. M. Rama Rao published transcripts of their texts together with summaries of their contents, but without facsimiles in the *Journal of Indian History*, Vol. XLIII, pp. 733 f. He also discussed the problems of Vishṇukuṇḍin history presented by these new grants. Subsequently, Dr. Ajay Mitra Shastri discussed the contents of the grants in the same *Journal*, Vol. XLIV, pp. 683 f. and proposed alternative schemes of Vishṇukuṇḍin Chronology based on their evidence. Dr. Rama Rao examined the theories of Dr. Shastri in the same *Journal*, Vol. XLVI, pp. 217 f. As the grants are very important for the history of the Vishṇukuṇḍins, they require to be examined further from all points of view. I too had a great desire to study them, but as their facsimiles were not available to me, I refrained till now from doing so. There are several passages in Dr. Rama Rao's transcripts whose wording seems to be incorrect;[1] but in the absence of the facsimiles it is not possible to say if the mistakes occur in the original plates. However, I am making a few tentative suggestions for the emendations of the texts which appear to be necessary for the interpretation of the two grants. For convenience of reference

* *Journal of Indian History*, Vol. L, pp. 1 f.

1. See *e.g* lines 16-17 *Śrīmān Vikramendra-bhaṭṭāraka-varmaṇāgata-kālabhāvinaḥ* should be *Śrīmān Vikramendra-bhaṭṭārakavarmānāgata-kāla-bhāvinaḥ*.

I call them here (1) Indrapura grant of Vikramendravarman, and (2) Indrapura grant of Govindavarman.

When I first read the texts of the grants in Dr. Rama Rao's article some years ago, they appeared *prima facie* spurious. The first of them is dated in the Śaka year 488, Kārttika *va. di.* 8, that being the eleventh regnal year of Vikramendravarman II. Now, the Śaka era was introduced in the Andhra Pradesh by the Early Chālukyas of Bādāmi, when they conquered the country in the first quarter of seventh century A.D. It was introduced in Kaliṅga much later, in the second half of the ninth century A.D.[1] The date of the first Indrapura grant is earlier by about fifty years than the date of the conquest of Andhra by the Early Cālukyas. Besides, all other known grants of the Vishṇukuṇḍins are dated in regnal years. We have indeed an earlier date of the Śaka era (*viz.* Śaka 380) from the eastern part of South India in the Jaina work *Lokavibhāga*; but it is proved that the date is spurious,[2] So the first Indrapura grant which bears a date of the Śaka era appeared suspicious. Again, that grant belongs to the reign of Vikramendravarman II, the great-grandson of Mādhavavarman I. The latter, who is known to have married a Vākāṭaka princess, was supposed to have come to the throne after the last Vākāṭaka king of the Vatsagulma branch, *viz.* Harisheṇa, closed his reign in Vidarbha in *circa* A.D. 500.[3] Mādhavavarman I had a long reign of about 50 years. His grandson Indrabhaṭṭārakavarman is known to have ruled for at least 27 years and his son Vikramendravarman II for at least 10 years. Even if we suppose that Vikramendravarman I, the son of Mādhavavarman I, did not come to the throne as he probably pre-deceased his father who had a long reign of about 50 years, the sum total of the duration of the reigns of Mādhavavarman I and Indrabhaṭṭārakavarman comes to 77 years. If Mādhavavarman I had come to the throne in *circa* A.D. 500, his great-grandson Vikramendravarman II could not have

1. *Studies in Indology*, Vol. IV, p. 196.

2. For a full discussion of this date, see *ibid.*, Vol. II., pp. 107 f.

3. *C.I.I.*, Vol. V, Introd., p. vi. Jaiswal placed the close of Harisheṇa's reign in A.D. 520, and Altekar in A.D. 510.

commenced his reign earlier than A.D. 577. So the Indrapura grant in the eleventh year of his reign dated Śaka 488 (A.D. 566-67) appeared spurious.

These arguments are not, however, irrefutable. For aught we know, the Śaka era may have been introduced in Andhra earlier than the advent of the Early Chālukyas. We have an analogous instance in the Hisse Borāḷā inscription[1] of the Vākāṭaka king Devasena, which is dated in the Śaka year 380, though all other known records of the Vākāṭakas are dated in regnal years. After all, the supposed date of the accession of Mādhavavarman I is conjectural. He may have come to the throne a few years earlier. So we must examine these Indrapura grants with an open mind. I have tried to do so here.

The first Indrapura grant of Vikramendravarman II gives the following genealogy of that Vishṇukuṇḍin king: *Mahārāja* Govindavarman—his son *Mahārāja* Mādhavarman I, who performed eleven Aśvamedhas and several other sacrifices such as Bahusuvarṇa, Pauṇḍarīka, Vājapeya *etc.* and married a Vākāṭaka princess—his dear son *Mahārāja* Vikramendra (I), who was a devout follower of the Buddha and a great poet—his son Indrabhaṭṭārakavarman, who became the lord of the entire Cakravartikshetra by his victories with many four-tusked elephants—and his dear son Vikramendrabhaṭṭārakavarman (II), who had several *Sāmantas*.[2] We are further told that he treated one Mādhavarāja as his own son. The latter had established his greatness by forcibly ousting several kings, and was endowed not only with a handsome form but also with several good qualities such as political wisdom and valour. It is not known in what connection his name is mentioned in this grant. We next get the information that the Paramabhaṭṭārikā-

1. *Ep. Ind.*, Vol. XXVII, pp. 1 f. It is possible that the use of the Śaka era in this case was due to the person who excavated the tank having come from Saurāshṭra, where the Śaka era was in vogue. It is noteworthy that he named the tank as *Sudarśana*.

2. Rama Rao thought that Mādhavarāja mentioned in line 20 of the first Indrapura grant was a *sāmanta*; but the expression *aśesha-kula-tilakāyamāna-* refers to the royal family of Śrī-Pṛthvīmūla, and not to Mādhavarāja.

mahādevī (*i.e.* the Crowned Queen) of the illustrious Govindarāja was born in the famous royal family of Pṛithvīmūla, which was the foremost among the feudatory families (of the Vishṇukuṇḍins) and whose matrimonial relation with the Vishṇukuṇḍins had been commended by all persons respected by the family of the latter. She had erected a monastery called Paramabhaṭṭārikāmahāvihāra at Indrapura. The king Vikramendrabhaṭṭāraka, after his victory over a Pallava king named Siṁha[varman], granted, when encamped at the Mahāvihāra, the village Iruṇḍera on the eighth *tithi* of the dark fortnight of Kārttika in the Śaka year 488, which was his eleventh regnal year. The charter was apparently written by one Mūlarāja, who had played an important role in restoring the fortune of his royal lord.

The second Indrapura grant is of the Vishṇukuṇḍin king Govindavarman. It gives the following genealogy : *Mahārāja* Indravarman—his son *Mahārāja* Mādhavavarman—his son *Mahārāja* Govindavarman, who made several grants to temples and *vihāras*. The last king made the grant of the village Dvārvembadala, also known as Peṇka, to the Paramamahādevīvihāra at the instance of his own Crowned Queen for the purpose of providing materials of the worship (of the Buddha), the food, raiment and medicines of the *bhikshus* and for the repairs of the *vihāra*, on the full-moon day of Vaiśākha in his thirty-seventh regnal year.

The first Indrapura grant summarised above gives the genealogy of the Vishṇukuṇḍins from Govindavarman to Vikramendravarman II as in other known grants of the Vishṇukuṇḍins, but the kings mentioned in the second Indrapura grant are apparently new. These two grants have posed the following problems :—

(1) Who was Mādhavarāja mentioned in lines 19-20 of the first Indrapura grants ? What part did he play in the making of the grant ?

(2) How were the kings mentioned in the second Indrapura grant, related to those in the first grant chronologically ?

(3) Was Govindarāja mentioned in line 28 of the first grant, different from or identical with Govindavarman mentioned in line 13 of the second grant ?

(4) How was Pṛithvimūla, the progenitor of the royal family in which the Paramabhaṭṭārikāmahādevī, the queen of Govindarāja, was born, related to the homonymous king known from the Godāvarī plates ?

We shall try to answer these questions serially.

(1) The text in lines 17 to 20 in the first Indrapura grant which describes the Mahāvihāra is obscure.[1] There is some lacuna. Perhaps it was intended to be stated that the grant was made at the instance of Mādhavarāja, who is described as treated by the ruling king Vikramendravarman II as his own son. Some expression like *anurudhya* has been inadvertently omitted after *Śrī-Mādhavarājaṁ .... naya-parākram-ādi-guṇa-sandohaṁ.* It was probably inteended to state that the king made the grant in order to please[2] or at the instance of Mādhavarāja.

(2) The kings mentioned in the second grant were closely related to those named in the first grant as will be clear from the following tables :—

(First Grant)	(Second Grant)
Indrabhaṭṭārakavarman	Indravarman
|	|
(son)	(son)
Vikramendrabhaṭṭārakavarman	Mādhavavarman
	|
	(son)
	Govindavarman

So Mādhavavarman was the brother of Vikramendravarman. He is evidently identical with Mādhavarāja mentioned in the first grant, at whose instance the first Indrapura grant was apparently made. Dr. Rama Rao's objection to Mādhavarāja being recognised as a Vishṇukuṇḍin prince has little weight. Not all Viṣṇukuṇḍin princes bore names ending in *varman*. See *e.g.* Vikramamahendra and Mañchaṇṇabhaṭṭāraka. Besides, Mādhavarāja may have been called Mādhavavarman after he came to the throne.

1. The expression *Śrī-Mādhavarāj-ābhidhānaṁ* is left unconnected in lines 19-20. The expressions in the accusative case in lines 21-23 qualify *Śrī-Pṛthvimūla-rāja-vaṁśaṁ* in line 23.

2. For *anurudhya* in this sense, see *ity-ādibhiḥ priya-satair-anurudhya mugdhām* etc. in the *Uttararāmacharita,* Act III. In the second grant also the person at whose instance it was made, *viz.* the queen of the reigning king Govindavarman, is mentioned.

The first Indrapura grant describes that Mādhavarāja had established his greatness by forcibly ousting other kings and that he was endowed with political wisdom and valour. Evidently, he had greatly helped Vikramendravarman in extending his dominion. So, though he was a brother, the latter treated him lovingly like his own son.

(2) The kings mentioned in the second Indrapura grant were closely related to the last two kings in the first grant. It seems that Mādhavavarman succeeded his brother Vikramendravarman. The latter may have died sonless. There is no reason to suppose that Mādhavavarman usurped the throne, as Rama Rao supposes. He was later succeeded by his own son Govindavarman.

(3) Govindarāja mentioned in the first grant was an earlier king[1] of the Vishṇukuṇḍin family, who is mentioned as the husband of the Paramabhaṭṭārikāmahādevī. The latter constructed the Paramabhaṭṭārikāmahāvihāra at Indrapura. This Govindarāja was identical with the homonymous father of *Mahārāja* Mādhavavarman I. It seems that Govindavarman was the first great king of the Vishṇukuṇḍin family who laid the foundation of its dominion. So he and his queen were held in great veneration. This is shown by the title *Paramabhaṭṭarikā* used in connection with the latter's name. On the other hand, Govindavarman mentioned in the second grant was a later king, being the nephew of Vikramendravarman II. The *mahāvihāra* to which the grants were made was, however, the same.

(4) Pṛithvīmūla in whose royal family the crowned queen of Govindarāja who constructed the Mahāvihāra at Indrapura, was born, was probably an ancestor of the homonymous king who was a contemporary of the Vishṇukuṇḍin king Indrabhaṭṭāraka mentioned in the Godāvarī plates. The first Indrapura grant states that the queen of Govindarāja was born in his lineage (*Pṛithvīmūlarājavaṁśaṁ...śriyā iva sāgaram alaṅkṛitavatyā*). She was *not* his daughter.

1. He cannot be identical with Govindavarman mentioned in the second Indrapura grant because the latter flourished in a later age and his wife could not nave been referred to in first grant as *Parama-bhaṭṭārikāmahādevī*.

So Vikramendravarman II was succeeded by Mādhavavarman (III), and the latter by his son Govindavarman (II). Vikramendravarman II ruled for at least 11 years. His last known date is Śaka 488 (A.D. 566-67). We do not know how long Mādhavavarman III reigned, but his son and successor Govindavarman II ruled for at least 37 years. Adding 37 to A.D. 566, we get A.D. 603. Vikramendravarman II, Mādhavavarman III and Govindavarman II must have reigned for some years more than what we know from their own or their successors' grants. So Govindavarman II was probably the Vishṇukuṇḍin king who was befeated and deposed by Pulakeśin II in *circa* A.D. 615.

How does this reconstruction of Vishṇukuṇḍin history affect the dates at present assigned conjecturally to the Vishṇukuṇḍin kings ? Supposing that Vikramendravarman I predeceased his father Mādhavavarman I (who had a long reign of about 50 years), the total known reign-periods of Mādhavavarman (about 50 years), Indrabhaṭṭārakavarman (27 years), and Vikramendravarman II (11 years) comes to 88 years. Deducting this from A.D. 566, the known date of Vikramendravarman II, we get the year A.D. 478, which is the latest limit for the accession of Mādhavavarman I. Harisheṇa, the Vākāṭaka king who had conquered Andhra and entered into a matrimonial alliance with the Vishṇukuṇḍin Mādhavavarman I, ruled probably from A.D. 475 to A.D. 500.[1] He was thus a contemporary of Mādhavavarman I and so the matrimonial alliance which probably took place in his reign is not unlikely.

Finally, let us see what light, if any, is shed on the epoch of the Gaṅga era by this construction of Vishṇukuṇḍin history.

From the Godāvarī plates of Pṛithvīmūla[2] we learn that *Adhirāja* Indra fought in company with other chiefs who were united to overthrow a certain Indrabhaṭṭāraka. Kielhorn's identification of the latter with the homonymous Vishṇukuṇḍin king is generally accepted. Dr. Rama Rao identifies *Adhirāja*

1. *C.I.I.*, Vol. V, Introd., p. vi.
2. *J B.B R.A.S.*, Vol. XVI, pp. 114 f.

Indra with the Gaṅga king Indravarman I of the Jirjingi plates, dated in the Gaṅga year 39, on the ground of similarity of description (*viz.* fighting with four-tusked elephants), and gives the following equation :—

> Accession of Indrabhaṭṭāraka=A.D. 528=39th year of the Gaṅga era.
>
> From this he concludes that the Gaṅga era commenced in (A.D. 528—39)=A.D. 489.

The argument is fallacious. The description of fighting with four-tusked elephants is conventional.[1] Still, the identifications based on the similarity of description may be correct. But the equation given above is not correct. The fight mentioned in the Godāvarī plates did not necessarily occur in the first year of Indrabhaṭṭāraka's reign. Similarly, it is not known for certain that it occurred in the 39th year of the Gaṅga era, the date of the Jirjingi plates of the Gaṅga king Indravarman I. So Rama Rao's conclusion that the Gaṅga era started in A.D. 489 is unwarranted.

Dr. Rama Rao says that there have been as many views about the epoch of the Gaṅga era as there are writers. This was true before the present writer fixed the epoch as A.D. 498-99, Chaitra *śu. di.* 1. All the known dates of the Gaṅga era can now be satisfactorily worked out with this epoch as shown elsewhere.[2] Now, with the new information supplied by the first Indrapura grant, Indrabhaṭṭārakavarman seems to have closed his reign in A.D. 555-56. He ruled for at least 27 years before this date. So his reign must have commenced not later than A.D. 528-29. That was the 30th year of the Gaṅga era according to my reckoning of that era. The Jirjingi plates of the Gaṅga king Indravarman are dated in the 39th year of the Gaṅga era. So he was a contemporary of the Vishṇukuṇḍin king Indrabhaṭṭārakavarman. The identification first suggested by Kielhorn is thus corroborated by the new Vishṇukuṇḍin grant of Vikramendrabhaṭṭāraka.

1. See a similar expression in two grants of the Sendrakas, *C.I.I.*, Vol. IV, pp. 112 and 119. See also *Ep. Ind.*, Vol. XXII, p. 95 and *ibid*, Vol. XXV, p. 30.
2. *Studies in Indology*, Vol. IV, pp. 178 f.

XIV. LOCATION OF VARDHAMĀNAPURA MENTIONED IN JINASENA'S HARIVAṀŚA

In the *Harivaṁśapurāṇa* (canto 66) of the Jaina author Jinasena there occur the following two verses about the date, the kings of the time ruling in the different directions and the places where he commenced and completed that work :—

शाकेष्वब्दशतेषु सप्तसु दिशं पञ्चोत्तरेषूत्तरां
पातीन्द्रायुधनाम्नि कृष्णनृपजे श्रीवल्लभे दक्षिणाम् ।
पूर्वां श्रीमदवन्तिभूभृतिनृपे वत्सादिराजेऽपरां
सौराणामधिमण्डले जययुते वीरे वराहेऽवति ॥
कल्याणैः परिवर्धमानविपुलश्रीवर्धमाने पुरे
श्रीपार्श्वालयनन्नराजवसतौ पर्याप्तशेषः पुरा ।
पश्चाद्दोस्तटिकाप्रजाप्रजनितप्राज्यार्चनावर्धने
शान्तेः शान्तगृहे जिने सुरचितो वंशो हरीणामयम् ॥

In these verses Jinasena tells us that when he commenced the work at Vardhamānapura in the Nannarāja-vasati of the Tīrthaṅkara Pārśvanātha and completed it at Dostaṭikā, in the quiet temple of the Tīrthaṅkara Śāntinātha, in the Śaka year 705 (A.D. 783-84), Indrāyudha was ruling in the north, the illustrious Vallabha, son of King Kṛishṇa, in the south, the king of Avanti in the east, and King Vatsarāja and Jayavarāha in the kingdom of the Sauras (*i.e.* in Saurāshṭra) in the west. [1]

I have shown elsewhere[2] that these kings can be identified as follows :—Indrāyudha was ruling at Kanauj in North India. Śrī-Vallabha, son of King Kṛishṇa, was the Rāshṭrakūṭa king Dhruva, son of Kṛishṇa I, who had usurped the throne from his brother Govinda II just three years before in *circa* A.D. 780. Jinasena has not named the king of Avanti,

1. There are other and incorrect interpretations of the third line of the first verse, for which see our *Studies in Indology*, Vol. IV, pp. 137 f.

2. *Loc. cit.*

but I have shown elsewhere[1] that he was probably Chandragupta, who, twelve years later, was defeated by the Rāshṭrakūṭa king Govinda III in the course of his northern campaign. Finally, Vatsarāja was the Gurjara-Pratīhāra king of Bhinmāl, and Jayavarāha was ruling in Saurāshṭra or Kāṭhiawāḍ.

Several years ago Dr. Hiralal Jain suggested that Vardhamānapura where Jinasena commenced and wrote a considerable portion of the *Harivaṁśa* was identical with Badhnāwar, about 15 miles north of Dhār.[2] Since then Dr. H.V. Trivedi has discovered several Jaina antiquities at the place. Dostaṭikā where Jinasena completed the *Harivaṁśa* lies about 10 miles to the west of Badhnāwar and is now known as Dotariā. Further, I have shown that a place of the name Vardhamānapura was situated in Mālwā in ancient times. The Paramāra king Jayavarman, a descendant of Udayāditya, brother of the famous Bhoja of Dhārā, is known to have issued a copper-plate grant from that place.[3] Kielhorn, who edited the grant, could not identify the place, but there is no doubt that it was situated in Mālwā. It is probably identical with modern Badhnāwar. The directions of the kingdoms where the kings mentioned by Jinasena were ruling in his time suit Badhnāwar very well, *viz.* Kanauj in the north, Mahārāshṭra in the south, Avanti (Ujjain) in the east, and Rājaputāna and Saurāshṭra in the west. Besides, there is likely to have been a Jaina temple called Nannarāja-vasati at Badhnāwar. It was evidently built by a king named Nannarāja and named after himself. We know from the discovery of a stone inscription at Indragaḍh, about 100 miles north of Badhnāwar, that a king named Nannappa was ruling in the reign in the Vikrama Saṁvat 767 (A.D. 710-11).[4] That inscription records the construction of a Śiva temple at Indragaḍh by the Pāśupata ascetic Dānarāśi in that year. All these pieces of evidence point unmistakably to the identification of Vardhamānapura with modern Badhnāwar.

1. *Studies in Indology*, Vol. IV, pp. 137 f
2. *Ind. Cult.*, Vol. XI, pp. 161 f.
3. *Ind. Ant.*, Vol. XIX, pp, 349 f.
4. *Ep. Ind.*, Vol. XXXII, pp. 121 f. ; *Studies in Indology*. Vol. II, pp. 185 f.

Dr. A.N. Upadhye, however, does not agree with this identification.[1] He would identify Vardhamānapura with modern Waḍhwāṇ in Saurāshṭra. He draws attention to the mention of Vardhamānapura in the Haḍḍālā (Saurāshṭra) grant of Dharaṇīvarāha, dated Śaka Saṁvat 836.[2] He has raised several objections against the identification of Vardhamānapura with Badhnāwar. They are stated and critically examined below.

Objection 1—The corruption of Vardhamāna into Badhnāwar is speculative acrobatics of vowel and consonant changes. The place is called Vardhanapura in the records found at Badhnāwar.

Answer—The name Vardhamānapura was current in the ancient period from the eighth to the eleventh century A.D. Later, it seems to have changed first to Vardhanapura and finally to Badhnāwar. Dr. Upadhye has not stated the dates, definite or approximate, of the records at Badhnāwar which give the place-name Vardhanapura. Probably they are of a later period[3]. In that case that form of the place-name is not surprising. In the corruption of the name from Vardhamānapura to Badhnāwar one syllable has been dropped. This is no 'acrobatic of vowel and consonant change'; for similar changes are noticed in other place-names also. Take, for instance, the name Maheshwar derived from ancient Māhishmatīpura.[4] In this place-name the *aksharas ma* and *ti* have been elided in course of time. The same has happened in the case of Badhnāwar. That there was a place named Vardhamānapura in Mālwā in ancient times has been shown above from a grant of Jayavarman, a king of Malwā. About this, more will be said later.

Objection 2—The identification of Dostaṭikā with Dotaria is tempting, but it cannot be proposed without first prov-

1. See his edition of the *Kuvalayamālā*, Vol. II, Introduction, pp. 105 ff.

2. *Ind. Ant.*, Vol. XII, pp. 193 f.

3. Some inscriptions from Badhnāwar giving the name of the place as *Vardhanapura* cited by Dr. Jain in *Ind. Cult.*, Vol. XI, pp. 167-68 are dated V.S 1216 and 1229.

4. The ancient name *Māhishmatīpura* is mentioned in some records at Maheshwar. See *Potdar Commemoration Volume*, pp. 317 f.

ing that Vardhamānapura is Badhnāwar.

Answer—This identification clinches the issue as we have proved above by several pieces of evidence that Vardhamānapura mentioned by Jinasena is Badhnāwar. No place like Dostaṭikā is known in the vicinity of Waḍhwāṇ.

Objection 3—In none of the epigraphs found at Badhnāwar is mentioned the Punnāṭa Saṅgha with which both Jinasena and Harisheṇa were associated.

Answer—This is only an *argumentum ex silentio*. The mention of the Saṅgha may be noticed later.

Objection 4—Badhnāwar records mention neither any local Varāha ruler nor any suzerain with a name ending in *-pāla* referred to by Jinasena and Harisheṇa.

Answer—Jinasena says only that a ruler named Jayavarāha was ruling in Saurāshṭra. He does not say that any ruler with a name ending in *varāha* or *pāla* was ruling from Vardhamānapura. So this objection has no force. As for the mention of Vinayādikapāla, I have shown elsewhere that the Pratīhāras may have extended their rule to Mālwa later.

Objection 5—Badhnāwar presumes an earlier form of the name to end in *pura*, but Jinasena mentions only Vardhamāna as the name of the place, *pura* being a mere descriptive appendage.

Answer—This is a flimsy argument. In fact Jinasena mentions *Śrī-Vardhamāne pure*, which is the same as *Śrī-Vardhamānapure*. This objection should rather go against the identification of Vardhamānapura with Waḍhwāṇ, as the latter place-name has no part corresponding to *pura*.

Objection 6—No specific evidence is put forward to prove that any of the known Nannarājas had built a temple at Vardhamāna(pura) or at Badhnāwar.

Answer—There may be no record found at Badhnāwar mentioning specifically a temple of Pārśvanātha built by a king named Nannarāja. But I have shown that a king of that name was ruling in Mālwā in an earlier age, as a stone inscription mentioning his rule and dated A.D. 710-11 has been discovered at Indragaḍh in the adjoining Mandasor district.[1] He may

1. *Ep. Ind.*, Vol. XXXII, pp. 112 f

have built that temple. On the other hand, there is no evidence that such a king flourished in Saurāshṭra in that age. So this argument proves fatal to the identification of Vardhamānapura with Waḍhwāṇ.

Objection 7—The inscription of Jayavarmadeva, a Paramāra king, no doubt, mentions Vardhamānapura, but the various places mentioned therein have not been identified. May be that Jayavarman was staying at Vardhamānapura (in Saurāshṭra) in the period of his exile.

Answer—The inscription of Jayavarmadeva certainly belongs to Mālwā[1] He was a Paramāra prince, being a descendant of Udayāditya, brother of Bhoja of Dhārā. It is a gratuitous assumption that he was in exile at the time of the grant; for he made the grant as *Paramabhaṭṭāraka, Mahārājādhirāja, Parameśvara* at Vardhamānapura. Though none of the places mentioned in the grant have yet been identified, I have noticed some of them in the vicinity of Badhnāwar.[2] The King was encamped at Vardhamānapura, which, as shown already, is identical with Badnāwar. The King states in the grant that he had made it when he was encamped at Chandrapurī. This place is clearly identical with Chandoriā, about 7 miles north of Badhnāwar. As the grant has not been found complete, the name of the donated village has been lost, but it was probably identical with Māyamoḍaka situated in the territorial division of Vaṭakheṭaka—36, to the residents of which the royal order was addressed. The donee had emigrated from Adriyalavidāvarī. Some of these places can be identified in the vicinity of Badhnāwar. The identification of Māyamoḍaka is uncertain unless it is Madarpāḍā, about 10 miles north of Badhnāwar. Vaṭakheṭaka may be Baḍmaṇḍal, about 4 miles north-east of the latter. Adriyalavidāwarī has now lost its earlier half portion. It may be identical with Biḍwaī, about 6 miles north of Badhnāwar. Most of these identifications are almost certain. They show that Badhnāwar probably represents ancient Vardhamānapura of Māḷwā. The grant could not have been made at Waḍhwāṇ as Jayavarma-

1. The plate was found at Ujjayinī. *Ind. Ant.*, Vol. XIX, p. 345.
2. See Survey of India Map No. 46 M.

deva had no authority over that region. The attempt to locate Vardhamānapura in Saurāshṭra is, therefore, futile.

As the identification of Vardhamānapura with Badhnāwar is thus certain, Dostaṭikā is undoubtedly the same as modern Dotariā.

Some of the objections raised by Dr. Upadhye are like a double-edged sword. They cut the ground under his own feet. Some of the important objections that can be raised against his own identification of Vardhamānapura with Waḍhwāṇ may be stated as follows :—

(1) The directions in which the different kings named in the *Harivaṁśa* were ruling do not at all suit Waḍhwāṇ. Vatsarāja was ruling at Bhinmāl or Jālor, which is not to the west but to the north of Waḍhwāṇ. Jinasena was evidently mentioning the directions with reference to the place where he composed the *Harivaṁśa*. He was not writing the geography of India.

(2) There is no evidence of a place like Dostaṭikā in the vicinity of Waḍhwāṇ.

(3) There is no evidence that any king named Nanna was ruling over the region round Waḍhwāṇ who could have constructed the Jaina temple Nannarāja-vasati.

These are very strong pieces of evidence which preclude the supposition that Vardhamānapura mentioned in Jinasena's *Harivaṁśa* was identical with Waḍhwāṇ in Saurāshṭra. On the other hand, there is overwhelming evidence to support the identification of the place with Badhnāwar, 15 miles north of Dhār.

XV. NEW LIGHT ON THE HISTORY OF THE ŚILĀHĀRAS OF NORTH KOṄKAṆ

There were three families of the Śilāhāras ruling in Mahārāshṭra. One of them was ruling over North Koṅkaṇ comprising the Ṭhāṇā and Kolābā districts, with its capital at Sthānaka (modern Ṭhāṇā). The second held sway in South Koṅkaṇ. It was ruling at first from Chandrapura (modern Chāndor in the Goā State), but later shifted its capital to Balipattana (modern Khārepāṭan in the Ratnāgiri district). The third occupied Kolhāpur, Sātārā, Sāngli and Belgaon districts. Its first capital seems to have been Karahāṭa (modern Karhāḍ in the Sātārā district), but later it was shifted to Kolhāpur, where several of its records have been found.

The ancient history of this dynasty has been dealt with by Pandit Bhagwanlal Indraji, Dr. Fleet, Dr. R. G. Bhandarkar and Dr. A.S.Altekar. We also have given it elsewhere. Dr. M. G. Dikshit discussed some aspects of it while editing some of its records. Still, there are not a few incidents and problems in it which are far from clear. It is proposed to discuss some problems in the history of the Śilāhāras of North Koṅkaṇ in the period of a century from A.D. 1025 to 1125.

The political history of the Deccan in this period is very much complicated. Scholars have advocated different views about them. Before discussing them, it is necessary to give the genealogical lists of the Śilāhāras of North Koṅkaṇ and of two other contemporary royal families which came into conflict with them, *viz.* the Later Chālukyas of Kalyāṇī and the Kadambas of Goā. They are given below with approximate dates :—

The Śilāhāras of North Koṅkaṇ

Arikesarin

Chhittarāja (1020-1035)	Nāgārjuna (1035-1045)	Mummuṇi (1045-1070)
	Anantapāla (1070-1125)	
	Aparāditya I (1127-1148)	

The Latter Chalukyas

Jayasiṃha II (1015-1043)
|
Someśvara I (1043-1068)
|
Someśvara II (1068-1076)
|
Vikramāditya VI (1076-1126)

The Kadambas

Shashṭha II (1005-1050)
|
Jayakeśin I (1050-1080)
|
Gūhalla III (1080-1100)
|
Vijayāditya I (1100-1104)
|
Jayakeśin II (1104-1140)

Śilāhāra inscriptions state that there was *dāyāda-vyasana* or a Civil War after the death of Mummuṇi. The Yavana soldiers devastated the country, persecuting gods and Brāhmaṇas. Then Anantapāla (or Anantarāja) destroyed the violent and vile Yavanas and inscribed his fame on the disc of the moon. Again, at the close of his reign an Asura (demon) named Chhittukka invaded Koṅkaṇ. Feudatories joined him. Then religion was destroyed, old people were persecuted, the subjects became dispirited and the prosperity of the kingdom came to an end. But, undaunted, Aparāditya rushed single-handed on horse-back to the battlefield and by the prowess of his arms and his sword he routed the enemy. The latter was then completely confounded and did not know whether to fight or to flee. Ultimately, he took refuge with the Mlechchhas.

The Śilāhāra records do not mention the enemies who brought these calamities on North Koṅkaṇ. We have to find them out in the light of contemporary records.

About the calamity which occurred after the death of Mummuṇi, scholars have put forward conflicting views. D.C. Ganguly has stated that it was the Later Chālukya king Someśvara I who then invaded the Śilāhāra kingdom and killed Mummuṇi. M.G. Dikshit says that Kadamba Jayakeśin I destroyed Mummuṇi. But neither of these views appears to be correct. It is true that Someśvara I defeated a Śilāhāra king. Contemporary inscriptions state indeed that he gathered several of his generals such as Kākatīya Prola, Kadamba Chāmuṇḍarasa of Vanavāsī, Yādava Ajjarasa, Haihaya Devarasa, Madhusūdana or Madhuva and Pulakeśin. With their large forces he invaded North Koṅkaṇ and destroyed its ruler. This invasion is referred to in several records. The first of them chronologically is the one dated Śaka 969 (A.D. 1047) discovered at Taḍkhel in Nānded district of the Marāṭhwāḍā division of Mahārāshṭra. So Someśvara's invasion of North Koṅkaṇ must have occurred some time before that date. Mummuṇi could not have been killed in this encounter; for he was reigning for as many as twenty-four years at least after this date. So the Śilāhāra king who succumbed to the attack on this occasion must have been some one else.

We conjecture that the king who was killed in this campaign was Nāgārjuna. The genealogy given above shows that Arikesarin had three sons, *viz.* Chhittarāja, Nāgārjuna and Mummuṇi and they reigned over North Koṅkan, one after another. Dr. Altekar's statement that Nāgārjuna seems to have died before Chhittarāja is incorrect. Both the Khārepāṭan and Vaḍavalī plates state clearly that he became *kshmāpati* (king) after Chhittarāja. The contemporary Sanskrit *Champū-kāvya Udayasundarīkathā* states explicitly that all the three brothers Chhittarāja, Nāgārjuna and Mummuṇi reigned, one after another. As a matter of fact, there is now no scope for doubt in this respect. A copper-plate grant of Nāgārjuna dated in the Śaka year 961 (A. D. 1039) has been discovered at Thāṇā, which leaves no doubt that he reigned, though for a short time.

The last known date of Chhittarāja is A.D. 1034 and the first known date of Mummuṇi is A. D. 1048. Nāgārjuna reigned in the interval. He may, therefore, be placed in *circa* A. D. 1035-1045. He may have fallen in the invasion of Koṅkaṇ by Someśvara in *circa* A.D. 1045. So his destruction at the hands of the Later Chālukyas is referred to in the Taḍkhel inscription dated A.D. 1047.

As Nāgārjuna's son Anantapāla (or Anantadeva I) was a minor, his uncle Mummuṇi seems to have got the throne evidently by the favour of Someśvara.

Mummuṇi had a long reign of about 25 years (A.D. 1045-1070). During his reign the Kadamba king of Goā Shashṭhadeva II (*circa* A.D. 1005-1050) was once sporting along the Koṅkaṇ coast. A graphic description of how Mummuṇi welcomed him is given in the Narendra inscription as follows :—"When the exalted valour of Chhaṭṭayadeva in his sport on the ocean reached him, Mummuṇi of Ṭhāṇeya, hearing of it, came into his presence and led him to his palace, and displayed intense affection; and he bestowed on him his daughter with much pomp, and gave to his son-in-law five lakhs of gold."

Mummuṇi continued to reign till about A.D. 1070. The Khārepāṭaṇ plates of his successor Ananatapāla state that there was a Civil War at the close of Mummuṇi's reign. Taking advantage of it, the country was overrun by the Yavanas who harassed the gods and Brāhmaṇas. Dr. M. G. Dikshit has interpreted this description to mean that the Kadamba king Jayakeśin murdered the king Mummuṇi in his invasion of North Koṅkaṇ. Says he, "In view of the long continued hostilities of the Śilāhāras and the Kadambas, the welcome extended by Mummuṇi to Shashṭha II and the marriage of his daughter with the Kadamba king must have been done by the Śilāhāra king most unwillingly and perhaps with a view to establish good political relations with the Kadamba king. Otherwise, he would not have willingly given his daughter to an aged king who had completed a reign of fifty years. But hostilities between the two royal families seem to have increased in course of time; for we find that Shashṭha's son Jayakeśin II (?) killed Mummuṇi some time after Śaka 982 (1060)."

There are several misstatements in Dikshit's interpretation. Jayakeśin I (not Jayakeśin II) is known to have killed a Śilāhāra king, but as shown above, he was not Mummuṇi but his elder brother Nāgārjuna. If Jayakeśin I had killed Mummuṇi, the Khārepāṭan plates of Anantapāla would have said so. They, however, mention no such incident, but only state that there was a Civil War (*dāyāda-vyasana*) after Mummuṇi's death.

The Chālukya king Someśvara I had made great preparations for the invasion of North Koṅkaṇ. He had called to his aid several of his feudatories such as Kākatīya Prola, Chāmuṇḍarasa, the Kadamba prince of Vanavāsī, Yādava Ajjavasa. Haihaya Devarasa, Madhusūdana and Pulakeśin. Inscriptions say that they exterminated a Śilāhāra king. A similar statement occurs also in the records of the Kadambas of Goa, which also must be with reference to the same event. The Degāṁve inscription describes Jayakeśin I as 'Death to the king of Kapardī-dvīpa' (*Kāpardika-dvīpa-nṛipāla-kālaḥ*). North Koṅkaṇ was known as *Kapardi-dvipa* or *Kavaḍīdvīpa* after the founder of the Śilāhāra family, Kapardin I. So there is no doubt that Jayakeśin I killed a Śilāhāra king. As he was a contemporary of Mummuṇi, several scholars such as Fleet, Dikshit and others have supposed that he killed Mummuṇi; but the reference is probably to the destruction of Nāgārjuna as shown above. Shashṭha II, the father of Jayakeśin I, was a feudatory of Someśvara I. As shown above, the latter had called several of his feudatories to join him in the campaign against North Koṅkaṇ. It is not likely that he had not asked Shashṭha II, the neighbour of the Śilāhāra king to take part in the invasion. Shashṭha seems to have sent his son Jayakeśin I in response to the summons. He seems to have taken a prominent part in killing Nāgārjuna. So he is described as 'Death to the king of Kapardi-dvīpa'.

Thereafter, Mummuṇi appears to have sought the alliance of the Kadamba king by welcoming him and offering him his daughter in marriage. We have no reason to suppose that this alliance came to an end in the course of one generation. The reference to a Civil War in the plates of Anantadeva I tells a different tale.

We have stated above that as Anantapāla was a minor at the time of Nāgārjuna's death, Mummuṇi sat on the throne. After his death, Anantadeva must have pressed his claim to the throne. Perhaps, Mummuṇi may have arranged that his son should succeed him as was done in similar circumstances by the Early Chālukya king Maṅgaleśa and the Yādava king Mahādeva. As Anantapāla refused to acquiesce in his supercession, there seems to have broken out a Civil War in the country. The exact nature of this Civil War was not understood by scholars till now. Some took the expression *dāyāda-vyasana* to mean that there was a war between the Śilāhāra families of North Koṅkaṇ and Kolhāpur. But they were not really *dāyādas, i.e.* claimants for common ancestral property. So this *dāyāda-vyasana* must be taken as a conflict between Mummuṇi's son and Anantapāla for the throne at Ṭhāṇā.

On this occasion the Kadambas of Goā appear to have espoused the cause of Mummuṇi's son. There were then several settlements of the Arabs on the western coast. The Paṇajī plates of Jayakeśin I mention the settlement of an Arab merchant (*Nauvittaka*) named Mānāliyam of Chemulya (Chaula near Alibag in the Kolābā district). Like the British and French merchants of later times, these Arab merchants also may have kept a small force for the protection of their settlements. In ancient times the *Śreṇīs* (guilds) were allowed to maintain such a force for the safety of their trade and commerce. It was called *Śreṇi-bala.* The Governments of the time were not loth to use it in case of need. In course of time these Arab merchants became powerful. Some of them who helped the Kadambas in times of need were even appointed ministers and received gifts of villages from them. Some Arab allies of the Kadambas seem to have taken part in this campaign in support of Mummuṇi's son. As was their wont, they seem to have harassed the gods and Brāhmaṇas in this conflict, as described in the abovementioned passage in the Karepāṭaṇ plates. But Anantapāla, the son of Nāgārjuna, inflicted a crushing defeat on these Yavana compatriots of the Kadamba king and inscribed his glory of the disc of the moon. The verse describing this is very incorrectly written in the Khārepāṭaṇ plates and was not, therefore, understood correctly by the editor K.T. Telang. The correct form of the verse will be as follows :—

जाते दायादवैरिव्यसनिनि समये यैरवाप्तप्रभावै-
र्ध्वस्ता देवद्विजातिप्रमथनविधिना कौंकणक्षोणिरेषा ।
तानुग्रान्पापराशीन्मुनयवनभटान्खड्गधाराम्बुराशौ
क्षिप्त्वोच्चैश्चन्द्रबिम्बे स्वकुलपतिसखो यः स्वकीर्तिं लिलेख ॥

(In this calamity of the Civil War Anantapāla overwhelmed with the flood of water in the form of the sharp edge of his sword the violent and sinful Yavana soldiers of Muna (?), who, having become powerful, had destroyed the Koṅkaṇa land, oppressing gods and Brāhmaṇas, and being the protector of the family, he engraved his fame on the disc of the moon.)

Anantapāla ruled for a long time from *circa* A. D. 1070 to A.D. 1125). At the close of his reign, the Kadambas again invaded North Koṅkaṇ. This invasion is thus described in the Vaḍavalī plates of his son and successor Aparāditya I—

आसीत्कोऽप्यसुरो जगद्दलयितुं छित्तुक्कनामान्तकः
तस्यैवं च समस्तमेव मिलितं सामन्तचक्रं ततः ।
ध्वस्ते धर्मधने गतेषु गुरुषु क्लिष्टे विमासंश्रये
शीर्णे जीर्णपुरप्रजापतिजने नष्टे च राष्ट्रोदये ॥
एकश्चैकतुरंगमश्च भुजयोर्द्वन्द्वं च खड्गश्च तं
द्राग्दृष्ट्वा कठिने रणे सरभसं तत्संमुखं धावितः ।
नायोद्धुं न पलायितुं किमपि वा ज्ञातं च तेन स्फुटं
संग्रामं परिहृत्य यस्य च भिया म्लेच्छाश्रये संश्रितः ॥

[There was a Yama-like demon named Chhittukka born for the destruction of the world. The whole circle of feudatory princes joined him (in the invasion of North Koṅkaṇ). When the wealth of religious merit was destroyed, the elders perished, the refugees were harassed, all townsmen and their servants were ruined and all prosperity of the kingdom came to an end—

he (Aparāditya), seeing that situation, rushed suddenly to that fierce battle, single-handed with only one horse (which he rode), his arms and his sword (to help him). (Then) the enemy did not know whether to fight or to run away. (Ultimately), being afraid of him, he sought refuge with the Mlechchhas.]

Dr. K. B. Pathak, who edited the Vaḍavalī plates, identified Chhittukka with Jayakeśin, but did not state on what grounds. While writing on the history of the Śilāhāras, Dr. A. S. Altekar, however, put forward a suggestion which is ingenious. The Kadamba king Jayakeśin II (A.D. 1104-1140) had two sons named Śivachitta and Vishṇuchitta, who succeeded him, one after the other. So their father Jayakeśin II may have been known as *Chhittukka*. He invaded North Koṅkaṇ and occupied it for some time. The Narendra stone inscriptions call him *Kavaḍīdvīpādhipati*. As we have seen before, North Koṅkaṇ was known as *Kavaḍī-dvīpa*. So there is no doubt that the Kadamba king occupied North Koṅkaṇ. The Śilāhāras naturally hated him. So he seems to have been described as an *Asura* (demon) in the passage cited above.

The Kadamba occupation of North Koṅkaṇ did not last long. The Narendra inscriptions dated A.D. 1125 and 1126 call Jayakeśin *Kavaḍī-dvīpādhipati*. Soon thereafter, Aparāditya appears to have driven him out; for his victory over the enemy has been mentioned in his Vaḍavalī plates dated in the next year A.D. 1127. In this he appears to have been aided by the Śilāhāras of Kolhāpur. The Kaśeḷī plates of the last Śilāhāra king BhojaII of Kolhāpur, dated Śaka 1113 (A.D. 1191), state that his father Vijayāditya had re-instated the deposed ruler of Sthānaka. The reference in this must evidently have been to the help which Vijayāditya rendered to Aparāditya I to regain his throne. This Aparāditya is well known as the author of a commentary on the Yājñavalkya-smṛiti.

We have thus tried to solve some problems in the history of the Śilāhāras of North Koṅkaṇ in the following manner—

(1) The Śilāhāra king who was killed by the Later Chālukya king Someśvara was not Mummuṇi as supposed so far, but Nāgārjuna.

(2) The Kadamba king Jayakeśin I killed not Mummuṇi, but his brother Nāgārjuna.

(3) The Civil War mentioned in the Khārepāṭan plates was between Anantapāla and Mummuṇi's son.

(4) Chhittukka was the Kadamba king Jayakeśin II. He occupied North Koṅkaṇ for about two years after the death of Anantapāla, but was ultimately driven out by Aparāditya I with the aid of Vijayāditya of the Kolhāpur branch.

XVI. AN ODD COPPER PLATE OF THE YĀDAVA KING RĀMACHANDRA

Several years ago Mr. S.N. Joshi of the Bhārat Itihāsa Saṁśodhaka Maṇḍal drew my attention to this incomplete grant which was then in the possession of Mr. G. N. Thatte, then Principal of the Arts and Science College at Auraṅgābād. Mr. Joshi sent me also a transcript of the record and asked me for some information about its contents. As the grant, incomplete though it is, has remained unpublished for a long time, I requested Mr. Thatte to let me edit it. He very kindly agreed to it and sent me the original copper plate. The inscription is edited here from that plate.

The grant must have originally consisted of three or four plates like the Purushottampurī plates of the same king, but now all of them except the first one are lost. The present plate is very massive, measuring 11.5" broad, 1' 5¼" high and ⅛ of an inch thick. It weighes six seers. The ends of the plate are not raised into rims for the protection of the writing; still, the record is in a good state of preservation, except in the last two or three lines, where a few *aksharas* have become indistinct. All of them, however, with the exception of ten in the right-hand corner, can be restored without much difficulty. The plate has, in the centre of the bottom, a large hole, .8" in diameter, for the ring which must have connected it with the other plates of the set, but neither the ring nor the seal which it may have carried is now forthcoming. There are thirty-three lines in all, inscribed on one side of the plate. The technical execution is good.

The characters are Nāgarī. They resemble those of the Purushottampurī plates. The only peculiarities that call for notice are that the medial dipthongs are in some cases denoted by a *pṛishṭhamātrā*; see *e.g. sevyatām* in line 3 and *Soma-vaṁśaḥ* in line 5 : the subscript member of the ligature *ṇṇ* is denoted by a horizontal stroke ; see *ev-āvatīrṇṇaḥ* in lines 17-18 ; the left member of *dh* is fully developed; still the horizontal stroke joining the two verticals of *dhā* is not discarded ; *v* and *b* are shown by their proper signs.

The language is Sanskrit and the extant record except for the opening *oṁ namaḥ Śivāya*, is in verse. There are twelve complete verses and a part of the thirteenth on the present plate. The orthography does not call for any remark.

The inscription refers itself to the reign of the Yādava king Rāmachandra. His genealogy is traced back to the Moon. The first historical person is Siṁha (or Siṁhaṇa). Verse 4, which occurs also in the Purushottampurī plates, states that he defeated Ballāla and the king of Andhra, exterminated Kakkalla, devoured in no time the lord of Bhambhāgiri, imprisoned the king Bhoja on the crest of a fortress, and vanquished Arjuna. The identifications of the kings defeated or exterminated by Simhaṇa have already been discussed by me in the introduction to my edition of the Purushottampurī plates. As shown there, Ballāla was the Hoysaḷa king Vīra-Ballāla II, who flourished from *circa* A.D. 1173 to 1220. The Andhra king was probably Gaṇapati of the Kākatīya dynasty. Kakkalla, as I have shown elsewhere, was probably the contemporary ruler of Varāṭa which seems to have been situated somewhere to the north of Mysore. Bhambhāgiri was the same as modern Bhāmer in the modern Pimpalner *tālukā* of the Dhuliā District. The ruler of Bhambhāgiri was Lakshmīdhara, who belonged to the Ābhīra race. Bhoja, who was confined on a hill, was evidently Bhoja II of the Śilāhāra dynasty of Kolhāpur. The hill where he was imprisoned is clearly the modern fort of Panhāḷā, not far from Kolhāpur. Finally, Arjuna is probably identical with the Paramāra king Arjunavarmadeva of Mālwā.

Verses 5 and 6 describe Jaitrapāla, the son of Siṁhaṇa, but the praise is wholly conventional. Verse 6 mentions at the end Kṛishṇa, the son of Jaitrapāla, but gives no historical information about him. The next verse (7) mentions king Rāma (*i.e.* Rāmachandra) as the son of Kṛishṇa and Lakshmī.

We learn here for the first time that Lakshmī was the name of his mother. All reference to Mahādeva, the brother of Kṛishṇa, who had usurped the throne is here omitted. The next two verses (8 and 9), which occur also in the Purushottampurī plates, describe the ruse which Rāmachandra resorted to in order to capture the impregnable fort of Devagiri. He entered it with a party of dancers who were his soldiers in disguise. When admitted inside, he rallied his foot-soldiers and attacked his antagonists who were apparently engaged in seeing the dance. The dancers also joined in the fight throwing off their ornaments etc. Rāmachandra thus appears to have obtained an easy victory over his cousin Āmaṇa, the son of Mahādeva. Verse 9 contains an interesting comparison of Rāmachandra with Śarvavarman, the author of the Kātantra system of Sanskrit grammar. The next verse which is new runs as follows :—

रामेण कार्मुकं भंक्त्वा महादेवस्य नंदनम् ।
प्राप्ता जनकजा लक्ष्मीर्निर्जितोऽर्जुनकीर्तिदः ॥

"Just as in times of yore, Rāma, having broken the favourite bow of Mahādeva, obtained Sītā, the daughter of Janaka, and vanquished Paraśurāma who had deprived Sahasrārjuna of his glory, even so King Rāmachandra, having defeated (Āmaṇa) the son of Mahādeva, obtained the royal fortune of his father (Kṛishṇa) and subjugated the ally of Arjuna (*i.e.* the contemporary Kalachuri king), who traced his descent from Sahasrārjuna), who had made him famous." That Rāmachandra defeated a Kalachuri king of Ḍāhala is also known form the Purushottampurī plates, but who his ally was is not known.

The next verse (11) contains an interesting comparison of king Rāma with the Moon, whom he is said to have surpassed.

रामः सोम इति द्विराजमथवा राजात्र रामोऽधुना
न स्थानान्न परोदयान्न समयाद्रामेऽल्पता तेजसः ।
सोमे सा शिवरात्रिरात्मनि कलाशेषे तिथौ तापसे
रामे राजनि राजति प्रतिजनं सर्वाः शिवा रात्रयः ॥

"There are two kings—Rāma and the Moon. Or, rather, Rāma alone is the king ; for he does not suffer any dimunition of valour as the Moon suffers loss of lustre due to position, or the rise of his enemy or unfavourable time. When the Moon is reduced to a single digit, the *tithi* becomes Śivarātri, but only to him who practises a vow, while so long as this our King Rāmachandra shines, all nights become Śivarātris (auspicious nights) to all men."

The next verse (12) contains a beautiful example of the figure *Sasandeha*. It runs as follows :—

रामोऽयं भृगुनन्दनो यदि कथं कर्णेन नो वंचितो
रामोऽयं रघुनन्दनो यदि कथं भ्रान्तो न मार्गे क्वचित् ।
रामोऽयं यदुनन्दनो यदि कथं सर्वैरशेषो गुणै-
रामोऽयं स्वसमः स एव कवयः किं साम्यतः भ्राम्यथ ॥

"If this Rāma is identical with (Paraśurāma) the son of Bhṛigu, how has he not been deceived by his ears (i.e. by his spies) as Paraśurāma was deceived by Karṇa? If he is the same as god Rāmachandra, how is he not bewildered in regard to the right course of policy as Rāma was as regards his way ? If he is (Balarāma) the beloved of the Yādavas, how is it that he is endowed with all merits while Balarāma had several faults ? O poets, this Rāma is only like himself. Why do you fatigue yourselves by seeking his likeness (in others) ?"

The subsequent portion of the grant is not forthcoming. So all information about its date, the occasion and the object of the grant *etc.* is lost. The verses in the eulogistic portion are, however, in the best *kāvya* style of the age, being full of interesting figures like Ślesha, Sasandeha, Vyatireka etc. They show that the Yādava court gave liberal patronage to good Sanskrit poets.

वाचन

१. ॥ ओं नमः शिवाय ॥ निरतिशयनिरंतानंदचित्सत्स्वरूपप्रबलवि-
२. मलसत्व(स्व)स्वीकृतिव्यक्तशक्तिः । परमरमणमंगं मंगलानां निधा-

३. नं दधदधरितसेव्यः सेव्यतां शाङ्‌र्गपाणिः[1] ॥१॥ लक्ष्मीनारायण-

४. क्रीडासरःक्षीरसमुद्रजं(जम्) । लीलांबुजं विजयते विधुस्त्रिभुवन-
श्रियाः[2]

५. ॥२॥ निःसीमः सोमवंशः स जयति जगति प्रोल्लसत्कीर्तिवल्लिर्मु-
क्तारत्ना-

६. नि तत्राप्युदर्दधिरदधो वृष्णयः स्वच्छवृत्ताः । तेष्वप्येकावलीसद्
गुण-

७. घटिततनुःकंठकांतिः कवीनां तस्यामप्येष चिंतामणिरधिचितद-

८. चिर्नायकः सिंहभूपः[3] ॥३॥ बल्लालो विजितः पराजयभुवं संभा-
वितोंध्राधि-

९. पः कक्कल्लो दलितः क्षणेन गिलितो भंमागिरेरीश्वरः । दुर्गाप्रे
विनिब-

१०. ध्य भोजनृपतिर्ध्वस्तोर्जुनो निर्जितः सिंहेनेति निशम्य के भुवि भयं
भे-

११. जुनं भूमीभुजः[4] ॥४॥ तत्पुत्रो जैत्रपालः कुलकुमुदविधुर्वीर-
लक्ष्मीप्र-

१२. सादप्रासादो रूपसंपत्सुसमितसुषमाकंदकंदर्पदर्पः । यः कर्ण्णः किं

१३. दधीचिः किमु किमुत शिबिः किन्नु जीमूतवाहः सत्वो(त्वो)द्रेकैक-
सीमा पुनर-

१४. भवदिति व्यक्ततर्कव्यंतर्कि[5] ॥५॥ आज्ञापंचदशाश्चतुर्दश कलाः

१५. कीर्तीर्व्यधानीज्जगद्भेदाद्भेदवतीर्निधाय गिरिशे यः षोडशीं
माव-

१६. नां (नाम्) । यस्मिन्नुद्गत एव तापतपसी प्राणे(ण)श्यतां प्राणिनां
राजा शुद्धरुचिः

१७. स कृष्ण उदभूत्तस्माद्गुणांभोनिधेः[6] ॥६॥ जयति जगति रामः
काम ए-

१८. वावतीर्ण्णः पुनरपि यदुवंशे कृष्णलक्ष्मीतनूजः । न हि कथमपि के-

1. Metre : *Mālinī*
2. Metre : *Anuṣṭubh*
3. Metre : *Sragdharā.*
4. Metre : *Śārdūlavikrīḍita.*
5. Metre : *Sragdharā.*
6. Metre : *Śārdūlavikrīḍita.*

१९. त्रिविक्रमो वीक्ष्यते स्म क्षितिनिपतित एव वीक्ष्यते वीरवर्गः[1] ॥७॥ आ-

२०. दौ देवगिरिप्रवेशनमथो वृ(नृ)त्तप्रकारेक्षणं पश्चात्स्वैरपदातिमेलन-

२१. मथालंकारविक्षेपणं(णम्) । अन्विष्टार्थविरोधिदूरकरणं तस्माद्ग्रासा-

२२. दनं श्रीरामेण कृतं ततस्तत इति श्लोकोस्य लोकोत्तरः[2] ॥८॥ श्रीरामः

२३. शर्ववर्मा पदघटनलघूपायदृग्दुर्गवृत्तिव्याख्याताशेषसूत्रो वि-

२४. करणविलसद्धातुनिष्पादितार्थः । वर्ण्णानां व्युत्क्रमेण व्यवहरणमपा-

२५. कृत्य संदर्शिताध्वा जेता दिव्याकृतीनां शिशुरपि तदिह स्पृश्यते नापश-

२६. ब्दैः[3] ॥९॥ रामेण कार्मुकं भंक्त्वा महादेवस्य नंदनं(नम्) । प्राप्ता जनकजा ल-

२७. क्ष्मीर्निर्जितोर्जुनकीर्तिदः[4] ॥१०॥ रामः सोम इति द्विराजमथवा राजाथ

२८. रामोधुना न स्थानान्न परोदयान्न समयाद्ग्रामेल्पता तेजसः । सोमे सा

२९. शिवरात्रिरात्मनि कलाशेषे तिथौ तापसे रामे राजनि राजति प्रति-

३०. जनं सर्वाः शिवा रात्रयः[5] ॥११॥ रामोयं भृगुनंदनो यदि कथं कर्ण्णेन नो वं-

३१. चितो रामोयं रघुनंदनो यदि कथं भ्रांतो न मार्गे क्वचित् । रामो-

३२, यं यदुनंदनो यदि कथं सर्वैरशेषो गुणै रामोयं स्वसमः स एव

३३. कवयः किं साम्यतः भ्राम्यथ ॥१२॥ संतः स . . . . .

1. Metre : *Mālinī.*
2. Metre : *Śārdūlavikrīḍita.*
3. Metre : *Sragdharā.*
4. Metre : *Anushṭubh.*
5. Metre of this and the next verse : *Śārdūlavikrīḍita.*

SECTION III

NUMISMATICS

XVII. THE IDENTITY OF THE SĀTAVĀHANA KING ŚIVAŚRĪ PUḶUMĀVI*

It is well known that the list of the Sātavāhanas given in the Purāṇas contains many discrepancies. No two Purāṇas agree in regard to the number, names and reign-periods of the kings of the family. The Purāṇas are, however, in most cases our only source of information about the names, succession and reign-periods of these kings. We must, therefore, try to reconcile the available evidence as far as possible. It is proposed to state the conflicting evidence in regard to one of the kings and to suggest a way of reconciling it.

Pargiter has critically edited this portion of the Purāṇas and given the various readings in each case. He gives the following text regarding the well-known king Gautamīputra Sātakarṇi and his successors[1] :—

राजा श्रीगौतमीपुत्र एकविंशत्समा नृपः ।
अष्टाविंशः सुतस्तस्य पुलोमा वै भविष्यति ।
शिवश्रीर्वै पुलोमा तु सप्तैव भविता नृपः ॥

These lines state that Gautamīputra was succeeded by his son Pulomā and the latter by Śivaśrī Pulomā. In the list of Sātavāhana kings[2] Pargiter gives the name of the third king as Śivaśrī only, omitting Pulomā given in the constituted text. Again, Pargiter found in a manuscript of the *Vāyupurāṇa* (*e* Vā) a king named Sātakarṇi in the following line[3] :—

एकोनत्रिंशति भाव्यः सातकर्णी ततो नृपः ।

He was puzzled as to the position of this Sātakarṇi in the list. His name was mentioned only in one manuscript of a Purāṇa (viz. *e* Vā), but Pargiter was not inclined to omit him altogether for 'a line found in only one MS. should not be

* *Journal of the Numismatic Society of India*, Vol. XXXI, pp. 151 f.

1. Pargiter, *D.K.A.*, p. 42.
2. *Ibid.*, p. 26.
3. *Loc. cit.*

rejected straight away."[1] But as no other Purāṇa mentioned his name, he gave the line and also the name of the king in brackets. He was confronted with another difficulty. If this Sātakarṇi is included, the total number of kings in the list becomes thirty-one, but many Purāṇas say that there were only thirty kings of the Andhra (*i.e.* Sātavāhana) family.

Pargiter tried to solve this difficulty in the following manner. In a MS. of the *Vishṇupurāṇa* (viz. *l* Vsh) he found the line stating the succession of Pulomā as follows : *tasy-āpi Sātakarṇiḥ tataḥ Śivaśrīḥ*.[2] This line showed that Pulomā was succeeded by Sātakarṇi and the latter by Śivaśrī. Pargiter identified Śivaśrī with Śivaśrī Pulomā of his constituted text given above. The admission of these kings made the total number of the Andhra (*i.e.* Sātavāhana) kings thirty-one, which was against the consensus of the Purāṇas, but Pargiter supposed that the total 30 is a round number.[3]

The evidence of the finds of coins seems to support the view of Pargiter. In the hoard of Sātavāhana coins found at Chāndā in Vidarbha, there were some coins the legend on which Hoernle conjecturally read as *[Si]vasiri-Puḷumāvisa*, but he admitted that the first akshara *si* of *Siva* was uncertain.[4] He thought it not improbable that the intended word was *raño*, not *Siva*. Rapson suggested that the traces read as *Siva* might only be the traces of some symbol, perhaps a conch-shell.[5] But such a symbol is not known to occur in that place on any Sātavāhana coin. Again, M. F. C. Martin has stated that among the coins which he purchased from P. Thoburn, there was one from the Chāndā hoard which has the legend *Siva-siri-Puḷumāvisa* quite clear.[6] Besides, in the Tarhāḷā hoard[7] there were as many as 32 coins with the legend (incomplete in many cases) *Raño Siva-siri-Puḷumāvisa*.[8] So Altekar's conjecture that the coins Śivaśrī may be of Gautmīputra Siva-śrī

1. *D.K.A.*, p. 37.
2. *Ibid.*, p. 42, n. 1.
3. *Ibid.*, p, 37.
4. *J.A S.B.*, for 1903, p. 117.
5. *Ibid.* for 1903, p. 306.
6. *Ibid.* for 1934, Num. Suppl. Art 413.
7. *J.N.S.I.* II, pp. 3 f.
8. *J.N.S.I.* Vol. II. pp. 46 f. ; *Studies in Indology*, III, Vol. p. 40.

Sātakarṇi cannot be accepted. We have indeed silver coins of Vāsishṭhīputra Sātakarṇi.[1] Again, he is named in a Kānheri cave inscription, from which we learn that he was a son-in-law of the Śaka Satrap Rudradāman I. So there is no doubt that he reigned and was different from Puḷumāvi. I have ascribed some potin coins from the Tarhāḷā hoard to him.

Should we then accept the reading in the *Vishṇupurāṇa* and hold that Puḷumāvi was succeeded by this Sātakarṇi and the latter by Śivaśrī, who is identical with Śivaśrī Pulomā of Pargiter's constituted text ? This can also be supported by the conjecture that this Śivaśrī Pulomā was perhaps the grandson of Puḷumāvi, the successor of Gautamīputra Sātakarṇi; for in India a grandson is often named after his grandfather.

This reconciliation of available evidence does not, however, appear convincing. In the first place, the admission of these two kings, *viz*. Vāsishṭhīputra Sātakarṇi and Śivaśrī Puḷumāvi will increase the total number of Sātavāhana kings to thirty-one, which would conflict with the consensus of the Purāṇas. Secondly, this Śiva-śrī Puḷumāvi, if he was a son of Vāsishṭhīputra Sātakarṇi, would be only a nephew of Vāsishṭhīputra Puḷumāvi, and not his grandson. Besides, the mere addition of Śiva-śrī would not make him different from Vāsishṭhīputra Puḷumāvi; for we know that *Śiva-śrī* was prefixed to the names of some other kings also. We have a coin of the Sātavāhana king Āpīlaka with the legend *Siva-siris-Āpīlakasa*.[2] We have also the name *Śiva-Skanda*[3] in the list of the Andhra (*i.e.* Sātavāhana) ktngs, given in the Purāṇas.[4] So it would seem that Pulomāvi prefixed *Śiva-śrī* to his name in the legend of some of his coins, though he issued a few other coins without that epithet.

So we should accept the reading in another Ms. of the *Vishṇupurāṇa*, *viz*. *Sātakarṇī Śivaśrīḥ*[5] (not *tasy-āpi Sātakarṇiḥ tataḥ Śivaśrīḥ*) in the MS. of *l Vsh*. given above. This would

1. *J.N.S.I.*, Vol. XI, pp. 59f.
2. *J.R.A.S.B.*, Vol. III, Num. Suppl. pp. 93 f.
3. Pargiter gives the reading *Skandha*, but it is evidently a mistake for *Skanda*.
4. *D.K.A*, p. 42.
5. *Ibid*.. p. 42, n. 1.

show that like Āpīlaka, Puḷumāvi and Śiva-Skanda, Sātakarṇi also prefixed *Śiva-śrī* to his name. As a matter of fact, we have coins with such a legend, *viz. Śiva-sirisa Sātakaṇisa.*[1] This would keep the total number of the Sātavāhana kings to 30 as stated in several Purāṇas.

But then the question arises, How do you explain the line in the constituted text—

Śiva-śrīr-vai Pulomā tu sapt-aiva bhavitā nṛipaḥ ? The answer is not difficult to give. A MS. of the *Matsyapurāṇa* (*viz.* j *Matsya*) gives the reading *Śiva-śrīr vai Pulomāt tu sapt-aiva bhavitā nṛipaḥ.*[2] This reading would show that Śivaśrī (*i.e.* Śivaśrī Sātakarṇi or Vāsishṭhīputra Sātakarṇi) would reign for seven years after Pulomā. The ablative form *Pulomāt* from *Pulomā* is not unlikely; for, as Pargiter has shown,[3] the text of these dynastic lists in the Purāṇas was originally in Prakrit and was later rendered into Sanskrit.

The foregoing discussion has shown that—

(1) *Śivaśrī* was prefixed to the names of several Sātavāhana kings;

(2) Some of these kings issued some coins with this prefix to their names and some other coins without it;

(3) Puḷumāvi, the son and successor of Gautamīputra Sātakarṇi, was succeeded by his brother Vāsishṭhīputra Sātakarṇi.

(4) This Vāsishṭhīputra Sātakarṇi was succeeded not by Śivaśrī Puḷumāvi,[4] but by Śiva-Skanda. The coins of this Śiva-Skanda have been found in the Tarhāḷā hoard, with the legend *Śiva-Khada-Sātakaṇisa.*

(5) The total number of the Andhra (*i.e.* Sātavāhana) kings was thirty, not thirty-one.

1. Rapson, *B.M.C*, *A.W.K.* etc. p. 29.
2. *D.K.A.*, p. 42, n. 2.
3. *Ibid.*, Introduction. p. x.
4. If we adopt the reading *Śivaśrīr vai Pulomāt tu*, it may be objected that Śivaśrī was only an epithet and would not necessarily denote Śivaśrī Sātakarṇi. This is true. It would have been better to read *Sātakarṇiḥ Pulomāt tu*, but we have no manuscript giving such a reading.

XVIII. WĀṬEGAON HOARD OF SĀTAVĀHANA COINS*

(PLATE I)

Wāṭegāon is a small village about sixteen miles, as the crow flies, south by west from Wāḷwā, the chief town of the Wāḷwā tālukā of the Sāṅglī district in Western Mahārāshṭra. In the first week of August 1961 some boys discovered this hoard near the house of one Maruti Vithu Mane while planting flower-plants in a low ground. According to the report of the Collector of the Sāṅglī district, who subsequently acquired it, the hoard then consisted of 700 coins in a fair condition and about 35 more in a broken condition. Later, the Collector sent the coins to the Department of Archaeology and Archives, Mahārāshṭra, where I had a look at them in 1963. The coins were later taken away by an Officer of the Department of Education for study. They were with him for more than eight years. Recently, after his retirement, he returned them to the Department of Archaeology and Archives, Bombay. The hoard has not, so far as I know, been noticed anywhere. I, therefore, requested Dr. A. U. Shaikh, Secretary to the Government, Ministry of Education, Mahārāshṭra, to allow me to study it. I am grateful to him for giving me the necessary facilities for doing so and for permission to publish the results.

When the hoard reached me, it consisted of 684 coins, of which 682 are of lead, and two of copper, one of them being in a broken condition. I do not know what became of the other coins of the hoard. All the coins are roundish in shape and have on the obverse the figure of an elephant facing right or left with the trunk uplifted and the legend encircling it. As the blanks of these coins were in almost all cases smaller than

*_Journal of the Numismatic Society of India_, XXXIV, pp. 205 f.

their dies, no coin gives all the letters of the legend entire and legible. One has to put together a number of coins of a similar type in order to decipher completely the legend on them. The reverse of all the coins has the well-known Ujjain symbol, which has, in some cases, a crescent over one of its circles.

This is the second large hoard of Sātavāhana coins from Mahārāshṭra to be published.[1] Thirty-three years ago, in 1939, a larger hoard consisting of more than 1500 potin coins of the Sātavāhanas was discovered at Tarhāḷa in the Mangruḷ tālukā of the Akolā district of Vidarbha. I have described it in the *J.N.S.I.*[2] It contained the coins of several Sātavāhana kings, the names of two of whom, *viz.* Skanda Sātakarṇi and Vijaya Sātakarṇi, were read for the first time, and those of three more, *viz.* Kumbha Sātakarṇi, Karṇa Sātakarṇi and Śaka Sātakarṇi became known for the first time. I, therefore, expected to see similar coins of known and unknown kings in the present hoard. However, as I began to decipher the legends on these coins, the conviction forced itself on me that the hoard contains the coins of only two kings, *viz.* Vāsishṭhīputra Śiva-śrī Puḷumāvi and Vāsishṭhīputra Skanda Sātakarṇi. With this clue, I could satisfactorily decipher the legends of all the coins except in those cases where the obverse has become smooth or worn out, or the legends were too fragmentary; but I am convinced that even in these cases the coins belong to one or the other of these two kings only.

Of the 684 coins of this hoard, two are of copper. They appear to have been imported from some other place since all the rest are of lead. One of them is slightly rusted and has a fragmentary legend, *viz. taka* on the back of the elephant facing right on the obverse and the Ujjain symbol on the reverse. The coin is evidently of some Sātavāhana king whose name ended in *Sātakarṇi*. In the absence of the complete legend it

1. Two earlier hoards of ancient coins discovered at Brahmapurī, a suburb of Kolhāpur, contained some Sātavāhana coins. That discovered in 1873 contained copper and lead coins of the Sātavāhanas, of which 381 copper and 1 lead have been noticed by P. L. Gupta in *Prince of Wales Museum Bulletin* (*PWMB*). V. 65. Rama Rao has noticed 8 coins of the Sātavāhanas from the second hoard of 1877 in *J.N.S.I.*, XVII, 81-82.
2. Vol. I 83.

is not possible to identify him definitely, but he is probably Gautamīputra Sātakarṇi, the predecessor of the two kings whose coins are comprised in the present hoard. The other copper coin is in a broken condition. Of the remaining 682 coins of this hoard, 369 are of Vāsishṭhīputra Śiva-śrī Puḷumāvi, and 191 are of Vāsishṭhīputra Skanda Sātakarṇi. The remaining 122 coins could not be definitely identified as their obverse has become worn out or their legends are too fragmentary.

I describe below five good specimens of the coins of each of these two kings.[1]

The complete legends on the two types of coins are as follows :—

(1) Śiva-śrī-Puḷumāvi—*Raño Vāsiṭhi-putasa Siva-siri-Puḷumāvisa.*

(2) Skanda Sātakarṇi—*Raño Vāsiṭhi-putasa Siri-Khada-Sātakaṇisa.*

Each of these legends consists of seventeen *aksharas*. They both encircle the figure of the elephant with the trunk uplifted on the obverse. The elephant faces right on some coins of Puḷumāvi, and left on some others. It faces right on all coins of Skanda Sātakarṇi. All coins have the Ujjain symbol on the reverse, but in some cases we notice a crescent on one of its circles. The characters of the legend are of the Brāhmī alphabet of about the second century A.D. On some coins of Skanda Sātakarṇi, the *akshara kha* in the royal name *Khada* shows a hollow triangle at the bottom caused by a leg of the elephant.[2] In one case the *aksharas pu* and *ḷu* are found stamped in the reverse form. The language is Prakrit. The form *raño* meaning 'of the king' is found used in all cases in place of *raṇa* noticed on some coins of the Tarhāḷā hoard. Another noteworthy difference is that the legend on these coins completely encircles the elephant, whereas on the coins of the Tarhāḷā hoard it commences behind the hind legs of the elephant, and ends near his uplifted trunk. Again, it is noteworthy

1. For the photographs, size and weights of these coins I am indebted to V.P. Rode, Curator of the Central Museum, Nagpur.

2. See the form of *kh* in Coins 2 and 4 of Skanda Sātakarṇi described below.

that the legends contain the matronymic *Vāsithiputa* (son of a lady of the Vasishṭha *gotra*), which is not noticed on any coin of the Tarhāḷā hoard. Recently I have shown elsewhere[1] that Śiva-śrī Puḷumāvi and Śrī Paḷumāvi are identical. Śiva-śrī as a prefix of the royal name was affected by some Sātavāhana kings such as Siva-siri Āpīlaka, Siva-siri-Puḷumāvi and Sivasiri Sātakarṇi.[2] The Purāṇas wrongly give Śiva-śrī itself as the name of an Andhra (*i.e.* Sātavāhana) king.[3]

I. COINS OF ŚIVA-ŚRĪ PUḶUMĀVI

	Size (diameter) in cm.	Weight in grams.	Device	Legend
(1)	1.2	8.600	Elephant rt.	(xii)—*Raño Vasaṭha-[putasa] [Sava]-sara-Puḷumavasa.* (**Pl. I,1**)
(2)	1.3	6.750	Elephant left	(viii)—*Raño [Vasa]-ṭhaputasa Savasara-Puḷumavasa.* (**Pl. I, 2**).
(3)	1.1	2.400	Elephant left	(vii)—*[Raño] Vasa-ṭhaputasa [Savasara]-Puḷumavasa.* (**Pl. I, 3**).
(4)	1.1	5.030	Elephant rt.	(iii)—*Raño Vasatha-. . . . Puḷumavasa.* (**Pl I, 4**).
(5)	0.9	4.748	Elephant rt.	(iv)—*Raño Vasaṭha-putasa Sava-sara-Puḷumava [sa].* (**Pl. I, 5**).

II. COINS OF SKANDA SĀTAKARṆI

The name of this king was read on his coins for the first time when I published his coins from the Tarhāḷā hoard in

1. See, above, pp. 163 f.
2. *Śiva* was also prefixed to his name by the Pallava king Sivaskandavarman, *E.I.*, VI. 86 f, and ibid, I, 5 f. See also the name Sivākhada-nāgasiri (Lüders' *List*, 1186).
3. Pargiter, *Dynasties of the Kali Age* (*D.K.A.*), 36.

J.N.S.I. There was indeed a coin of this king in the previously discovered Chāndā hoard; but as its legend was fragmentary, Hoernle, who deciphered the coins of that hoard, read its legend as *ya(ga)da-Sāta.* Vincent Smith has catalogued a coin of this king from the Indian Museum, but he read its legend as *Sara-Chaḍa-Sātakaṇi.* That reading is certainly wrong. There also the correct reading is *Sara-Khada-Sātakaṇi.*[1] So also probably is that of the coins described by Edward Thomas in the *Indian Antiquary.*[2] Pargiter, who collated several MSS. for the Andhra dynastic list, gave the king's name as *Skandha Sātakarṇi.*[3] This is certainly wrong though the reading is given by some MSS. of the Purāṇas. The correct royal name *Skanda* is given by the MS *e-Vāyu,* which, in this as in several other cases,[4] has preserved the original reading.

Though the coins of the Tarhāḷā hoard gave the royal name Khada (Skanda) on some coins, it mentioned no matronymic of the king. *It is known for the first time from the coins of this hoard.* Like Puḷumāvi, he also is described as *Vāsiṭhi-puta* (son of a lady of the Vasishṭha *gotra.*)

	Size, (diameter) in cm.	Weight in grams	Device	Legend
(1)	1.1	4.380	Elephant rt.	(iii) *Raño Vasaṭha-putasa Sara-Khda-* **Pl. I**, 6).
(2)	0.9	6.550	Elephant rt.	(xi) *Raño Vasaṭha-putasa sara-Khada-Satakaṇisa.* (**Pl. I, 7**)
(3)	0.9	5.350	Elephant rt.	(iv) *Raño Vasaṭha-puta...Khada-Sata-kaṇisa.* (**Pl. I, 8**)
(4)	0.8	8.850	Elephant rt.	(xi) *Raño Vasa*[*tha*]-*puta*[sa] *sara-Khada-Satakaṇasa.* (**Pl. I, 9**)

1. *J.N S.I.*, II, p. 89.
2. These coins are said to have been from the Brahmapurī hoard (*J.N. S.I.*, XVII.59). E. Thomas read their lengends as *Raño Vāsithi-putasa sara Yasatasa* (*I.A.*, VI. 277 and IX, 63), but that reading was probably incorrect. They were probably coins of Khada Sātakaṇi.
3. *D K.A.* 42.
4. See *C.I.I*, IV. Intro., xxvi.

(5) 0.8 6.340 Elephant rt. (xii) *Raño Vasaṭha-putasa sara-Khada-* [*Sata*...] (**Pl. I, 10**)

Most of the Purāṇas mention no reign-period of this king. Their reading *Śiva-Skandaḥ Sātakarṇir-bhavit-āsy-ātmajaḥ samāḥ*[1] is evidently defective as no number of regnal years (*samāḥ*) is mentioned therein. As elsewhere, the MS. *e-Vāyu* has a better reading, *viz*. *Śiva-Skandaḥ Sātakarṇir-bhavishyati samās-trayaḥ*,[2] but its statement that king Skanda Sātakarṇi ruled for only three years is obviously incorrect in view of the large number of his coins found in different parts of South India and the several issues of them as indicated by the different commencement of the legends on them.[3] He evidently ruled for a much longer period. The reign-periods mentioned in the Purāṇas have been proved to be wrong in some other cases also.[4]

The fact that the present hoard has coins of only two Sātavāhana kings, *viz*. Vāsishthīputra Śiva-Śrī Puḷumāvi and Vāsishṭhīputra Skanda Sātakarṇi, is also suggestive. The hoard contained no lead coins of any earlier Sātavāhana king. This can be interpreted to mean that that country of Kuntala, in which Wāṭegāon is situated, was first brought under the control of the Sātavāhanas in the reign of Puḷumāvi. The Nāsik Cave Inscription of Puḷumāvi's reign (19th regnal year)[5] mentions only Asika (Ṛishīka, Khāndesh), Asaka (Aśmaka, Ahmadnagar district), Mūlaka (with its capital at Pratishṭhāna in the Aurangābad district) and Vidarbha as Southern countries included in the dominion of Gautamīputra Sātakarṇi, though it describes in a general way that his horses had drunk the water of the three oceans. Kuntala, in which Waṭegāon is situated,[6] is

1. *D.K.A*, p. 42.
2. *Ibid.* 42, n. 7. This reading is grammatically incorrect as in several other Purāṇic passages; for the word *samā* is fem. The correct reading would be *samās-tisraḥ*.
3. See that the legend commences at different places on the coins of Skanda Sātakarṇi illustrated above.
4. The Purāṇas give a reign of 21 years only to Gautamīputra(Sātakarṇi) (*D.K.A*, 42), but the Nāsik Cave inscription (*E.I.*, VIII. 78 f) records his twenty-third regnal year.
5. *E.I.*, VII. 60 f.
6. I have shown elsewhere (*Studies in Indology*. Vol. 1, second ed., p. 9) that the upper Kṛishṇā valley was included in Kuntala. This is also

not included in this list of Southern countries under Gautamīputra Sātakarṇi's rule. It seems that it was Puḷumāvi who first extended his rule to that country[1] and Skanda Sātakarṇi, continued to govern it after him. As the hoard seems to have been buried during or soon after the reign of Skanda Sātakarṇi, we do not know from it how long it continued in the possession of the Sātavāhanas.[2]

We have now three Sātavāhana kings[3] who have the matronymic *Vāsishṭhīputra*, viz. Śiva-śrī Puḷumāvi, Sātakarṇi (V) and Skanda Sātakarṇi. The Purāṇas name them in the following order.

राजा श्रीगौतमीपुत्र एकविंशत्ततो नृपः ।
अष्टाविंशः सुतस्तस्य पुलोमा वै भविष्यति ॥
शिवश्रीर्वै पुलोमास्तु[4] सप्तैव भविता नृपः ।
शिवस्कन्दः सातकर्णिर्भविष्यति समास्त्रयः ॥[5]

This passage states the king in this order : Gautamīputra (Sātakarṇi IV),[6] his son Pulomā (*i.e.*) Puḷumāvi of the coins

shown by the explicit statement that Karahāṭa—4000 (modern Karhāḍ in the Sātārā district) was included in the Kuntala country. See *An. Rep. Ind. Epi.* for 1953-54. No. 18. Similar statements occur in other inscriptions also. See *Karṇāṭaka Inscriptions*, II, 79 f. The Rāshṭrakūṭa king Mānāṅka, who was ruling from Mānapura (modern Māṇ in the Sātārā district) is described as *Śrimat-Kuntalānāṁ praśāsitā* in the Pāṇḍaraṅgapallī Grant (*E.I.*, XXXVII. 9 f.). In view of this D.C. Sircar's translation of the above description of Mānāṅka as 'the chastiser of the Kuntalās' is absurd. Wāṭegāon is some miles south of Karhāḍ.

1. A stray coin of Gautamīputra was found at Brahmapurī (*J.N.S.I.*, XVII, No. 75, p. 81) as it was at Wāṭegāon. Other coins with the legend *Sātakaṇisa* may or may not be his.
2. The coins of Skanda, Yajña Sātakarṇi, Rudra Sātakarṇi etc. found at Brahmapurī shows that the Sātavāhana rule continued in Kuntala for a long time. (*P.W.M.B.*, V, 65).
3. One more, *viz.* Vāsishthīputra Sri Chandra Sāti, is known from coins found in Andhra and an inscription from Kodavolu (Lüder's *List* No. 1341). He is the same as Chandra Svāti of the Purāṇas.
4. For this emendation suggested in Pargiter's text, see *J.N.S.I.*, XXXI. 154. The reading occurs in a MS. of the *Matsyapurāṇa.*
5. Pargiter's reading *Śiva-Skandhaḥ Sātakarṇir-bhavitāsy-ātmajaḥ samāḥ* would make Skanda a son of Śivaśrī Puḷumāvī, but the matronymie *Vasishthīputra* applied to Skanda makes this impossible.
6. *D.K.A.*, 42. I have called Gautamīputra as Sātakarṇi IV, as he was preceded by three kings of that name.

with or without the prefix Śiva-śrī), Śiva-śrī (*i.e.* Vāsishṭhīputra Sātakarṇi V of the coins) and Śiva-Skanda (*i.e.* Skanda Sātakarṇi of the coins). From the inscription of Gautamī Balaśrī also we know that Puḷumāvi was a son of Gautamīputra Sātakarṇi; for the latter aged Queen-mother describes herself as *Mahārāja-mātā* and *Mahārāja-pitāmahī*; for she was the mother of Gautamīputra Sātakarṇi and the grandmother of Puḷumāvi. Puḷumāvi was evidently the eldest son of Gautamīputra Sātakarṇi from his queen Vāsishṭhī (a lady of the Vasishṭha *gotra*). Sātakarṇi (V) and Skanda Sātakarṇi, who also were Vāsishṭhīputras, were evidently his uterine brothers. According to the Purāṇic list, Siva-śrī [Sātakarṇi (V)] succeeded Puḷumāvi, and he was followed by Skanda Sātakarṇi. The present hoard, however, shows that Skanda Sātakarṇi succeeded Puḷumāvi at least in Kuntala; for if Sātakarṇi (V) had preceded him, his coins would, in all probability, have been found in the present hoard. The coins of Skanda have been found in Vidarbha also. So he seems to have been governing both Vidarbha and Kuntala, and probably Western Mahārāshṭra also.[1] His coins have not yet been found in Andhra. On the other hand, the coins of Vāsishṭhīputra Sātakarṇi have been found in Andhra.[2] There is no doubt that Andhra was included in the dominion of both Gautamīputra Sātakarṇi and Puḷumāvi. Was then the Sātavāhana empire divided between the two brothers Sātakarṇi V and Skanda Sātakarṇi after Puḷumāvi's death ? The absence of Sātakarṇi's coins in the present hoard and that of Skanda Sātakarṇi's coins from Andhra seem to point to this conclusion. Sātakarṇi's silver coins have been found in Western India as well as in Andhra[3]

1. His coins have been found at Brahmapurī as shown above.
2. In his *Sātavāhana Coins in the Andhra Pradesh Museum*, 50-51 f. Rama Rao ascribes several coins to this Sātakarṇi, but none of them has the matronymic *Vāsishṭhīputra*. However, some of them may have belonged to him. The matronymic is not noticed in the case of Puḷumāvi's coins also.
3. One of his silver coins was found in Hyderabad (*J.N.S.I.*, XXI, 9). Another was purchased there (*Ibid.*, XXVII, 32). A third is in the Prince of Wales Museum, Bombay (*Ibid*, XI, 59). A fourth was found in Saurāshṭra (*Ibid.*, XXI, 107).

and an inscription of a minister of his queen who was a daughter of Mahākshatrapa Rudra[dāman I] has been discovered at Kānheri in North Koṅkaṇ.[1] Perhaps Sātakarṇi V extended his rule to Vidarbha, Kuntala and Western Maharashtra after the death of Skanda Sātakarṇi.[2]

The present hoard has thus thrown much additional light on the history of the Sātavāhanas.

1. Lüder's *List*, No. 994.
2. Some, if not all, Brahmapurī coins with the legend *Sātakaṇisa* may have been issued by him (*P.W.M.B.*, V, 65).

XIX. TWO KSHATRAPA COINS FROM VIDARBHA*

(PLATE I)

Coins of the Western Kshatrapas are found from time to time in Vidarbha[1]; and I have published some such finds of the coins of later Kshatrapas from Vijayasena to Rudrasena III. Recently some coins of the Western Kshatrapas have been sent to me by my friends for decipherment and publication. Two of them are being published here.

1. A COIN OF KSHATRAPA VIŚVASENA

This coin was received from Y.K. Deshpande, who had obtained it from a friend at Bhātkuli, a village near Amarāvatī in Vidarbha.

Findspot—Bhātkuli; Weight 1.7 gm.; Size 1.3 cm.

Obv.—Bust of king to right ; no letters round the edge; symbols of date behind the ear cut off.

Rev.—Three-arched hill, with a crescent on the left. No star on the right. Only part of the following legend legible—*Rajña* (*Mahakshatrapa-Bhartṛidama-putrasa*) *Rajña Kshatrapasa Viśvasenasa*.

(Pl. I, 11).

I have published another coin of this kshatrapa found at Kuṇḍinapura in Vidarbha in the *J.N.S.I.*, but his name was not fully legible thereon. The *aksharas* of his name are quite clear on the present coin. As on other coins of his reign he bears on this coin also the lower title *Kshatrapa*. The date on the obverse is cut off.

II. A COIN OF KSHATRAPA RUDRASENA III

This coin was sent to me by M.R. Joshi of Akolā, who had obtained it form I. M. Khan of Bāsim (Vāśīm) in the Akolā District of Vidarbha.

* *Journal of the Numismatic Society of India*, Vol. XXX, pp. 92 f.

1. *Ibid.*, XXXI, pp. 113 f. ; XXIII, pp. 225 f. ; XXVII, pp. 94 f.

Findspot—Bāsim : Weight 1.75 gm. Size 1.4 cm.

Obv. : Bust of king as above. Behind the ear, traces of the symbols for 200 30 and 4 or 5. Of these, the first is probable, the slanting stroke, turning the imperfectly preserved symbol for 100 into one for 200, being quite clear. The next symbol, though partially cut at the top, is also probable, judging by the traces left. The next or unit symbol is, however, uncertain. Its lower trace, still visible, indicates that it is either 4 or 5.

Rev. : A Three-arched hill, with a crescent on the left and a star on the right. Only part of the legend round the edge legible—*Svāmi-Jīva*[*dāma-putrasa*] *Rajña Kshatrapasa Rudrasenasaḥ*.[1]

(*PL*. II. 1)

When I first deciphered the legend on this coin, I read the reigning Kshatrapa's name as *Rudrasena*. Later, I noticed that no Kshatrapa ruler of the name Rudrasena, son of Svāmi Jīvadāman, has been mentioned by Rapson in his *Catalogue* of Kshatrapa coins in the British Museum. The only reigning Kshatrapa who was a son of Jīvadāman, mentioned in that *Catalogue* is Rudrasiṁha.[2] On the corresponding Kshatrapa coins deciphered by Bhagvanlal Indraji,[3] H.R. Scott[4] and D.R. Bhandarkar[5] also the name of the Kshatrapa was read as *Rudrasiṁha*. Rapson states that on some coins[6] the letter *ha* appears in its old horizontal form which shows the Kshatrapa name to be clearly *Rudrasiṁha*. On some other coins, however, the letter read by him as *ha* appears like a vertical, and, therefore, may be read as *na*. In that case, the name of the reigning Kshatrapa would be *Rudrasena*. It is noteworthy that only one of the coins on which he noticed the old form of *ha* has been illustrated in Plate XVI attached to his Catalogue,[7] but on

1. The sign of *visarga* appears on some coins of this type.
2. Rapson, *B.M.C*, pp. 170 f.
3. *Bombay Gazetteer*, I, part i, p. 40.
4. *J.B.B.R.A.S.*, Vol. XX, p. 207.
5. *A.R.A.S.I.*, for 1913-14, p. 241.
6. See coins Nos. 768, 779 and 781 in the *B.M.C.*
7. *viz.* coin No. 779.

this coin the letter is far from clear. In the Uparkot hoard deciphered and described by H.R. Scott, there were some coins of this type, on which the Kshatrapa name was read by him as *Rudrasiṁha*, but on the coins illustrated by him (*viz.* Nos. 6 and 7 in the Plate attached to his article) the letter read by him as *ha* appears to be *na*.[1] D.R. Bhandarkar also gives the Kshatrapa name as *Rudrasiṁha* only in his article on the Sarvāṇiā hoard, but the name is not legible on the only coin (viz. No. 12 in his Plate) illustrated by him.[2] Recently, A.K. Narain has published a coin on which the letter appears in a vertical form and so he read the name as *Rudrasena*.[3] Altekar also agreed with him, but he was unable to decide whether the Kshatrapa's name was *Rudrasiṁha* or *Rudrasena*. Katare has published another coin of this Kshatrapa,[4] on which he reads the disputed letter as *ha* and takes the name to be *Rudrasiṁha*. He says, "The vertical of the letter (*ha*) at the top is bound by a horizontal stroke and its lower portion is elongated downward with a slight bend toward the right." He has illustrated the coin, which appears quite clear in the Plate. The vertical stroke is, no doubt, more elongated than usual for *na*, but it is doubtful if this in itself is sufficient for the letter being read as *ha*. The bend, very slight, is noticed in the upper part, not at the bottom as it should be if the letter was intended to be *ha*.

Rapson states clearly that the letter on some coins (which he has specified in his *Catalogue*) is of the old horizontal type. In view of his long experience in the decipherment of ancient coins we cannot doubt its veracity. But if the old form of the letter was restored, as he says, in the time of Rudrasiṁha II, it looks strange that the old degenerate form of the letter also appears on some of his coins. It is, again, noteworthy that the old form of the letter appears only on the undated coins described in his *Catalogue*. On some of the coins, illustrated in the *Catalogue*, the form is vertical and so the letter would naturally be read as *na*. As Rapson found the letter *ha* clear on

1. *J.B.B.R.A.S.*, XX, plate facing p. 210.
2. *A.R.*, *A.S.I.*, for 1913-14, plate LXVII.
3. *J.N.S.I.*, XII, pp. 167-169.
4. *Ibid*, XVI, pp. 207-209, Pl. I, No. 27.

some coins, he read the reigning Kshatrapa's name as *Rudrasiṁha* (II) on all coins. Again, it is noteworthy that the disputed letter appears in the vertical form in that Kshatrapa's name on the coins of his son Yaśodāman. It would, therefore, appear that the coins in question have to be referred to two Kshatrapas —some with the horizontal *ha* to Rudrasiṁha II and others, with the so-called vertical degenerate form of it, to Rudrasena (to be called Rudrasena III).

The certain dates on the coins of Rudrasiṁha II, read by Rapson, range from Śaka 229 to 231. Some other dates such as Śaka 232 or 233 and 235 or 239 were proposed to be read by him, but the unit figure in these cases was uncertain. H.R. Scott read the dates on two coins Rudrasiṁha II in the Uparkot hoard as 227 and 229.[1] D.R. Bhandarkar read some later dates in the Sarvania hoard as 227, 234, 235, 236, 237 and 238,[2] but these are likely to be the dates of Rudrasena III's reign. We have a certain date (viz. Śaka 239) for Yaśodāman, the son of Rudrasena III.[3] It would seem, therefore, that at the end of the reign of Viśvasena, son of Bhartṛidāman, there was a revolution in the kingdom. Rudrasiṁha, son of Swāmi Jīvadāman who bears no royal title, usurped the throne and ruled for a short period, perhaps from Śaka 227 to Śaka 231. He was succeeded by his brother Rudrasena III to whose reign the coins ranging in dates from 234 to 238 should be ascribed. He was followed in Śaka 239 by his (not Rudrasiṁha's) son Yaśodāman II. This appears to be the only satisfactory way of reconciling the conflicting evidence of these coins.

Consequently, on this correction in the attribution of the coins, some changes in the numbering of subsequent rulers will also have to be made. As suggested by A.K. Narain[4], Rudrasena III in Rapson's *Catalogue* will now be Rudrasena IV and Rudrasena IV will be Rudrasena V. Narain also suggested that Rudrasiṁha III should be named Rudrasiṁha II, but as we have seen that there are some coins on which Rapson read the name Rudrasiṁha clearly, that change should be avoided.

1. *J.B.R.A.S.*, XX, p. 207.
2. *A.R.A.S.I.*, 1913-14, p. 241.
3. Rapson, *B.M.C.*, p. 175.
4. *J.N.S.I.*, XII, pp. 168 f.

XX. DAHĪGAON HOARD OF KSHATRAPA AND TRAIKŪṬAKA COINS*

(Pl. II, 2)

This hoard was found while digging the ground for the construction of the quarters for a Grāma-sevaka at Dahīgaon, a village in the Malkāpur Tālukā of the Bulḍhāṇā district in Vidarbha fourteen years ago, on 30.11.1958. It was found by one Dipa Maruti Koli of Dahīgaon. The hoard was seized by the Police Patel of Dahīgaon and was deposited in the Sub-Treasury at Malkāpur. Later, it was acquired by Government and was recently sent to the Director of the Department of Archaeology and Archives. At my request Dr. A.U. Shaikh, Secretary to the Government, Ministry of Education, sent the hoard to Nāgpur and gave me the necessary facilities for its examination and publication, for which I am grateful to him.

The Tahsildar, Malkāpur, reported that the hoard consisted of 35 silver coins. Actually, it contains thirty-six coins, one of them being in a broken condition, which may not have been counted. This is the second hoard of Kshatrapa coins to be discovered in Vidarbha. The first hoard of this type was discovered at Sonpur in the Chhindwārā district (comprised in ancient Vidarbha) many years ago. It consisted of 633 coins and was examined by G.V. Acharya, whose report has been published in the *Numismatic Supplement* XLVII of *J. A. S. B.*, 1937-38. This is a much smaller hoard, but has a special importance of its own as will be shown below.

Stray coins of the Kshatrapas have been discovered in several districts of Vidarbha such as Akolā, Amrāoti, Yeotmāḷ and Wardhā of modern Vidarbha and also in the Seoni and Chhindwārā districts now comprised in Madhya Pradesh. I have published several such coins in the Volumes of the *Journal of the Numismatic Society of India*[1] but it is now for the first time

* *Journal of the Numismatic Society of India*, Vol. XXXV, pp. 118 f.

1. *JNSI*, XXII, 112 f.; XXIII, 335 f.; XXVII, 94 f.; XXX, 92 f.; XXXI, 22 f. Also *Studies in Indology*, IV, 215 f.

that a hoard of such coins is coming to notice in modern Vidarbha.

As stated before, the hoard contains thirty-six coins, of which ten belong to the Traikūṭaka king Dahrasena and the remaining twenty-six to various Western Kshatrapas as stated below. The latter are, however, much worn and as in almost all cases the blank was smaller than the die, only a few letters have come out on them. The identification of the issuer is doubtful in many cases. I give below the legends of the ten coins which could be identified either definitely or conjecturally :—

(1) Saṅghadāman (one coin) —*Rajña Kshatrapasa Rudrasiṁha-putrasa Rajña Kshatrapasa Saṁgadamasa.*

It is noteworthy that the name of this Kshatrapa appears as *Saṁgadāman*, not as *Saṁghadāman* as given by Rapson. He had a very short reign of about two years[1] and so his coins are rare. I therefore publish here his coin in the present hoard in an enlarged size (PL. II, No. 2)

(2) Vijayasena- (one coin) —*Rajña Maha-Kshatrapasa....putrasa Rajña Maha-Kshatrapasa Vijayasenasa*

(3) Dāmajadaśrī (two coins) —(1)........*Damajadaśriya.*

(2) ....*Kshatrapasa Damajadaśriya.*

(4) Bhartṛidāman (two coins) —(1) *Rudrasena-putrasa Rajña Maha-Kshatrapa [Bhartṛidāmnaḥ*]*

(2) *Rudrasena-putrasa Rajña......*

(5) Viśvasena (three coins) —(1) ...*Kshatrapasa Bhartṛidama-putrasa....[Viśvasenasa*]*.

(2) ....*Kshatrapasa Bhartṛidama-putrasa......*

(3) *Rajña Mahā-Kshatrapa[sa......] Viśvasenasa.*

1. *H C.I.P.*, II. 187.

(6) Rudrasiṁha II[1] (one coin) —*Svāmi-Jīvadama-putrasa Rajña Kshatrapasa [Rudrasiṁhasa*]*

The identification of the remaining sixteen coins is uncertain for want of a clear and sufficient legend. All the ten coins of the Traikūṭakas belong to Dahrasena and have the usual legend. It need not be given here.

As one tries to decipher the legends on these coins, one thing strikes him, *viz.* that the coins of the Kshatrapas appear to be much worn and were evidently long in circulation before they were buried. Those of the Traikūṭaka king Dahrasena, on the other hand, appear quite clear and had apparently been not much in circulation. No certain date appears on the coins of the Kshatrapas. So they do not add to our knowledge of their history.

The six Kshatrapa kings whose coins are comprised in the present hoard were ruling from *circa* A.D. 222 to A.D. 316. The coins of one more king, *viz.* Rudrasena IV, son of Rudradāman II, have been discovered in Vidarbha.[2] The latest date on his coins is Śaka 312 (A.D. 390-91).

The finds of these Kshatrapa coins in Vidarbha have posed a problem which scholars have attempted to solve in different ways. Some thought that Vidarbha was then comprised in the dominion of the Western Kshatrapas and so their coins have been found there ; but apart from these coins, there is no vestage of Kshatrapa rule in Vidarbha. Besides, Vidarbha was ruled by powerful Vākāṭaka kings like Vindhyaśakti, Pravarasena I and Pṛithivīsheṇa I in that period. So it appears unlikely that the Western Kshatrapas could get a foothold in Vidarbha in that period. Dr. Altekar thought that these coins represented the tribute which the Kshatrapas paid to the Vākāṭakas.[3] This theory also is unlikely ; for some of these are of *Mahākshatrapas* who do not appear to have submitted to the Vākāṭakas in any period. As I have shown elsewhere,[4] the Vākāṭakas, who had no currency of their own, seem to have allowed these silver coins of the Kshatrapas to circulate

1. As his name does not occur on this coin, the issuer of this coin may have been Rudrasena III. See above, pp. 176 f.
2. *J.N S.I.*, XXVII, 95; Num. Suppl. XLVII, 96.
3. *The Vākāṭaka-Gupta Age*, 55.
4. *J.N.S I*, XXIV, 27 f. ; *Studies in Indology*. IV, 223 f.

in their dominion as they allowed the gold coins of the Guptas to be current therein.

As stated before, the present hoard contains ten coins of the Traikūṭaka king Dahrasena, who ruled over Gujarat, Koṅkaṇ and Western Mahārāshṭra. It is now for the first time that Traikūṭaka coins have been found in Vidarbha. The Bulḍhānā district in which the present hoard was discovered was probably included in the dominion of the Vākāṭakas; for, as shown elsewhere,[1] Narattaṅga-Vārī where the Vākāṭaka king Pravarasena II made a grant in his twenty-third regnal year is situated in the adjoining Akolā district. Traikūṭaka Dahrasena was a contemporary of Vākāṭaka Narendrasena, son of Pravarasena II.[2] He was a powerful king, who performed an Aśvamedha as stated in his Pārḍī plates[3] dated Kalachuri Saṁvat 207 (A.D. 457). He must have raided and also occupied distant countries in the course of his *digvijaya*. On the other hand, Narendrasena was a weak prince. We know that his kingdom was invaded by the Nala king Bhavadattavarman ruling over the country now included in the Bastar district of Madhya Pradesh. He occupied a considerable portion of Eastern Vidarbha and made Nandivardhana, the erstwhile capital of the Vākāṭakas, the seat of his government.[4] In this period the Vākāṭakas were reduced to great straits as acknowledged in their own grants.[5] Taking advantage of this debacle of the Vākāṭakas, Dahrasena seems to have raided and occupied some portion of Western Vidarbha comprising *inter alia* the Bulḍhānā district. This is shown by the present hoard discovered in a village of that district.

Dahrasena could not have retained his hold over Vidarbha for a long time. He was soon driven out by Narendrasena's son Pṛithivīsheṇa II, who, in his grants, is said to have raised his sunken family.[6] We know that he drove out Bhava-

1. *C.I.I.*, V, 49.
2. Dahrasena ruled in *c.* A.D. 440-465 and Narendrasena in *c.* A.D. 450-470. *C.I.I.*, IV, xlii and V, vi.
3. *C.I.I.*, IV, 22f.
4. *E.I.*, XIX, 100 f.
5. Pṛithivīshena II is described as *dvi-magna-vaṁśasya uddhartā* and the Bālāghāṭ plate (*C.I.I.*, V, 81) and *magna-vaṁśasya uddhartā* in the Māhurzaṛī plates (*Vidarbha Saṁsodhana Maṇḍala Vārshika*, 1971, p. 76.
6. *Loc. cit.*

dattavarman's son Arthapati from Eastern Vidarbha and even carried the war into the enemy's territory ; for he davastated his capital Pushkarī.[1] He may have freed the western part of Vidarbha also from the clutches of the Traikūṭaka king Dahrasena. This is shown by the Traikūṭaka coins in the present hoard, which, unlike the coins of the Kshatrapas, are in a good condition. They seem to have been buried during or soon after Dahrasena's expulsion from Vidarbha. No other Traikūṭaka coins have been found in Vidarbha.

The elder branch of the Vākāṭaka family to which Narendrasena belonged came to an end with the death of Pṛithivīshena II. Its dominion was thereafter annexed to that of the Vatsagulma branch.[2] Harishena, the last known king of that branch, soon took revenge for Traikūṭaka aggression in Vidarbha by defeating the king of Trikūṭa, who was probably Vyāghrasena, the son and successor of Dahrasena. This is stated in the now sadly mutilated inscription of his minister in Ajaṁṭā Cave XVI.[3]

The find of Traikūṭaka coins in the present hoard has thus shed some additional welcome light on the history of the Vākāṭakas and the Trikūṭakas in the second half of the fifth century A.D.

1. *E I*.. XXI, 155.
2. *C I.I.*, V. xxviii.
3. *Ibid.* V, 108.

XXI. THE FIND OF A VISHṆUKUṆḌIN COIN NEAR NĀGPUR*

[Pl. II, 3]

I obtained this coin from Mr. P.G. Velankar [of the Training College, Nāgpur, who informed me that it was found in a large mass of scrap iron brought to Nāgpur from some neighbouring place. It has been lying with me for some time. In the meantime some stray coins of the Vishṇukuṇḍins and also a hoard of their coins have been discovered at Pavnār in the Wardhā District[1] and Nagar[2] in the Bhaṇḍārā District of Vidarbha. Still, the present coin deserves publication in view of its clear type which suggests a somewhat different interpretation of its reverse side. I describe the coin below.

Metal : alloyed copper of reddish black colour.

Shape : round. Diameter : 1.83 cm. . Weight : 8 grams.

Obverse : A well-executed figure of a lion, facing right, mouth wide open and tail curled up, a fore paw raised, with a *ka*-like symbol in front and a partial *ya*-like symbol on the back, inside a circular border.

Reverse : A vase placed on a stand of two horizontal lines cut in the middle by a vertical one, with the

* *Journal of the Numismatic Society of India*, Vol. XXXIII, pp. 126 f.

1. S.B. Deo and Dhavalikar, *Paunar Excavations*, p.13; *J.N.S.I.*, XXVIII, pp. 164 f.

2. I did not find this village in the *List of Villages* published by the Mahārāshṭra Government. Perhaps it is identical with the village Nangapura in the Gondiā Tehsil of the Bhaṇḍārā District. This coin, which closely resembles the coin described here, was attributed to the Pallavas, but it is probably of the Vishnukuṇḍins as the Pallavas are not known to have extended their sway to Vidarbha.

figure of a *triśūla*[1] on either side, inside a rayed circle.

(Pl. II. 3)

Such coins were previously ascribed to the Pallavas,[2] but it has now been shown that they probably belong to the Viṣṇukuṇḍins. Some of them have been discovered at Nevāsā in Western Mahārāshṭra.[3] I am glad to find that these finds of Vishṇukuṇḍin coins in Vidarbha and Western Mahārāshṭra have remarkably corroborated the theory first propounded by me that the Vishṇukuṇḍin king Mādhavavarman I conquered Dakshiṇa Kosala, Vidarbha and Mahārāshṭra.[4] As suggested in the story of Viśruta in Daṇḍin's *Daśakumāracarita*, he may have espoused the cause of the last known Vākāṭaka king Harisheṇa's son, when the latter was attacked and killed by the ruler of Vanavāsī (North Kanara) helped by the rebellious feudatories of Vidarbha.[5] Mādhavavarman may have placed Harisheṇa's grandson on the throne of Vidarbha for some time after driving out the enemies, but later, he seems to have occupied the country himself.[6] He then extended his sway to Western Mahārāshṭra as shown by his copper-plate grant found at Khānāpur in the Sātārā District of Western Mahārāshṭra[7] and the description of his grandson as *Tṛikūṭa-Malayādhipati*.[8] There is, of course, a mountain named Trikūṭa in the eastern part of the Deccan also, but the mention of Trikūṭa with Malaya in the afore-cited expression points to its location in Western Mahārāshṭra. The mountain Trikūṭa situated west of Nāsik is well known. It is mentioned by Kālidāsa in the *Raghuvaṁśa*, and the *Trikūṭa-vishaya* named after

1. This is usually taken as a lamp-post, but the three pronged top cut by the circular border at the sides shows that the symbol represents a *triśūla*. The Vishṇukuṇḍins were worshippers of Śrīparvata-svāmin (Śiva) and had a lion as their *lāñchhana*.
2. See the reference in *J.N.S.I.*, XXVI, p. 241, notes 2 to 4.
3. Sankalia, *From History to Pre-History at Nevāsā*, pp. 199 f.
4. See my articles reprinted in the *Studies in Indology*, Vol. I, pp. 193 f. and pp. 241 f.
5. *Ibid.*, Vol. I, pp. 182 f.
6. *Loc. cit.*
7. *Ep. Ind.*, XVII, pp. 312 f
8. *Ibid.* XVII, p. 338.

it has been noticed in a copper-plate grant found at Anjaneri near Nāsik.[1] The discovery of a hoard of Vishṇukuṇḍin coins at Paunār[2] and that of stray coins in the excavations at Nevāsā[3] corroborate the recónstruction of the history of Vidarbha and Western Maharashtra stated above.[4]

1. *C.I.I.*, IV, p. 151.
2. *Paunar Excavations*, pp. 15 f.
3. Sankalia, *From History to Pre-History at Nevāsā*, pp. 199 f.
4. D.C. Sircar's remark (*HCIP*, IV, p. 210, n.) that 'Mādhavavarman of the Khānāpur plates can hardly be regarded as belonging to the Vishṇukuṇḍin family' is thus disproved by the discovery of Vishṇukuṇḍin coins in Western Mahārāshṭra.

XXII. NUMISMATIC NOTES

(Pl. III, 1-3)

During the last thirty years D.C. Sircar has been indulging in rancourous attacks on my readings and interpretations of inscriptions and coins in and out of season. Many of my friends have inquired of me the cause of it. I told them that I do not know any. So far as I know, I have not given him any offence. Perhaps it is a case of *Svabhāvo dur-atikramaḥ*. In self-defence I have answered his criticism point by point, but still he repeats it again and again. In his recently published *Studies in Indian Coins* (p. 42) he says, "Another weakness of our students is that they show scant regard for truth and are inclined to stick to their suggestions, based on insufficient study or data, even after they are shown to be totally wrong." This is perfectly true, but it applies more to Sircar himself than to others as I shall show presently.

As Sircar is determined to criticise almost every view of mine, be it right or wrong, he sometimes makes himself ridiculous. Several years ago I showed from new readings and interpretations of some passages in a grant found in a village near Kolhāpur and first published by M.H. Krishna that an early Rāshṭrakūṭa family founded by Mānāṅka was ruling over the Southern Maratha Country, contemporaneously with the Vākāṭakas, who held Vidarbha. I showed that in the first line of the record Mānāṅka is described as *Vidarbh-Āśmaka-vijetā śrīmat-Kuntalānāṁ praśāsitā*. I interpreted this to mean that Mānāṅka had conquered Vidarbha and Aśmaka and was the ruler of Kuntala (modern Southern Maratha Country).[1] As Sircar was determined to lose no opportunity to differ from me and criticise my views, he took the statement to mean that Mānāṅka had defeated both the branches of the Vākāṭaka family—one ruling from Nandivardhana (Vidarbha), and the

* *Journal of the Numismatic Society of India*, Vol, XXXII, pp. 65 f.

1. *A.B.O.R I.*, XXV (1944). pp. 36 f.

other from Vatsagulma (Aśmaka).[1] I had then to point out that the country under the rule of the Vatsagulma branch was also included in Vidarbha.[2] Further, he interpreted *Kuntalā-nām praśāsitā* in that grant as meaning that Mānāṅka was 'the chastiser of the Kuntalas.[3] This was a strange interpretation. I showed that it was totally wrong for the following reasons : Firstly, though the root *śās* in Sanskrit means both (i) to punish and (ii) to rule, it is used in the latter sense when the object is some territory and in the former sense when it is a living being. I cited several passages to support my view.[4] Secondly, Kuntala did not, in ancient times, comprise only the modern Kannaḍa-speaking territory but also the upper Kṛishṇā valley which included the dominion of Mānāṅka. In support of this I cited an inscriptional passage.[5] Thirdly, the *Daśakumāracharita*, in its eighth *uchchhvāsa*, says that the ruler of Kuntala was a feudatory of the contemporary king of Vidarbha, while it refers to the ruler of the southern Kannaḍa country as Vānavāsya (the ruler of Vanavāsī, modern Banavāsī in the North Kanāra District)[6]. Fourthly, Hāla, the author of the *Sattasaī* in Māhārāshṭrī Prakrit, ruling from Pratishṭhāna (moderu Paiṭhaṇ in the Aurangabad District), is called 'the lord of Kuntàla.'[7] Fifthly, the *Udayasundarīkathā* of Soḍḍhala, who flourished in the first half of the eleventh

1. *Vākāṭaka-Gupta Age* (1946), pp. 81, n. 1 ; *H.C.I.P.*, III (1954), p. 200.
2. *I.H.Q.*, XX, pp. 309 f.
3. *H.C.I.P.*, III, p, 200.
4. (A) For *śās* to govern, see—
   (i) सत्पुत्रः पार्थिवेन्द्रस्य प्रशशास धर्मेण मेदिनीम् । *C.I.I:*, V, p. 108.
   (ii) कुमारगुप्ते पृथिवीं प्रशासति । *Ibid.*, III. p. 82.
   (B) For *śās* to chastise, see—
   राज्ञः प्रवरसेनस्य शासनं रिपुशासनम् । *Ibid.*, V, p 8.
5. विख्यातकृष्णवर्णे तैलस्नेहोपलब्धसरलत्वे ।
   कुन्तलविषये नितरां विराजते मल्लिकामोदः ॥ *E.I.*, XIII, p. 153, Karahāṭa—4000 (modern Karhāḍa in the Sātārā District was included in Kuntala. *Ar. Rep. Ep.* for 1953-54, No. 18.
6. *Daśakumāracharita* (*B.S.P.S.*, p. 138).
7. हाल इति शातवाहनस्य कुन्तलाधिपस्य नाम । See Bhuvanapāla's commentary on the *Sattasai*, V. 1.

century A.D., explicitly states the Pratishṭhāna on the Godāvarī was the capital of the Kuntala country.[1] There is thus overwhelming evidence supporting the view that the Southern Maratha Country, over which Mānāṅka was ruling, was known in ancient times as Kuntala. If the expression *Kuntalānām praśāsitā* is interpreted as 'the chastiser of the Kuntalas', it would be describing Mānāṅka as chastising his own people ! No king in his senses would ever think of doing so. The expression must, therefore, be understood to mean 'the ruler of the Kuntala country.' This was pointed out to Sircar long ago. Still, he persists in interpreting the expression as 'the chastiser of the Kuntalas.'[2] Ordinarily, no person who has good knowledge of Sanskrit would ever think of taking the expression as Sircar has done.

Sircar holds me to ridicule because some of my readings of coin-legends are wrong. I shall show in the sequel that his criticism is ill founded in many cases; but even supposing that all my readings of coin-legends are completely erroneous, it would only show that others who had better means of reading and interpreting them have improved on my attempts.[3] The reading and interpretation of coin-legends are not easy tasks. What Sircar says about the reading of inscriptions is even more true in the case of that of coin-legends. "The correct reading of a word in a damaged passage of an inscription," says he, "may baffle the decipherer for fifty times and occur to him in his fifty-first attempt or not all. Sometimes a damaged passage cannot be deciphered without the help of a similar passage elsewhere." This is even more true in the case of coin-legends, because each coin does not contain its legend completely or even distinctly. One has, therefore, to revise his readings when better material becomes available. In this connection I would invite attention to the following remarks of Kielhorn : "The task of the critic is much easier than that of the editor. The

1. कुन्तलेषु तटे गोदावरीति महासरितः प्रतिष्ठानं नाम नगरम् । p. 21; प्रतिष्ठाननगरीपरमेश्वरः कुन्तलानामधीश्वरो राजा सातवाहनो भवान् । p. 89.
2. *H:C.I.P.*, Vol III, p. 200.
3. I have accepted the correction in respect of the interpretation of a coin-legend in *J.N.S.I.*, XVIII, p. 122. Still, Sircar harps on it in his *Studies in Indian Coins*, pp. 140 f.

editor, unless he be ready to delay the publication of his work *ad infinitum*, must, within a limited time, make up his mind on whatever difficulties he may meet with; while the critic may concentrate his attention on certain select passages, and trust to continued study and accident for clearing away the difficulties offered by them."[1] When Kielhorn pointed out some mistakes in the readings and interpretations in *C.I.I.*, III, at Fleet's request, he did not indulge in any carping criticism. Sircar would do well to bear in mind these noble words of Kielhorn when he is tempted to ridicule others for their mistakes.

And who does not commit mistakes ? The history of Indian epigraphic research will show that several great scholars such as Cunnigham, Bühler, Fleet, Rapson, Hoernle, R.G. and D. R. Bhandarkar, R. D. Banerjee and K.P. Jaiswal, committed mistakes which they themselves or others corrected later. There has been no greater epigraphist than Kielhorn, but even he sometimes committed mistakes either because of bad or insufficient material or want of sufficient time. I have myself pointed out some of his mistakes in *C.I.I.*, IV[2] and *J.N.S.I.*[3] But I cannot even dream of claiming better knowledge than he or any of the other scholars whose mistakes I may have corrected. I am a humble worker in the field. In pointing out what I consider inaccuracies in the writings of others I have always observed proper decorum. In this connection I may be permitted to reproduce here what R.C. Majumdar wrote to me when I sent him an article pointing out a different interpretation of the description of Prabhāvatīguptā, *viz. sāgra-varsha-śata-jīva-putra-pautrā*. He wrote to me on 10-1-1945, "I fully appreciate your criticism of my paper on Vākāṭaka chronology. I am glad to find in you one who can offer strong criticism without any shade of rancour or bitterness, and, I presume, can also accept criticism in the same spirit. Unhappily, my experience does not show that there is a large number of such free and friendly critics, and I, therefore, welcome your letter

1. *I.A.* p. XX, p, 188.
2. *C.I.I.*, IV. Introd. x; pp. 410, notes 1 and 2.
3. *J.N.S I.*, XXV, pp. 238. f.

all the more."[1] It requires a large heart to appreciate merit in the writings of others.

Has Sircar himself committed no mistakes ? Let us see. In his *Select Inscriptions* (first ed., p. 193 ; second ed., p. 200) he gives the following note on the expression *Jīva-sutāya rāja-mātuya vachanena* in the Nāsik Cave Inscription of Gautamīputra Śātakarṇi—Regnal Year 24—"The word *Jīva-sutā* suggests that the king was ill and the people had to be assured against the death. The next king was possibly on his way to the throne, but the queen-mother, who might have been in power for some time, had to refer to the dying king's name. This illness apparently proved fatal to Gautamīputra." The ridiculous nature of this note will be evident to those who know that *jīva-sutā* (having a living son) was regarded as a sign of good fortune in the case of women, and the expression is used generally in the description of women in the *Ṛigveda, Mahābhārata, Rāmāyaṇa* and other works of Sanskrit literature.[2] It also occurs in the aforecited description of Prabhāvatīguptā, though in a somewhat altered form.

But, it may be said, this mistake occurs in the interpretation of an inscriptional passage and not in the decipherment of a coin-legend in which Sircar's authority is unquestioned. Let me, therefore, take an example from his latest work *Studies in Indian Coins*. In Plate XV of this book he has illustrated a coin (No. 18), which he describes as follows in 'the Key to Plates' (p. 382)—

1. Scholars may contrast the tone in Sircar's criticism of my readings and interpretations in *E.I.*, XXXV, 69 f. with that in my rejoinder in the same journal, XXXVII, pp. 45 f.

2. (1) वयं जीवा जीवपुत्रा अनागस: ।

Ṛigveda X, 36. 9. This is said of men.

(2) जानासि मे जीवपुत्रे भावं नित्यमविग्रहे ।
क्रोशतो न च गृह्णीते वचनं मे सुयोधन: ।।

Mahābhārata, V, 144. 2.

(3) जीवपुत्रे निवर्तस्व पुत्रं रक्षस्व चाङ्गदम् ।
अन्तको रामरूपेण हत्वा नयति वालिनम् ।।

Rāmāyaṇa, IV. 19. 11.

"XV/18. Early Kalachuri Kṛishṇarāja. Silver (20-Rati Rūpaka)—31 grains=2 grammes.

Obverse : head of king to right.

Reverse : humped bull, couching, to right; legend around—*Parama-Maheśvara-Mahādevyoḥ pād-ānudhyāta-śrī-Kṛishṇarājaḥ* "the illustrious Kṛishṇarāja meditating on the feet of the Supreme Maheśvara and Mahādevī (Śiva and Durgā).

Cf. Rapson, *I.C.* IV. 17."

This coin has a long history, which N.L. Rao has given in *J.N.S.I.*, XVI, pp. 107 f. I have also given it in *C.I.I.*, IV, pp. clxxx f. This type was first noticed by Bhau Daji, who read the legend on it as *Rāja Parama-Maheśvara Manasa Nṛipa Deva Dhyāna Śrikasa* (?). He referred it to a king of the 4th cent. A.D. Later, Cunningham read the legend as *Parama Māheśvara-Mahāditya-pād-ānudhyāta-śri-Kṛishṇarāja* (*A.S.R.*, IX, p. 30). Fleet first gave the correct reading in (*I.A.*, XIV, p. 68) as *Parama-Māheśvara-mātā-pitṛi-pād-ānudhyāta-śrī-Kṛishṇarāja*. I have given the same reading in *C.I.I.*, IV, Introd. p. clxxxi, and Pl. A, No. 3. N. L. Rao has given an enlarged photograph of the coin in *J.N.S.I.*, XVI, parts i-ii, Pl. V, No. 1. That coin is well preserved and all the letters of the legend are perfectly clear in the plate. Sircar knows of this article of N.L. Rao as he has referred to it in f.n. 1 on p. 239 of his *Studies in Indian Coins*. Still, he has chosen to follow Rapson in the wrong reading given by him. Rapson had doubts about the correctness of his reading; for he has prefixed '(apparently)' to his reading; but Sircar has none. He translates *Parama-Maheśvara-Mahādevyoḥ pād-ānudhyāta* as 'meditating on the feet of the Supreme Maheśvara and Mahādevī (Śiva and Durgā).'[1]

Anybody can convince himself from the enlarged photograph published by N.L. Rao about the correctness of the legend first given by Fleet. Apart from it, even a tyro in the

1. Sircar seems to have become wiser after he wrote the article on Kalachuri Kṛishṇarāja in *H.C.I.P.* III; for he says on p. 195, "The greatness of the family was established by Kṛishṇarāja, whose silver coins bearing the legend *paramamāheśvara-Kṛishṇarāja*...were discovered not only in the Nasik District etc." Here he has taken the legend to be *paramamāheśvara*.

interpretation of epigraphic records knows that *parama-Māheśvara*, which occurs frequently in epigraphs in the description of Śaiva kings, means 'a devout worshipper of Maheśvara' and not 'Supreme Maheśvara'. Again, Kalachuri Kṛishṇarāja is described in the records of his successors as 'devoted to Paśupati' only and not as 'meditating on the feet of the Supreme Maheśvara and the great goddess (Durgā)'. This should convince any unbiassed student that Rapson's reading adopted by Sircar is quite wrong. There may have been some excuse for adopting the reading before Fleet published his version and N. L. Rao published an enlarged photograph of the coin. Now there is none.

If Sircar's reading and interpretation of this coin are proved to be incorrect, I should consider myself to be in good company.

Sircar takes great pleasure in holding me to derision for my readings and interpretations of the Mahisha coins. He made the first attack on me in his Presidential address to the Numismatic Society of India in 1955.[1] I did not attend that meeting, but some members who did so told me later that his criticism of my views was in bad taste. I answered it point by point in *J.N.S.I.*, XVIII, pp. 116 f. Sircar again attacked my view in *E.I.*, XXXV, pp. 1f. That Journal is generally devoted to the publication of inscriptions, but Sircar did me special honour by discussing in it the coins attributed by me to the Mahisha kings. In that article also he has repeated his previous objections to my readings and interpretations without caring to notice my answers to them in my afore-mentioned article in *J.N.S.I.* I refuted his criticism again in a subsequent part of the *E.I.*, XXVII. pp. 45-49. In his recently published book *Studies in Indian Coins* he has again repeated his criticism of my views almost *verbatim* from *J.N.S.I.* and *E.I.*, without caring to examine my refutation of his criticism in the two journals. In my afore-mentioned article in *E.I.*, XXXVII, pp. 45f. I have shown how his own readings and interpretations of some crucial coins of the family were incorrect and unsatisfactory. His repetition of the same old objections without caring

1. *J.N.S.I.*, XVIII, pp. 1 f.

to examine the evidence against them throws lurid light on his professed search for truth. Like the schoolmaster in Goldsmith's *Deserted Village*, 'even though vanquished, he could argue still'. As readers of his book are likely to carry a wrong idea about the coins in question, I propose to answer again, though briefly, his objections to my readings and interpretations of their legends and also to examine critically those offered by him.

I give below Sircar's objections and my answers to them.

Objection I—We know that the names of the Śaka rulers of ancient India did not usually begin with the tribal designation *Śaka*, while there are names like Śakasena and Śakasāta or Śaka Sātakarṇi among people who were not Śakas. It is impossible to be confident without further evidence that a Śaka is referred to.

Answer—There are instances of the tribal designation *Śaka* being prefixed to the names of Śaka kings. See e.g. *Śaka-Nanda-putreṇa Mahādaṇḍanāyakena Śaka-Śridharavarmaṇā* in the Kanakhera inscription[1] As for the further evidence required, see the symbols of thunderbolt and arrow on the coins of Śaka Māna. Rapson calls them 'the distinctive badge of the Kshaharātas' who were Śakas. These symbols do not occur on the coins of Śaka Sātakarṇi or any other non-Śaka ruler.

Objection II—It is equally impossible to be definite that the Purāṇic Śakyamāna (which has other variants) really refers to a Śaka named Māna in view of the fact that the tribal name Śaka, quite well known to Purāṇic Chroniclers, would not, in that case, have possibly been modified in the context.

Answer—Unlike the sacred Vedas, the Purāṇas have not been preserved in their original form. They contain gross mistakes in regard to personal names. If Sircar wants an instance of the tribal name *Śaka* being corrupted into *Śakya*, he will find it in the variants given by Pargiter. Instead of the

1. *C.I.I.*, IV, p. 15 and p. 609.

reading *Śak-āshṭādaś-aiva tu* adopted by Pargiter, some manuscripts of the *Matsyapurāṇa* read *Śakyāś-ch-āshṭādaś-aive tu.*[1]

Objection III—On some coins attributed to the same ruler, the legend was originally supposed to read *Mahāsenāpatisa radaji-putasa Sagamāna-chuṭukulasa,* in which *radajiputasa* was later corrected to *bharadaja-putasa,* although the intended reading of the expression is no doubt *bharadajiputasa* i.e. *Bhāradvāji-putrasya.* It may be pointed out that the matronymic *Bhāradvājī-putra*' born of a lady belonging to the Bhāradvāja *gotra*' does not appear to suit a Śaka king very well.

Answer—The reading *radaji-putasa* was given first from a coin with a fragmentary legend. Since then we have a well-preserved coin of Śaka Māna with the complete legend and the medial vowels in it clearly marked. There is no sign of medial ī on *ja* in this legend. So the reading is *Bhāradvāja-putrasya.* We have several instances of patronymics used in the inscriptions and coins of the Śakas. See e.g. the Kanakhera inscription mentioned above. Besides, even granting that the intended reading is *Bhāradvājī-putrasya,* why should the matronymic be unsuitable in the case of a Śaka king when we find a similar one viz. *Māḍharī-putra* used in the case of an Ābhīra king ?[2] We know that many Śakas adopted Indian names in that age.

Objection IV—The author's interpretation of *chuṭukulasa* (found to be *chuṭukasa* on some specimens) of *sagamāna-chuṭukulasa* as 'of Śaka Māna who is of the Chuṭu family' is obviously unwarranted. It is also difficult to believe that one and the same person described himself on some of his coins as a scion of the Mahisha dynasty and on others as that of the Chuṭu family.

Answer—There is nothing strange in this. Māna called himself Mahisha because he ruled over the Māhishaka country. Notwithstanding this, he may have belonged to the Chuṭu family. Do we not know that the Vākāṭakas, who belonged to the Vishṇuvṛiddha *gotra*, and the Chālukyas, who were of the

1. Pargiter, *Dynasties of the Kali Age* (D.K.A.), p. 4ˀ, n. 12.
2. *C.I.I.*, IV, p. 3.

Mānavya *gotra*, both styled themselves as Hāritīputras in their grants ?

Objection V—Although the existence of a Chuṭu family of Sātakarṇis ruling from Banavāsī in the North Kanara District was accepted by scholars, it was not a Śaka dynasty.

Answer--The epithet *Chuṭukula* may have been assumed by the prince of the Banavāsī inscription in imitation of that adopted by a well-known ruler of the neighbouring country. We have several instances in ancient history of such senseless imitations. See e.g. the epithet *Hāritīputra* adopted by several southern royal families, though all of them were not descendants or disciples of the sage Hārīti.

I had asked Sircar to give his own readings and interpretations of the legends of these coins. He has given them in his article in *E.I.*, XXXV, pp. 69 f. and repeated them in his *Studies in Indian Coins* (pp. 126 f.), without meeting the objections raised by me against them in my rejoinder in a subsequent part of *E.I.*, (VII, pp. 45 f.). I shall state below his readings and interpretations and examine them critically.

Though several coins of Māna and other kings of the Mahisha family have been published in *J.N.S.I*, we need to examine only three crucial coins here. Their photographs or ink impressions are given in Plate III, Nos. 1-3 for ready reference. The first two of them are smaller and rectangular in shape, though the incuse on them shows that their die was circular. The legends on these coins are complementary to each other. They have the figure of an elephant with uplifted trunk to right as on several coins of the Sātavāhanas, with a *svastika* in the field on the back of the elephant. As the blank of these coins was smaller than the die, some of the *aksharas* have not come out at the lower left and the upper right corner. The legend of No. 1 reads *gamānamahasa* and that of No. 2 *Raño Sagamāna-ma*. The two fragments of the legend show that the complete legend must have been *Raño Saga-Māna-Mahasasa*. The last *akshara* is supplied here so that the expression would be in the genitive corresponding to *raño*. The letters are bold and the coins show that the legend could not have had any more *aksharas*.

Sircar reads the legend on the two coins mostly as I do, but he takes the first two *aksharas* of the legend of No. 2 as a hill symbol. Again, he takes *mahasa* at the end as part of *Mahāsenāpati*. Both these suppositions are unwarranted. If there had been a hill symbol in the beginning of the legend, it would have been very unusual. We have hundreds of coins of the Sātavāhanas with the device of the elephant with uplifted trunk, but nowhere does any symbol occur below the tail of the elephant. Such a symbol may occur in the field over the back of the elephant. See the *svastika* on the back of the elephant. Again, if *mahasa* had been part of *Mahāsenāpati*, the legend must have had *Chuṭukulasa* also after it as on Coin No. 3 illustrated below; for *Sagamāna Mahāsenāpatisa* (which Sircar takes to mean 'of the Mahāsenāpati of the Sagamas') would not contain the name of any issuer of the coin. We must, therefore, suppose that the legend was *Sagamāna Mahāsenāpatisa Chuṭukulasa* on these small coins also. It will, however, be noticed that the letters on these coins are very bold, while the size of the coins is small. *So such a large legend is not likely in the case of these coins*. The legend begins in the lower left corner and must have ended in the upper right corner as on several elephant-type coins of the Sātavāhanas. What Sircar takes to be a hill symbol is really the word *raño*. Any unbiassed scholar can convince himself from the photograph of Coin No. 2. The *aksharas raño* are quite clear. So the legend of these coins is *Raño Saga-Māna-Mahasasa* meaning that 'this coin is of the king Śaka Māna Mahisha.' For the interpretation of this legend the following line of the Purāṇas renders great help :

Śakyamān-ābhavad-rājā mahishīṇāṁ mahīpatiḥ.[1]

This line as it stands yields no satisfactory meaning. Pargiter translates it as follows :—'Śakyamāna was king of the mahishīs.'[2] This makes no sense. We must, therefore, suppose that the correct original reading of the line was—

Śaka-Māno-bhavad rāja Mahishāṇāṁ mahīpatiḥ

Thus emended, the line yields a satisfactory sense. It would mean that 'there flourished the Śaka king Māna, the Lord of

1. *D.K.A.*, p. 51.
2. *Ibid.*, p. 73.

the Mahisha country.' This Mahisha is undoubtedly the Māhishaka country mentioned in the epics and the Purāṇas as situated in the neighbourhood of Vidarbha, Ṛishīka, Kaliṅga and Āndhra.[1] It is noteworthy that some of the coins of this king were found in the excavations at Kondapur in the Central Deccan.

Sircar has no satisfactory explanation to offer about this hemistich in the Purāṇas.

I have shown above that the legend on Coin No. 1 had at most only one *akshara* more at the end, which has not come out on the face of that coin, viz. *sa*. Fortunately, we have a coin the legend of which supports this conjecture. In *J.N.S.I.*, XI, pp, 1 f. I have published a coin found in the excavation at Kondapur. Its legend is *ṇa-Mahasasa*. There are traces of an *akshara* like *ma* in the beginning. So the legend is probably *Māṇa-Mahasasa*. This Māṇa is probably the same as Māna of the two coins discussed here, notwithstanding a slight difference in their names. The legend of this coin shows that Coin No. 1 also had a similar legend, viz. *Raño Saga-Māna- Maha sasa*.

We shall now take Coin No. 3. It has a clear and complete legend which I read as follows : *Mahāsenāpatisa Bharadaja-putasa Saga-Māna-Chuṭukulasa*. The legend means 'This coin is of the Mahāsenāpati Śaka Māna, son of Bhāradvāja, of the Chuṭu family.' Sircar's reading is mostly the same as mine, but he reads *Bharadaji-putasa* in place of *Bharadaja-putasa*. This coin, which has all medial vowels clearly shown, has no sign for medial *i* on the letter *ja*. As I have shown, there are several patronymics in the inscriptions and coins of the Śakas. So we need not suppose that the intended reading was *Bhāradvājī-putrasya*.

Sircar, again, interprets the legend differently. He takes it to mean '(This coin is) of the *Mahāsenāpati* Chuṭukula of the Sagamas (i.e. of the Sagama family).' This interpretation is open to the following objections—Firstly, no such family as Sagama is known to history. Sircar blames me for 'creating' the families of the Mahishas and the Sebakas. If one talks in this manner, all researches in ancient Indian history are 'crea-

1. See the passages cited in my article in *J.N S I.*, XI, p. 4.

tions'; for we had no history worth the name before. The Mahisha and Sebaka families are no 'creations'; for their coins have clearly shown that they ruled in ancient times. But the so-called Sagama family is in fact a creation of Sircar; for we have no proof of its existence in the past. Sircar interprets *Sagamāna Chuṭukulasa* on the analogy of *Pallavāṇa Sivakhaṁdavamo* in the Hirahadgalli plates of Śivaskandavarman. This interpretation is, however, open to the following objections: (i) The latter expression occurs in a copper-plate grant where there is no dearth of space. No such partitive genitive is known to occur on a coin. (ii) the family name generally occurs after the personal name. Cf. *Raño Siri-Yaña Satakaṇisa*; *[Pa]kasasiva Sebakasa* etc. If Sagama had been the family name and Chuṭukula the personal name of the king who issued these coins, the legend on his coins would have been *Chuṭukula-Sagamasa*. Secondly, Chuṭukula is not a personal name but a family name since it is added to such personal names as Viṇhukaḍa. See the Malavali inscription of Hāritīputra Viṇhukaḍa Chuṭu-Sātakarṇi. Rapson also says that *Chuṭu* like *Sātavāhana*, is the name of a clan.[1] Sircar's attempt to prove that Chuṭukula was a personal name is futile.

These coins were, therefore, issued by the Śaka king Māna, son of Bhāradvāja, of the Chuṭu family. He was previously a feudatory of the Sātavāhanas and so he uses the subordinate title *Māhasenāpati* on some of his coins. Later, he threw off their yoke and assumed the independent title *Rājan*. That he belonged to the Śaka race is shown by the device of thunderbolt and arrow on his coins. This was a distinctive sign of the Kshaharātas, who were Śakas. Māna uses it on his coins probably because he was a descendant of Nahapāna. It is noticed on the coins of no other family of ancient times. Sircar has not been able to account for the occurrence of these symbols on the coins of the so-called Sagama King Chuṭukula.

Sircar's objection that no inscriptions of the Śaka king Māna have been discovered applies equally to his so-called Sagama king Chuṭukula. Māna's case is similar to that of

1. Rapson, *Coins of the Andhras* etc., p. liii.

Rāmagupta. Until the beginning of 1967, only the copper coins of Rāmagupta were found but no inscriptions of him were known. So some scholars like Sircar were objecting to his recognisation as a Gupta king. Fortunately, three epigraphs mentioning clearly *Mahārājādhirāja* Rāmagupta have recently been discovered near Vidiśā, which leave no doubt about his existence in the Gupta age. Let us hope that some inscriptions of the Śaka king Māna and his descendants will also be discovered hereafter in the Deccan. If they are discovered, the manner of their dating may throw some light on the question of the spread of the Śaka era in Southern India. I have put forward a theory in this respect, but it remains to be corroborated by the discovery of records actually dated in that era.

Sircar's objections to my attribution of some other coins to king Sebaka are equally flimsy. Another coin of that king has recently been published by M.G. Dikshit in *J.N.S.I.*[1] Sircar will have to show how he reads the legends of these coins before he can accuse us of 'creating' these kings.

I regret very much that I have to waste my time in controverting again and again Sircar's fantastic objections to my readings and interpretations of these coins ; but I have to do so because he shows scant regard for truth and repeats his arguments again and again even after they have been proved to be wrong.

1. *J.N.S.I.*, XXX, pp. 186 f.

SECTION IV

MISCELLANEOUS

XXIII. LOCATION OF RĀVAṆA'S LAṄKĀ

This subject has become very controversial during the last more than fifty years. As far back as 1919, at the first session of the All-India Oriental Conference held at Poona, Sardar Madhavrao Kibe first propounded his theory that Rāvaṇa's Laṅkā was situated near Amarakaṇṭak on the Vindhya mountain.[1] This theory was then based on the mention, in the Kishkindhā Kāṇḍa of the *Rāmāyaṇa*, of the countries to which Sugrīva directed the monkeys to search for Sītā. Later, Kibe supported this theory with more arguments in several articles in different journals.[2] It received further support from Rai Bahadur Hiralal, a renowned Indologist of Madhya Pradesh, who adduced some more evidence[3]. A similar view was advocated by Paramaśiva Iyer[4] and G. Ramdas[5] on additional grounds. Latterly, H. D. Sankalia has put forward the same view in several articles in Marathi and English and also in his brochure *Rāmāyaṇa and Laṅkā*. This view has not yet been critically examined by any scholar. It is proposed to discuss it here in view of its importance for the history and culture of India.

Really speaking, there is no difference of opinion on this point among our ancient writers. Whoever wrote on the life of Rāma in ancient days has assumed that Rāvaṇa's Laṅkā was situated in the island of Ceylon (now Śrī Laṅkā). The oldest of these authors is Kālidāsa. In the description of the journey in an aerial car from Rāvaṇa's capital to Ayodhyā in the thirteenth canto of the *Raghuvaṁśa* he has assumed this

1. *Proceedings and Transactions of the First Oriental Conference*, Vol. I, p. cxxvi.
2. *I.H.Q.*, Vol. IV, pp. 694 f.; *F. W. Thomas Felicitation Volume*, pp. 144f.; *P. K. Gode Volume*, pp. 93 f.
3. *Ganganatha Jha Commemoration Volume*, pp. 151 f.
4. See his *Rāmāyaṇa and Laṅkā*.
5. *I. H. Q.*, Vol. IV, pp. 339 f.; Vol. V, pp. 281 f.

identification. We have shown elsewhere from indications in the *Uttara-Rāma-charita* that Bhavabhūti, who flourished later, believed that the hermitage of Agastya was situated not in Madhya Pradesh but near modern Nevāse on the bank of the Godāvarī in the Ahmadnagar district.[1] He evidently held the view that the river Godāvarī and the places Kishkindhā, Pampā and others were situated in South India. The same view was shared by subsequent Sanskrit playwrights like Murāri, Rāja-śekhara, Jayadeva and others as shown by their description of Rāma's journey from Laṅkā to Ayodhyā.[2] So there is unanimity on this point among our ancient writers.

But some modern scholars have advocated different views on this matter. Jacobi, an eminent German Orientalist, thought that Laṅkā was situated in Assam. This is *prima facie* such a strange and inconceivable view that it needs no refutation. As stated above, Kibe located it near Amarakaṇṭak. Paramaśiva Iyer has attempted to identify it with the hill near the village Indrāṇā, about eighteen miles north of Jabalpur, and Sankalia has supported his view. Though the views of Kibe and Iyer are not identical, they agree in placing Laṅkā in Central India. We now proceed to examine critically the arguments they have advanced in support of their respective theories.

Argument I—Description of the Way from Chitra-kūṭa to Kishkindhā

Kibe has stated this way as follows, citing passages from the *Rāmāyaṇa*—

"When Rāma arrived at the Chitrakūṭa hill near the river Mandākinī, he learned about the harassment caused to the sages by the Rākshasas such as Khara and others. So he and others proceeded to the Daṇḍakāraṇya. There Rāma killed Virādha and then they proceeded to the hermitage of Śara-bhaṅga. Śarabhaṅga advised them to proceed to the hermitage of Sutīkshṇa, and he himself entered fire. After taking leave of Sutīkshṇa, Rāma and others had to go a long distance to reach a large lake extending over a *yojana*, known by the name of Pañchāpsaras. Thereafter, they spent ten years in wandering,

1. See our *Studies in Indology*, Vol. I (second ed.), pp. 283 f.
2. See our *Bhavabhūti*, pp. 378 f.

staying four, five, six or ten months in different places. Then they returned again to Sutīkshṇa's hermitage. After spending some time there, Rāma asked the sage the way to the hermitage of Agastya. The sage replied, "At a distance of four *yojanas* from here lies the hermitage of Agastya's brother. Agastya's own hermitage is one *yojana* further on. After going to that hermitage, Rāma asked Agastya about a quiet place for their residence. Then the sage said, "You should stay at the place called Pañchavaṭī, two *yojanas* from here, which is full of shady trees and abounds in roots and fruits." While at Pañchavaṭī, Rāma killed Khara and other Rākshasas. After the abduction of Sītā, Rāma and Lakshmaṇa repaired to Pampā, where they met Sugrīva. The latter told Rāma, "This is a secure place called Malayagiri, ruled by Vālin. You will have no fear here". Then they stayed on the Ṛishyamūka hill. Not far from it lay Kishkindhā, the capital of Vālin. And to its west there spread a sea of red water :—

ततो रक्तजलं भीमं लोहितं नाम सागरम् ।

After the death of Vālin, Sugrīva sent troops of monkeys in all directions to search for Sītā. But none of them could find any trace of her. Ultimately, Hanumān came to the Vindhya mountain, where he met Sampāti, the elder brother of Jaṭāyu. Sampāti said to him—

इतो दूरे समुद्रस्य संपूर्णे शतयोजने ।
तस्मिल्लंकापुरी रम्या निर्मिता विश्वकर्मणा ॥

"At a distance of full hundred *yojanas* from here, in the midst of the ocean, there lies the beautiful city of Laṅkā planned by Viśvakarman."

After stating the above short account of Rāma's journey from Chitrakūṭa to Kishkindhā, Kibe has calculated the distrance between them as follows :—Rāma took one whole day to traverse the distance from Chitrakūṭa to Sutīkshṇa's hermitage. So the distance between the two places was from 12 to 18 miles. From there Śarabhaṅga's hermitage lay at a distance of one day's journey, that is about 18 miles. Agastya's brother's hermitage was 6 *yojanas* or 24 miles away.

From there Agastya's own hermitage lay 8 miles distant and Pañchavaṭī was further at a distance of half a day's journey or 8 miles. Pampā lake was six miles from there and Kishkindhā was just near it. So the distance between the Chitrakūṭa hill and the city of Kishkindhā was about 22 *yojanas* or 88 miles (or 100 miles at most). This is the actual distance of Pampā (a lake near Govindagaḍa in the former Revā State) from Chitrakūṭa. Rāvaṇa's Laṅkā was not far from it.[1]

Examination of the Argument

The description of the journey of Rāma and others in the Āraṇya and Kishkindhā Kāṇḍas of the *Rāmāyaṇa* is very brief. It names very few places. For instance, it contains no reference to Rāma's crossing of the Vindhya mountain, while going to the hermitage of Agastya, but it is explicitly stated that the hermitage was situated on the bank of the Godāvarī. Both the *Rāmāyaṇa*[2] and the *Mahābhārata*[3] narrate the legend of Agastya's journey to South India. When Vindhya began to rise higher and higher, obstructing thereby the path of the luminaries in the sky, Agastya proceeded to the South in response to the prayers of gods. When he approached Vindhya, the latter lay low before him. Agastya then repaired to the bank of the

1. *P. K. Gode Volume*, pp. 93 f.
2. See—

    नाम्ना चेयं भगवतो दक्षिणा दिक्प्रदक्षिणा ।
    प्रथिता त्रिषु लोकेषु दुर्धर्षा क्रूरकर्मभिः ।।
    मार्गं निरोद्धुं सततं भास्करस्याचलोत्तमः ।
    संदेशं पालयंस्तस्य विन्ध्यशैलो न वर्धते ।।

    Rāmāyaṇa (Cr. Ed.), Āraṇyakāṇḍa, X, 82-84. The references to the *Rāmāyaṇa* given hereafter are to this critical ed. pub. by the Oriental Institute, Baroda.
3. See—

    तच्छ्रुत्वा वचनं विप्रः सुराणां शैलमभ्यगात् ।
    सोऽभिगम्याब्रवीद्विन्ध्यं सदारः समुपस्थितः ।।
    मार्गमिच्छाम्यहं दत्तं भवता पर्वतोत्तम ।
    दक्षिणामभिगन्तास्मि दिशं कार्येण केनचित् ।।
    यावदागमनं मह्यं तावत्त्वं प्रतिपालय ।
    निवृत्ते मयि शैलेन्द्र ततो वर्धस्व कामतः ।।

    Mahābhārata, (Cr. Ed.), III, 102, 10-12.

Godāvarī where he established his hermitage. Later, he went further south. Several Sanskrit works contain references to his hermitage on the Malaya mountain,[1] but in the age of the *Rāmāyaṇa* he was staying on the bank of the Godāvarī. We do not, however, find any reference to Agastya's hermitage north of the Vindhya as we have none to the Godāvarī also. Hiralal has stated that there is a small stream named Godā which flows about 11 miles south of Chitrakūṭa and later disappears in a well (!) like the ancient river Sarasvatī.[2] But this insignificant stream cannot be the Godāvarī of the *Rāmāyaṇa*. Like Vindhya, the Godāvarī has an important place in that Epic. It cannot be identical with this streamlet. Besides, the Godāvarī, according to Kibe, was flowing about 80 miles south of Chitrakūṭa. It cannot be identified with the streamlet flowing 11 miles south of the hill and losing itself in a well!

Besides, as we have shown elsewhere, the distances mentioned in the *Rāmāyaṇa* do not correspond to realities. For instance, according to the description in the *Rāmāyaṇa*, Chitrakūṭa lay at a distance of 10 *krośas* from the hermitage of Bhāradvāja,[3] whereas the actual distance of it from Allahabad where the hermitage was situated is not less than 75 miles.[4] Again, the location of several places mentioned in Rāma's journey to the south is uncertain. So we cannot be sure that such places as Pampā and Kishkindhā were situated in Central India.

Mankad, Editor of the Kishkindhākāṇḍa in the Critical

1. See e.g. Uddaṇḍin's *Mallikā-Māruta* summarised in our *Bhavabhūti*, pp. 394 f.
2. *Gaṅgānāth Jhā Commemoration Volume*, p. 157.
3. See—

   दशक्रोश इतस्तात गिरिर्यस्मिन्निवत्स्यसि ।
   महर्षिसेवितः पुण्यः सर्वतः सुखदर्शनः ॥
   गोलाङ्गूलानुचरितो वानरर्क्षनिषेवितः ।
   चित्रकूट इति ख्यातो गन्धमादनसंनिभः ॥

   Rāmāyaṇa, Ayodhyākāṇḍa, 48, 25-26.
4. The distance between Allahabad and Māṇikpur by rail is 104 Kms. and that between Manikpur and Chitrakūṭa, again by rail, is 40 Kms. —total 144 Kms. or 90 miles. The distance between Allahabad and Chitrakūṭa as the crow flies will be somewhat less, say 80 miles.

Edition of the *Rāmāyaṇa*, also held the view that Laṅkā was situated in Central India. But the mention of the Godāvarī presented an insuperable objection to it. To get over it he had recourse to a novel plea. In his Introduction to that *Kāṇḍa*, he says, "In the Kishkindhākāṇḍa, the Godāvarī is mentioned in eleven places, but except in two places, there is another reading, *viz. Mandākinī* in place of it. So the name of the Godāvarī seems to have been substituted in place of the Mandākinī in all passages."[1] This is a strange way of ascertaining correct readings ! In critical editions of Sanskrit works, correct readings are determined on the evidence of Mss., not on calculations like this. Besides, Pusalkar has shown[2] that the Godāvarī finds mention in as many as thirteen passages of the Kishkindhākāṇḍa and in four passages of the Araṇyakāṇḍa. In twelve passages out of these, there is no *v. l.* for *Godāvarī*. Only in five passages *Mandākinī* occurs for *Godāvarī*. In these latter passages, *Godāvarī* clearly appears the better reading on Ms. evidence and so it has been adopted in the Critical Edition by Mankad himself. Even if correct readings are determined on the basis of calculation, *Godāvarī* will have to be accepted in preference to *Mandākinī*.

Nowhere do we get any reference to the Godāvarī flowing in North India. The *Rāmāyaṇa* states that Agastya's hermitage was situated on the bank of that river and we know from both the *Rāmāyaṇa* and the *Mahābhārata* that the sage had established it there *after* crossing the Vindhya mountain. So Laṅkā could not have been in Central India.

Argument II—Mention of Vindhya, south of Kishkindhā.

Kibe had stated this argument when he first propounded his theory about the location of Laṅkā near Amarakaṇṭak. He drew attention to the following *ślokas* stating Sugrīva's directions to the monkeys going in search of Sītā in the south—

1. *Rāmāyaṇa*, Kishkindhākāṇḍa, Mankad's Introd., p. iv.
2. *J. O. I.*, Vol. XV, pp. 33 f.

ततः प्रस्थाप्य सुग्रीवस्तन्महावानरं बलम् ।
दक्षिणां प्रेषयामास वानरानभिलक्षितान् ॥

* * *

सहस्रशिरसं विन्ध्यं नानाद्रुमलतावृतम् ।
नर्मदां च नदीं दुर्गां महोरगनिषेविताम् ॥
ततो गोदावरीं रम्यां कृष्णवेणीं महानदीम् ।
वरदां च महाभागां महोरगनिषेविताम् ॥

Sugrīva was ruling over Kishkindhā. If Vindhya and rivers like the Narmadā, the Godāvarī, the Kṛishṇā and the Varadā (modern Wardhā) lay to the south of Kishkindhā, the latter city must have been situated in North India.

Examination of the Argument

Kibe had advanced this argument when he first propounded his theory in 1919. Later, when he learned from Jacobi that these verses might have been interpolated, he gave it up and has not mentioned it in his subsequent articles. But these *ślokas* have been given in the Critical Edition of the Epic. So we must critically examine this argument also.

While asking the monkeys to search for Sītā in all directions, Sugrīva has mentioned the following countries lying there[1] :

(1) East—The rivers Bhāgīrathī, Sarayū, Kauśikī, Kālindī, Sarasvatī *etc.* and the countries of Videha, Mālava, Kāśī-Kosala, Magadha, Puṇḍra *etc.*

(2) South—Vindhya mountain, the rivers Narmadā, Godāvarī, Kṛishṇaveṇī and Varadā, the countries of Mekala, Utkala, Vidarbha, Ṛishīka, Vaṅga, Kaliṅga, Kauśika, Andhra, Chola, Pāṇḍya and Kerala, the mountains Malaya and Mahendra.

(3) West—Surāshṭra, Bāhlīka, Śūra, Ābhira, the confluence of the Sindhu and the ocean, the Western ocean *etc.*

(4) North—Himālaya, the countries of Bhārata, Kuru, Madraka, Kāmboja, Yavana, Śaka, Āraṭṭaka, Bāhlika, and Chīna, the mountains Kailāsa, Krauñcha *etc.*

On a close scrutiny of these mountains, countries and

1. Kishkindhākāṇḍa, cantos xxxix f.

rivers in the four quarters, it will be noticed that they are mentioned with reference to India as a whole and not as situated in the different directions of a particular place. So it would not be proper to suppose that Vindhya, the Narmadā, the Godāvarī *etc.* were situated to the south of Kishkindhā. However, if one stresses the description of Vindhya as situated to the south of Kishkindhā in the above passage, it can be easily shown that there was another Vindhya near the Malaya mountain in South India. In a sub-continent like India, it should not be surprising if we find more than one mountain, river or place of the same name. Take, for instance, the case of Rāmagiri. I have shown elsewhere that there are several hills of this name in different parts of South India such as Vidarbha, Bastar District of Madhya Pradesh, former Sirgujā State, Orissa *etc.* Which of these was intended by Kālidāsa as Rāmagiri in the *Meghadūta* must be determined from the description of the Cloud-Messenger's way described in that *kāvya*[1]. Besides the Kishkindhā of the *Rāmāyaṇa* there was, in ancient time, another homonymous city near the village Kalyāṇapur, about forty-five miles south of Udaipur in Rājasthān.[2] Nay, there was even another Laṅkā in South India. In several inscriptions of the Kadambas and the Śilāhāras the Goā region is called Siṁhala.[3] None would identify Rāvaṇa's Laṅkā with it. These instances show what risk lies in identifying places merely on the evidence of similarity of their names.

Many years ago Pargiter had shown that there was a mountain called Vindhya in South India. This is also corroborated by a close study of the *Rāmāyaṇa*.

As directed by Sugrīva, Hanumān taking other monkeys with himself, proceeded to search for Sītā in the caves of the

1. See our *Studies in Indology*, Vol. I (second ed.), pp. 15 f.
2. We have edited the Dhulev plates of *Mahārāja* Bhetti found near this Kishkindhā in *E.I.*, Vol. XXX, pp. 1 f.
3. See—

   ततः सिलारवंशोऽयं सिंहलक्ष्माभृतां वरः ।
   प्रभूतभूतसौभाग्यभाग्यवानूर्जितोर्जितः ॥

   in the Khārepāṭaṇ plates of the Śilāhāra king Raṭṭarāja, *E. I.*, Vol. III, pp. 292 f.

Vindhya mountain in the South. In this passage the South is called 'the direction traversed by Agastya.'[1]

अगस्त्याचरितामाशां दक्षिणां यमरक्षिताम् ।
सहैभिर्वानरैर्मुख्यैरङ्गदप्रमुखैर्वयम् ।।

Later, they found themselves locked up in a large cave. Then a female hermit named Ratnaprabhā asked them to close their eyes and in a moment transported them all out of the cave and addressed them as follows :[2]

एष विन्ध्यो गिरिः श्रीमान्नानाद्रुमलतायुतः ।
एष प्रस्रवणः शैलः सागरोऽयं महोदधिः ।। (४, २२, १२)

(This is the beautiful Vindhya mountain, covered with various kinds of trees and creepers. Here is the Prasravaṇa mountain and here is the ocean of abundant water.)

This Vindhya mountain was near the shore of the Southern Ocean. The word *mahodadhi* used to denote the ocean shows that it was not a mere lake as thought by Kibe.

There is another indication of the situation of this Vindhya mountain on the shore of the Southern Ocean noticed in the Kishkindhākāṇḍa of the *Rāmāyaṇa*. While the monkeys were roaming on the hill in search of Sītā, they noticed the Vulture named Sampāti. He told them, "Formerly, while my brother Jaṭāyu and myself were flying against the Sun, my wings were singed by its burning rays, but those of my brother remained unscorched as they were covered by mine. I then fell on the Vindhya mountain and Jaṭāyu in Janasthāna (near Nāsik).

आशङ्के तं निपतितं जनस्थाने जटायुषम् ।
अहं तु पतितो विन्ध्ये दग्धपत्रो जडीकृतः ।।

This very *kāṇḍa* contains an indication of the situation of the Vindhya mountain where Sampāti had collapsed. Sampāti said further to these monkeys—[3] "As I have become incapable of moving about, my son Supārśva supports me by giving me food *etc*. One day he was late in coming. When he

1. *Rāmāyaṇa*, Kishkindhākāṇḍa, Canto LI, v. 7.
2. *Ibid*., Canto LII, v. 12.
3. *Ibid*., Canto LVIII, v. 8.

was asked the reason of it, he told me, "I went to the Mahendra mountain in search of flesh and stood there, guarding the only passage to the ocean. Then I noticed a huge dark-complexioned man carrying a woman resplendent like the Sun. I stopped him, but as he entreated me again and again, I allowed them to go. Later, I learned that he was Rāvaṇa and that he was carrying the lamenting woman Sītā.

This description in the *Rāmāyaṇa* shows that the aforementioned Vindhya mountain was situated near the Mahendra mountain. The latter is mentioned in several inscriptions as situated in South India. There is not an iota of evidence to indicate that it lay in North India. The adjoining Vindhya mountain was on the southern sea-shore. It must be taken to be different from the homonymous mountain north of the Narmadā.

Sankalia knows the situation of the Mahendra mountain, but he takes it to be a short off-shoot of the Vindhya mountain going by the name of the Eastern *ghāṭ*. Would he call Sahyādri another offshoot of the Vindhya ? How strange that he connects these southern ranges of hills with the northern Vindhya !

Argument III—Existence of the descendants of Rāvaṇa in Central India.

Kibe says[1] that there are at present four indigenous tribes in Central India, *viz.* (1) Rāvaṇa, (2) Vānara, (3) Raghu and (4) Komara. Some Goṇḍs of Central India regard themselves as descended from Rāvaṇa. This indicates their habitation there in ancient times. So Rāvaṇa's capital Laṅkā must have been situated nearby—near modern Amarakaṇṭak.

Examination of the Argument—Such inferences will lead us to absurd conclusions. In the mediaeval times it became a fashion to trace one's descent from an eponymous hero or a famous royal family. Some royal families called themselves solar, and others lunar. The Pratīhāras took pride in tracing their descent from Lakshmaṇa, the *Pratīhāra* or door-keeper of Rāma. Some rulers called themselves *Pāṇḍava-vaṁśīs* or descendants of the Pāṇḍavas, while others in the Reva State

1. *F. W. Thomas Volume*, p. 144.

regarded themselves as *Kaurava-vaṁśīs*. The Early Gurjaras of Gujarat proudly mentioned their descent from Karṇa of the *Mahābhārata* fame. The Goṇḍs were non-Āryans. So they took pride in their supposed descent from Rāvaṇa. They had, however, as little connection with the latter as these others had from their supposed ancestors.

Argument IV—Realistic Interpretation of the epic descriptions.

If we interpret the descriptions in the *Rāmāyaṇa* from a realistic point of view they will point to the location of Laṅkā in Central India. It is stated in the Kishkindhākāṇḍa that Supārśva, the son of Sampāti, saw Rāvaṇa carrying Sītā in his arms as he was guarding the pass of the Mahendra mountain. So Rāvaṇa was an ordinary human being. The *Rāmāyaṇa* describes that the ocean which was crossed by Hanumān extended a hundred *yojanas*. If we identify Laṅkā with Ceylon, the distance between the latter island and Rāmeśvara should be a hundred *yojanas* or 450 miles. Such is not the case, however. So a *yojana* probably means 200 yards. Hanumān may have swum across such 100 *yojanas*. He may have walked some distance where the water was shallow, and rested himself on rocks jutting out of it elsewhere. In other parts of the lake where the water was deep, he may have swum across. In this way he crossed the lake, not the ocean. If we interpret the descriptions in the epic in a rationalistic manner, Laṅkā will have to be located on the Indrāṇā hill, about 18 miles north of Jabalpur.

Examination of the Argument

The *Rāmāyaṇa* is a *Mahā-kāvya*. The statements and descriptions in it are full of poetic fancy. They cannot be taken literally. We have shown this elsewhere from the mention of the distance of the Chitrakūṭa hill from the hermitage of Bhāradvāja mentioned in it. The Epic describes that Rāvaṇa was ten-headed, that Hanumān swam the distance of 450 miles, that Rāma journeyed from Laṅkā to Ayodhyā in an aerial car together with Bibhīshaṇa, Hanumān and others, and that several missiles like *Agnyastra*, were used in the Battle of Laṅkā. These descriptions cannot be taken literally. Again, it is not correct to say that Rāvaṇa was always going on foot. He sometimes flew in the sky. So Sītā is said to have thrown her ornaments to Sugrīva and others sitting on the Ṛishyamūka hill.

Besides, the *Rāmāyaṇa* names the mountain where Rāvaṇa was stopped by Supārśva at Mahendra, not Vindhya. That it was situated in South India has been shown above. Vindhya, which adjoined it, must be taken as a mountain lying near the southern tip of Bhārata. So Laṅkā which was to the south of this second Vindhya cannot be placed in Central India.

Some Miscellaneous Arguments

Sankalia has advanced some other minor arguments to substantiate the theory of Laṅkā being in Central India. They are as follows :— (1) Rāma is said to have pierced seven Sāla trees with his arrow. In the Battle of Laṅkā monkeys and Rākshasas uprooted and threw Sāla trees on one another. These trees are noticed only in such parts as the Amarakaṇṭak table-land, the region of Chhota Nagpur *etc.* (2) Laṅkā is a word of the Muṇḍa language. (3) Rāvaṇa was of the Goṇḍ aboriginal tribe.

Examination of the Arguments

These are flimsy arguments. One cannot be sure that South India had no Sāla trees in ancient times because they are not noticed there nowadays. On the other hand, the description of the ocean in the Rāmāyaṇa, *viz.* that it had salt water (*lavaṇāmbhas*), that its tides were caused by the rise of the moon,[1] that it contained large hills, alligators, Nāgas *etc.* would not suit any lake, however large, supposed to have existed in Central India. If one emphasizes the existence of Sāla trees as a valid argument, he must attach equal import-

1. उपायो दृश्यतां कश्चिल्लंघने लवणाम्भसः ॥
Rāmāyaṇa, Kishkindhākāṇḍa, Canto LVII, v. 31. See also—
चण्डनक्रग्रहं घोरं क्षपादौ दिवसक्षये ।
चन्द्रोदये समाधूतं प्रतिचन्द्रसमाकुलम् ॥
Yuddhakāṇḍa, Canto IV. v. 78.

ance to the afore-cited description of the ocean. Otherwise, it would be a cause of *ardhajaratīya-dosha*.

(2) The word Lankā may have been derived from a non-Aryan language. It may have been current in Ceylon also. This cannot falsify the story of the *Rāmāyaṇa*.

(3) The word Rāvaṇa can be derived in the Sanskrit language. In the *Gaṇa-pāṭha* attached to Pāṇini's sūtra शिवादिभ्योऽण् । (IV. 1.112) it is stated that *Viśravas* is changed to *Viśravaṇa* or *Ravaṇa* before the affix *aṇ* signifying a descendant. So we get *Vaiśravaṇa* meaning Kubera, and *Rāvaṇa*, the name of the famous Rākshasa, both being sons of the sage Viśravas. Since these words occur in the *Gaṇa-pāṭha*, this derivation is at least as old as the 6th century B.C.[1]

Though Rāma, Hanumān and Rāvaṇa were human beings, they possessed superhuman strength and powers. Vālmīki has described their actions from that point of view. It is objectionable to utilise only the portion of the description that suits one's theory and ignore the rest.

What is true in regard to description of individuals is also true in respect of town-planning, food and drink.[2] These descriptions are imaginary and exaggerated. To indulge in fanciful and exaggerated description is ingrained in the nature of Sanskrit poets. Even the great Kālidāsa, who flourished in the Historical Age, describes that Daśaratha ruled for nearly ten thousand years, in the following verse of the *Raghuvaṁśa* (X, 1) :

पृथिवीं शासतस्तस्य पाकशासनतेजसः ।
किञ्चिदूनमनूनर्द्धेः शरदामयुतं ययौ ॥

So when we find the *Rāmāyaṇa* describing large and straight roads running parallel to each other, we must not jump to the conclusion that the passage belongs to the age succeeding the establishment of Indo-Greek Kingdoms in the North-West Province.[3] Similarly, we must not see in the description of the reception of Bharata's soldiers with abundance of wine and women in the hermitage of Bhāradvāja the reflex of the social

1. See the Gaṇapāṭha on Pāṇini, IV. 1. 112.
2. See Sankalia's वाल्मीकि रामायण (एक पुरातत्त्वीय अध्ययन), p. 34.

condition in India after the influx of Roman wine-jars. Wine was not introduced in India first by the Romans. *Ṛigveda Sūkta* X. 34 describes how a Gambler in repentence ascribes his miserable condition to his addiction to wine. So the Poet could well have described the scenes of revelry in the hermitage of Bhāradvāja by his imagination.

Sankalia divides the *Rāmāyaṇa* story into four parts. He thinks that the oldest part of it goes back to the 6th or the 7th century B.C. and the latest to the 5th or the 6th century A.D. Some portion of the *Rāmāyaṇa* must indeed have been as old as the 6th century B.C. The *Mahābhāshya* of Patañjali (2nd cen. B.C.) cites the beautiful hemistich एति जीवन्तमानन्दो नरं वर्षशतादपि from the Sundarakāṇḍa of the *Rāmāyaṇa*. That some other portions of it are as late as the 1st or the 2nd century A.D. is clear from the mention in it of the foreign invaders of India such as the Śakas and the Pahlavas. But the *Rāmāyaṇa* must have attained its present form before the third century A.D. at the latest. The Rāma story given in the plays of Bhāsa (3rd century A.D.) and Kālidāsa (4th century A.D.) is as in the present version of the epic. It may have received minor additions here and there, but the main features of the story have not undergone any change. Sculptures of the Rāma story are not noticed before the Gupta age, but that does not prove non-existence of the Rāma saga in the earlier age.

We shall not be able to form an idea about the original form of the Rāma story from archaeological evidence. Excavation has not so far revealed any remains of the age of Rāma and there is no prospect of it hereafter also. The *Rāmāyaṇa* is regarded as the First Poem (*Ādi-kāvya*). It contains marvellous descriptions originating from the fertile imagination of a great Poet. The epic mentions some southern as well as some northern countries. We cannot say that the southern countries like Vidarbha were unknown in the fifth or sixth century B.C., for they are mentioned in the Vedic literature also. So the beginning of the Rāma saga can date even earlier than the sixth cen. B.C.

Sankalia has remarked that as the *Rāmāyaṇa* mentions articles of iron such as weapons, the box of Śiva's bow with iron wheels *etc.* its date must lie between 500-400 B.C. and 300-400 A.D.[1] But *ayas* (iron) was known to the Vedic Aryans also. *Ṛigveda*, I, 116, 15 tells us that when Viśpalā's leg had been cut off in battle like the wing of a bird, the Aśvins gave her an iron one (*āyasi jaṅghā*) in stead. Some scholars propose to take *ayas* in such passages as meaning 'copper', but without reason. All ancient and modern interpreters have understood it here in the sense of iron. If iron was used for such purposes, it is unlikely that it was not used for fabricating weapons, wheels of boxes, chariots *etc.*

The foregoing discussion must have made it plain that Rāvaṇa's Laṅkā was not situated in Central India, and that some portions of the *Rāmāyaṇa* were not composed after our contact with Roman Civilization as contended by Sankalia.

1. See Sankalia's book *loc cit.*

XXIV. ARE THE CAVES AT DHĀRĀSIVA BUDDHIST OR JAINA ?*

(Plate IV)

Dhārāśiva is an old town about 37 miles north of Sholāpur in the Marāṭhwāḍā Division of Mahārāshṭra. Some years ago its name was changed to Usmānābād by Usman Ali, a Nawab of Hyderabad. It is now the chief town of the Usmānābād District of the Marāṭhwāḍā.

About two miles north-east from the town there are a few caves in a ravine facing the west, which have long been known to Archaeologists. They have been described by Burgess in the *Archaeological Survey of Western India*, Vol. III, pp. 4 f. and in the *Cave-Temples of India*, pp. 504 f. Burgess ascribed them to the Jaina religion. After describing the image in Cave II, he says, "The details of this image, and all the arrangements of this and the neighbouring caves, are so exactly like those of Bauddha *Vihāras* that any one who had not seen other Jaina caves of a similar sort, might easily be led to suppose that these were Bauddha excavations. But a careful study of the Bauddha and Jaina groups at Elurā suffices to show that these are cave-temples of the Digambara or naked Jains, and perhaps among their earlier attempts at such works, when they began by imitating the Buddhist excavations."[1] Recently Dr. M. K. Dhavalikar has attempted to show that they belong to the Bauddha and not to the Jaina religion.[2] It is proposed to examine this question in the present article.

My attention was drawn to this problem as I was studying recently the history of the Śilāhāras, who were ruling over North and South Koṅkaṇ and the Kolhāpur region from the

* *Journal of Indian History*, Vol. LI, pp. 31 f.

1. *Archaeological Survey of Western India*, (*A.S.W.I*), Vol. III. p. 7.
2. *Journal of the Asiatic Society of Bombay* (*J.A.S. Bom.*), (New Series), Vols. XIX-XX, 183 f.; *J.I.H.*, Vol. XLVI, pp. 405 f.

ninth to the thirteenth century A.D.; for these kings proudly mention their *biruda Tagara-pura-parameśvara* (the lord of the city of Tagara) in their inscriptions. In accordance with the interpretation of similar expressions such as *Ujjayinī-puravar-ādhīśvara, Kālañjara-puravar-ādhīśvara etc.* this *biruda* must be taken to mean that they originally hailed from the city of Tagara, and not that they were then ruling at Tagara. Tagara was a flourishing city in the early centuries of the Christian era. Mercantile articles from several southern places such as Nāgārjunakoṇḍa, Viṇukoṇḍa, and Veṅgī were first taken to Tagara and then transported *via* Paiṭhaṇ and Nāsik to Ujjayinī in the north or to Broach in the north-west. Tagara has been mentioned as a famous emporium in the *Periplus of the Erythrean Sea*[1] as well as by Ptolemy.[2] Like the ancient cities of Ujjayinī, Tripurī and Kauśāmbī, Tagara also had coins struck in its name. One such tiny coin of the first or second century A.D. has recently been discovered in Marāṭhwādā.[3]

The location of Tagara was not certain for a long time. Being misled by the distance and bearing of the city from Broach and Paiṭhaṇ mentioned by the afore-mentioned Greek writers, scholars have variously identified it. It was taken to be identical with Devagiri by Wilford, with Junnar by Bhagvanlal Indraji, with Dhārūr in the Bhīr District by R.G. Bhandarkar, with Tavangir, 12 miles north of Kanakagiri by V.K. Rajwade, and with Karavīra (Kolhāpur) by Fleet. Fleet ultimately suggested its identification with Ter in the Usmānābād District[4] which has met with general acceptance. Ter is only about 10 miles north of the caves. It has remains of ancient Buddhist and Hindu temples. In the excavations recently made there by Mr. B. N. Chapekar several pieces of pottery, coins and terra-cotta figurines dating from the second century B.C. to the third century A.D. and thus belonging to the Sātavāhana period have come to notice.[5] Besides, some Sanskrit, Marathi and Kannada inscriptions dating from the eleventh to the fourteen-

1. R.C. Majumdar, *Classical Accounts of India*, p 376.
2. *Ibid.*, p. 304.
3. *J.N.S.I.*, Vol. xxxiii, pp. 37 f.
4. *J.R.A.S.* 1901, pp. 537 f.
5. See his *Report on the Excavations at Ter.*

th century A. D. have been found there. These antiquities support the identification of Tagara with Ter. Sanskrit *nagara* is changed to *ner* in course of time. See e.g. Pimpaḷner (from Pippalanagara) and Saṅgamner (from Saṅgamanagara). So *Tagara* seems to have been changed to *Ter*. Besides, the place is called Terapura or Terāpura in ancient Sanskrit and Apabhraṁśa works as shown below.[1] So there is now no doubt about the identification of Tagara with Ter in the Usmānābād District.

As stated before, Ter lies about 12 miles north-east of Dhārāśiva. The caves of Dhārāśiva have been described in some Jaina works published during the last fifty years. In 1924 Dr. Hiralal Jain discovered a manuscript of the Apabhraṁśa work *Karkaṇḍachariu* in the Jain Bhāṇḍār at Kārañjā in Vidarbha. He edited it subsequently in the Kārañjā Jaina Series. Its author Kanakāmara tells us that the minister who patronised him diverted the mind of king Karṇa.[2] This king is probably identical with the homonymous Kalachuri king who flourished in the period A.D. 1041-1073.[3] So the Apabhraṁśa work belongs to the eleventh cen. A.D. It gives the following story of king Karkaṇḍa :—

Karkaṇḍa was the king of the country of Aṅga in North India. He ruled from Champā, modern Bhāgalpur. His dominion comprised almost the whole of Bhārata, but the rulers of the southern countries of Chōla, Chēra and Pāṇḍya did not acknowledge his suzerainty. So he started with a large army to subjugate them. On his way he encamped at Terāpura. There a local ruler named Śiva met him and told him about the wonderful cave-temple on the hill nearby. His curiosity being aroused, he visited the site. He saw the image of Pārśvanātha in the cave. He also noticed another image of the Tīrthaṅkara on the top of the hill. He brought it down and installed

1. The *Bṛihatkathākośa* uses the expression *Ter-ākhya-nagara* (56, 352) and *Ter-ākhya-pura* (56, 390), which may indicate the name of the town to be *Tera* or *Terā*. But in 56, 396 Harisheṇa uses *Tera-pattana*, which shows that the name intended was *Tera* not *Terā*. The *Karakaṇḍachariu*, however, gives the name a *Terāpura* in 4.3.1.
2. *Karkaṇḍachariu*, 10.29.6.
3. *C.I.I.*, Vol. IV. Introd., pp. xciii f.

it in the cave. He then noticed a knob or protuberance (*granthi*) on the *siṁhāsana* of the original image in the cave.[1] Thinking that it was marring the beauty of the image, he called an artisan and asked him to chisel it off. The latter told him that the *granthi* was blocking a spring of water inside. If he chiselled it off, the stream of water would inundate the whole cave. But the king insisted on getting the *granthi* chiselled off. As soon as it was done, a large stream of water gushed forth and filled the whole cave. The king felt distressed, but he was consoled by a heavenly being who came there from above. He gave him the following account of the cave :

"In the southern Vedyardha[2] there ruled two Vidyādhara brothers named Nīla and Mahānīla. Having been ousted by their enemies, they fled to the south and established themselves at Terānagara. They were converted to Jainism by a Muni. Thereafter, they got the cave excavated and installed the image of Pārśvanātha therein. As for the other image of Pārśvanātha found on the hill, Karkaṇḍa was told that it had been brought there by two Vidyādharas from the Pudi hill in Kerala. While going through the air they noticed the cave. To see it they alighted on the hill, and keeping the image there, they went down to see the cave. When they came back, they found that their image could not be moved at all. So they left it there and went away."[3]

Karkaṇḍa got two more caves excavated on the hill. He then invaded Siṁhala and on his return from there he defeated the rulers Choḷa, Cēra and Pāṇḍya and then went back to his own country.

The story of Karkaṇḍa occurs also in the Sanskrit work *Bṛihatkathākośa* of Harisheṇa. It is similar to that given above, differing from it in one or two particulars. According to it, the image of Pārśvanātha found on the hill-top had been brought from Laṅkā.[4]

1. *Karkaṇḍachariu*, 4.12.1. Dhavalikar has not noticed this account in the work. He thinks that it occurs only in the *Bṛihatkathākośa*.
2. This means in the country to the south of Kailāsa.
3. *Karkaṇḍacariu*, 5.8. 4 f.
4. *Bṛihatkathākośa*, 56, 397-98. Again, the *Karkaṇḍachariu* states that Karkaṇḍa excavated only two caves on the hill, while the *Bṛihatkathākośa* says that he excavated three.

The *Bṛihatkathākośa* was composed at Vardhamānapura in the Śaka year 853, Vikrama year 989 (A.D. 931-32).[1] So it is earlier than the Apabhraṁśa work *Karkaṇḍachariu.* In fact, the story in the latter appears to be based on Sanskrit version in the earlier work. The mention of Terapura in the *Bṛihatkathākośa* is the earliest reference to that city so far known in Sanskrit literature.

The caves mentioned in both these works are undoubtedly those on the hill near Dhārāśiva. There are at present six caves on that hill, of which four are excavated facing west, and two more in another part of the hill.[2] Of the former, Cave No. II is noteworthy, though now in a dilapidated condition. It resembles the Vihāra caves Nos. XVI and XVII of the Vākāṭaka age at Ajantā.[3] (*See Plate IV*). The verandah in front of the cave measures 78 ft. in length and 10 ft. 4 inches in breadth. Its pillars, of which there were six or eight, have now fallen, bringing down the whole front except for a small fragment carved with the figures of the Jinas. The hall inside is 82 ft. in depth and from 79 to 85 ft. in width. It has 32 pillars arranged in two squares, one inside the other. The outer square has 20 pillars, and the inner one 12 pillars. The pillars in front of the shrine are round in shape with square bases and constricted cushion capitals, being decorated with horizontal bands of beads and festoons. There are twenty-two cells in the walls of the hall, 8 in each of the two side walls and 6 in the back wall, three being on each side of the shrine at the back. In the shrine, 19 ft. 3 inches wide, 15 ft. deep and 13 ft. high there is a large image of Pārśvanātha seated in the *dhyānamudrā*, with hands on the lap, the palms being turned up. On his *siṁhāsana* there appear two deer on each side of what appears to have originally been a wheel placed on its edge, but it has now almost completely disappeared. Over the head of the Tīrthaṅkara Pārśvanātha there are spread seven hoods of a serpent, with a small crown on each of them. There is a Chawri-bearer and, above, a flying Gandharva on each side of the Tīrthaṅkara. (*See Plate IV*).

1. *Bṛihatkathākośa*, Introd., p, 121.
2. *A.S.W.I.*, Vol. III, pp. 9 f.
3. *C.I.I.*, Vol. V, Introd.. pp. lxvi f.

It may be noted that in the floor of the cell in the north-west corner of the hall there is a hole which is always filled with water. It is probably connected with the cistern at the west end of the verandah in front of the hall.

A little to the east of this cave lies Cave No. III somewhat smaller in size, but otherwise resembling it. There is a similar figure of Pārśvanātha in the shrine, with the wheel on the *siṁhāsana* quite clear in front. No deer are, however, noticeable on the two sides of it. It is not known if they were carved before. There are four other caves excavated in the hill, but we need not notice them here as they are not relevant to the present discussion.

These caves have been described as of the Jaina religion in the Sanskrit work *Bṛihatkathākośa* and the Apabhraṁśa work *Karkaṇḍachariu*. I have cited above the opinion of James Burgess, who has described them fully in the *Archaeological Survey of Western India*, Vol. III, and rather briefly in the *Cave-Temples of India*. He also ascribes them to the Jaina religion. But recently Dr. Dhavalikar has put forward the view that they are Buddhist. He has advanced the following arguments in support of it :—

(1) Stylistically these caves resemble the Mahāyāna Bauddha caves of the Vākāṭaka age, which were carved towards the end of the sixth century A.D. On the other hand, they differ from the Jaina caves at Ellorā.

(2) In the fifth and sixth centuries A.D. to which these caves belong, Buddhism, not Jainism, was flourishing in the northern Daccan. It was only in the 9th century A.D. that Jainism flourished there when it received royal patronage, more particularly under the Śilāhāras.

(3) Literary evidence furnished by the *Bṛihatkathākośa* and the *Karkaṇḍachariu* indicates that Cave No. II was Buddhist, not Jaina. Karkaṇḍa is said to have installed another image of Pārśvanātha in that Cave. Where was the need of installing a new image of the Tīrthaṅkara if there was one there already?[1]

1. Karkaṇḍa may have installed it in the cell to the west of the verandah. For the image of Pārśvanātha found there, see *A.S.W.I.*, Vol. III. pl. III. fig. 2. This is a loose image.

So it seems that Karkaṇḍa, after worshipping the image, realised that he had committed a mistake, since it was an image of the Buddha. But it was not easy—nay, it was impossible—to install a new image in place of the old one, because the latter was carved out of the living rock. In fact, Karkaṇḍa did not install a new image. He only removed the *dharma-chakra* carved in front of the *siṁhāsana*. So we do not notice it now between the deer on the two sides. The version of the story of Karkaṇḍa in both the Jaina works supports this conjecture. It tells us that Karkaṇḍa got a knob (*granthi*) on the *siṁhāsana* of the Tīrthaṅkara image chiselled off. That knob was nothing else than a *dharmachakra* carved on the *siṁhāsana*. A similar *dharmachakra* is noticed on the *siṁhāsana* of the image in the adjoining Cave No. III. So both these images are of the Buddha.

(4) There is no doubt a seven-hooded *nāga* over the head of the image in Cave No. II, but representations showing *nāga*-hoods over the Buddha's head are not wanting in Buddhist art. In fact we have several representations of the Buddha in the *dhyānamudrā* with a seven-hooded serpent over his head discovered at Nāgārjunakoṇḍa.[1]

(5) Karkaṇḍa seems to have got excavated the rock-cut court in front of the cave and also the frieze of Jaina images on the facade of the verandah. This is of a later age—probably of the 9th century A.D. He may also have got excavated caves Nos. V and VI in another part of the hill.[2]

Dhavalikar has, therefore, come to the conclusion that Caves Nos. II and III were originally Buddhist. Later, in the 9th or 10th Century A.D., they were converted into Jaina Caves. We shall next proceed to examine his arguments to determine this matter.

(1) There is no doubt much similarity in the plans of the Mahāyāna caves (Nos. XVI and XVII) of the Vākāṭaka age at Ajaṇṭā and Caves II and III at Dhārāśiva. All of them have a verandah in front, a hall with cells on three sides behind it, a shrine at the further end, with an image on a *siṁhāsana* in it.

1. *Mem. A.S.I.*, No. 54, plates XXIII (b); XXXI (b).
2. *J.A.S. Bom.*, Vols. 39-40, p. 188.

But it would not be proper to infer from these similarities that they are all of the same faith. We can only conclude on the basis of this similarity that they were excavated in the same age. The similarity may be due to the employment of the same artisans by the princes or wealthy persons of the time for getting the Caves excavated. As Dr. U.P. Shah has observed, "no art is entirely Jaina, Buddhist or Hindu. The same artists who worked for one sect, were employed also by other sects in any particular unit of time and space.....Do we not find identical art style in the Jaina, Buddhist and Hindu specimens of the Kushāṇa period obtained from Mathurā ?"[1]

Dr. Burgess has shown that Jaina images are noticed on the frieze of the verandah of Cave No. II. Dhavalikar also has admitted it. We have no reason to suppose that this frieze only was carved three or four centuries after the cave behind it was excavated. It must have been carved along with the cave in the same period.

(2) That Jainism was not flourishing in North Deccan or Mahārāshṭra in the sixth and seventh centuries A.D. when these caves were excavated is irrelevant in the present discussion; for Tagara where the caves are situated was formerly not included in Mahārāshṭra, as it is now. It was Kannaḍa-speaking in those days. This is shown by the *birudas* assumed by the Śilāhāra kings of Tagara who founded principalities in the Koṅkaṇ and Kolhāpur regions in the ninth and later centuries by the favour of their Rāshṭrakūṭa and Chālukya suzerains. See, *e.g.*, the following *birudas*:[2] *Malagalagaṇḍa* (the hero among hill-chiefs), *Gaṇḍaragaṇḍa* (the hero of heroes), *Gaṇḍavaṅgara* (gold among heroes), *Nannisamudra* (an ocean of truth), *Villaviḍeṅga* (clever in the use of the bow), *Pusigaṅjuvāta* (who is afraid of falsehood) *etc.* These are all Kannaḍa *birudas*. Though the Śilāhāras of North Koṅkaṇ ceased to assume such *birudas* in later times, being naturalized in the Marathi-speaking country, the Śilāhāras of Kolhāpur continued to bear them

1. *Studies in Jaina Art*, p. 3.
2. See Janjirā plates of Aparājita, *Important Inscriptions from the Baroda State*, pp. 35 f.; Bhadānā grant of Aparājita, *Ep. Ind.*, Vol. III, pp. 267 f. *etc.*

to the last as appears clear from their inscriptions. Many of the records of these Later Śilāhāras of Kolhāpur are in the Kannaḍa language.[1] So these rulers must originally have been Kannaḍa-speaking in their home-town of Tagara. The history of Northern Deccan or Mahārāshṭra will not be of any use in finding out whether Jainism was flourishing in the country round Tagara. Unfortunately, we have no records from Tagara dating back to the sixth or seventh century A.D. But the Jaina religion was undoubtedly prevalent in Karṇāṭaka in that period. It had the support of the Kadambas and Early Chālukyas who were ruling in that age. It is well-known that the Chālukya Emperor Pulakeśin II gave liberal patronage to the poet Ravikīrti who erected a Jaina temple at Aihole in the Bijāpur District.[2] Aihole is only about 150 miles as the crow flies south of Dhārāśiva. So it is not unlikely that Jainism was flourishing at Tagara in the sixth or seventh century A.D. According to Jaina tradition, the Vidyādhara princes Nīla and Mahānīla were converted to Jainism and then they got these caves excavated. It is noteworthy that the Śilāhāras trace their descent from the Vidyādhara Jīmūtavāhana. It is not known if they had adopted the Jaina faith when in Tagara, but it is not unlikely that the caves were excavated with their royal patronage and so in course of time they came to be associated with the Vidyādharas.

(3) Dhavalikar has drawn attention to the *dharmachakra* carved on the *siṁhāsana* of the image in Cave No. III in support of his view that it is of the Buddha. A similar *dharmachakra*, now mutilated, was also carved between two deer on either side of the image in Cave No. II. The *dharmachakra* is a characteristic symbol of the Buddha image. After worshipping the image in Cave No. II, Karkaṇḍa realised that he had committed a mistake. So he got the *dharmachakra* chiselled off in order to convert the image into that of a Jaina Tīrthaṅkara. The knob (*granthi*) which, according to both the above mentioned Jaina works, was caused to be removed by Kar-

1. See *Ep. Ind.*, Vol. XIX, pp. 30 f.
2. *Ibid.* Vol. VI, pp. 1 f.

kaṇḍa was nothing else but this *dharmachakra*. So Dhavalikar takes this *chakra* placed edgewise on the *siṁhāsana* or pedestal of an image as the distinguishing mark of a Buddha image. We shall examine this argument at some length.

Gautama Buddha first preached his doctrine in the Deer Park at Sārnāth. This event is called *Dharmachakrapravartana* (Revolving of the Religious Wheel), and it is indicated by carving a deer on either side of a wheel placed edgewise on the pedestal or *siṁhāsana* of a Buddha image. This is no doubt a significant symbol of Buddhism. But it seems that it was adopted by the Jainas also in the beginning.[1] Caves Nos. II and III at Dhārāśiva are of this age. The Jainas also regard the wheel as a sacred symbol. Haribhadra's *Āvaśyaka Sūtra* has the following narrative about it.

Once upon a time Ṛishabhanātha, the Jaina Tīrthaṅkara, went to Takshaśilā. He reached the place in the evening. When Bāhubali, the ruler of the place, came to know of it, he thought of going next morning to have his *darśana*; but when he went there, he found that the Tīrthaṅkara had already left the place. Bāhubali felt disappointed. He consoled himself by erecting and worshipping a *chakra* there. This was the origin of the worship of the *chakra* in Jainism. Such a *chakra* of bronze fixed on a stick is preserved in the Patna Museum.[2]

The Jainas recognise twenty-four Tīrthaṅkaras. Their images are all alike, but they are distinguished by their cognisances carved on their *siṁhāsanas* or pedestals. In the Śaka and Kushāṇa periods these cognisances were not evolved. The images of the Tīrthaṅkaras had only the *dharmachakra* carved on their pedestals or *siṁhāsanas* and they were distinguished by their names incised on them. The cognisances were evolved later in the Gupta period.[3] Recently, two images of the Tīrthaṅkara Chandraprabha and one of Pushpadanta were discovered in the Vidiśā District of Madhya Pradesh. They have only the *dharmachakra* carved on the pedestal and are distinguished

1. Burgess also says that the caves at Dhārāśiva were imitated from the Buddhist caves.
2. *Studies in Jaina* Art, pl. VI, fig. 15.
3. *Ibid.*, pp. 14 f.

by the mention of their names in the inscriptions thereon. The cognisances are not carved on the two sides of their *Dharmachakra*.[1]

Later, these cognisances such as the bull in the case of Ṛishabhanātha or Ādinātha, the deer of Śāntinātha, the conch of Nemināthа, the snake of Pārśvanātha and the lion of Mahāvīra came into vogue. See, for instance, the image of Nemināthа at Rājgir.[2] The identity of the Tīrthaṅkara is suggested by the *dharmachakra* with the Chakrapurusha standing in front and a conch placed on either side of it. Recently, an image of a Tīrthaṅkara was discovered at Kheḍabrahma in North Gujarāt. It has on its *siṁhāsana* a *chakra* placed edgewise with a deer on either side exactly as in the case of a Buddha image.[3] It has been identified as an image of Śāntinātha. There is a similar image of Śāntinātha in the Faizabad Museum.

The *Dharmachakra* was thus not a distinguishing characteristic symbol of the Buddha image. It was used to signify the images of the Jaina Tīrthaṅkaras also. The identity of the Tīrthaṅkara was generally indicated by his cognisance carved in addition. In the case of the image in Cave No. II at Dhārāśiva the congnisance is the *nāga* or serpent which is shown as spreading his hood over its head. The image is, therefore, of the Tīrthaṅkara Pārśvanātha.

(4) But it may be said that 'the serpent hoods are seen over the head of the Buddha images also. Several such images have been discovered at Nāgārjunakoṇḍa. The image in Cave No. II at Dhārāśiva which has *nāga-hoods* over its head can, therefore, be taken to be that of the Buddha also.' This objection is, no doubt, relevant. It must be considered at some length.

The serpent-hoods spread over the head are not a distinguishing characteristic of a Buddha image as they are of the image of the Jaina Tīrthaṅkara Pārśvanātha. They are not noticed on *all* images of the Buddha. They are seen only in connection with an episode in the life of Gautama Buddha.

1. *J.O.I.*, Vol. XVIII. pp. 247 f.
2. *Studies in Jaina Art*, pl. VII, fig. 18.
3. *J.O.I.*. Vol. X, pp. 63 f.

Gautama spent five weeks at Gayā after he attained enlightenment. Then he went to the Nāga Muchalinda, who was dwelling in a lake nearby. To protect him from a storm which broke out at the time, the Nāga spread his hoods over his head. This episode is shown on the railing of many stūpas. The Nāga-hoods are shown over the head of the Buddha only in connection with this episode in the relics of Nāgārjunakoṇḍa.[1] He is shown as sitting on the coils of a serpent. Some Nāgas with similar hoods are shown humbly bowing to him. No such episode is intended to be represented in the caves Nos. II and III at Dhārāśiva. The images with nāga-hoods over their heads must, therefore, be taken to be those of the Jaina Tīrthaṅkara Pārśvanātha.

(4) On the frieze of the verandah are carved small images of Jinas, which leave no doubt that the cave behind is of the Jaina faith. We have no reason to suppose that this facade of the verandah was carved three or four centuries after the cave.

The foregoing examination of Dhavalikar's arguments must have shown that Caves Nos. II and III are of the Jaina faith. There is no evidence to attribute them to Buddhism. They were regarded as Jaina caves from the 9th to the 11th century as is clear from their description in the *Bṛihatkathākośa* and *Karkaṇḍachariu*.

We need not suppose that all the description of Cave No. II in the aforementioned two works is correct. Neither Harisheṇa nor Kanakāmara is likely to have personally seen them. The former was staying at Vardhmānapura which, as I have shown elsewhere,[2] was situated in Malwa. Kanakāmara may have been staying somewhere near Tripurī, the capital of King Karṇa mentioned in the *Karkaṇḍachariu*.[3] Both these authors lived far away from Dhārāśiva. Their description of Cave No. II at Dhārāśiva is evidently from hearsay or Jaina tradition. It is also imaginary to a great extent ; for they describe the image in the cave as inlaid with jewels and that on the hill-top as inlaid with gold and jewels. The hall of the

1. See *M.A.S.I.*, No. 54, pp. 28 and 32.
2. *Studies in Indology*, Vol. IV, pp. 137 f.
3. *Karkaṇḍachariu*, 10, 29.6.

cave had a thousand pillars! The story of water stream gushing out of a chiselled knob on the *siṁhāsana* of the Pārśvanātha image in Cave No. II is equally fanciful. It may have been suggested by the presence of a small hole in the cell in the north-west corner of the cave which is always filled with water. As Burgess conjectured, it has perhaps some connection with the cistern at the west end of the verandah. The cell in which the cistern has been excavated has two holes in the floor noticed by Burgess.[1] The miraculous story of the water stream inundating the whole cave may have owed its origin to the presence of these holes which are always filled with water.

The story that these caves were excavated by the Vidyādharas Nīla and Mahānīla, who hailed from the Himālayan region and were ruling from Tagara, may be equally imaginary. It occurs first in the Sanskrit work *Bṛihatkathākośa* (10th cen. A.D.) Nearly a hundred years before, the Śilāhāra kings had commenced their rule in North Koṅkaṇ. They state in their records that they had hailed from the city of Tagara. They also trace their descent from the Vidyādhara Jīmūtavāhana. This must have led to the tradition that the caves near Tagara were excavated by the Vidyādharas who had been converted to Jainism. We do not know whether the Śilāhāra kings ruling from Tagara were of the Jaina faith. The caves may have been excavated with their generous support. The tradition that the caves were excavated by Vidyādharas Nīla and Mahānīla after their conversion to Jainism is evidently due to the supposition that those who were responsible for the excavation must have been of the Jaina faith. It may be noted in this connection that a feudatory of the Śilāhāras of North Koṅkaṇ, *viz*. Chāmuṇḍarāja, who flourished in the first half of the eleventh century A.D., assumed the *biruda Tribhuvana-Nīla*. His father Vijjarāṇaka was known as *Āhava-Nīla*.[2] These *birudas* are reminiscent of the traditional rule of the Vidyādhara Nīla at Tagara: for like his Śilāhāra overlord, Chāmuṇḍarāja also bore the *biruda Tagarapura-parameśvara*, suggesting Tagara as his original home.

1. *A.S.W.I.*, Vol. III, p. 6.
2. *Ep. Ind.*, Vol. XXXII, p. 66.

XXV. WHO BUILT THE TEMPLE OF MAHĀLAKSHMĪ AT KOLHĀPUR AND WHEN ?

Kolhāpur is well-known throughout the country as Dakshiṇa-Kāśī (Southern Kāśī). The temple of Mahālakshmī there is counted among the 108 *Śākta-pīṭhas* of Bhārata. The *Devī Bhāgavata purāṇa* (VII. 38.5-6) enumerates the main *Śākta tīrthas* in the Mahārāshṭra in the following passage[1]—

कोलापुरे महास्थानं यत्र लक्ष्मीः स्थिता सदा ।
मातुः परं द्वितीयं च रेणुकाधिष्ठितं परम् ॥
तुलजापुरं तृतीयं स्यात् सप्तश्रृङ्गं तथैव च ॥

The *Devīmāhātmya* of the *Mārkaṇḍeya-purāṇa* describes the three forms of Śakti, *viz.* Mahākālī, Mahālakshmī and Mahāsarasvatī, corresponding to the three *guṇas* Tamas, Rajas and Sattva and their protection of the gods after exterminating of the *asuras* such as Mahishāsura, Śumbha, Niśumbha etc. This *māhātmya* is older than at least the eighth cen. A.D.; for as shown by me elsewhere[2] one of its verses has been cited in the Dadhimatī Māṭā inscription dated Harsha Saṁvat 189 (A.D. 795-96). The *Mārkaṇḍeya-purāṇa*, according to Pargiter, might date back to the sixth century A.D. In a cave-temple of the Udayagiri hill near Vidiśā, which belongs to the Gupta age, there is a beautiful sculpture of twelve-armed Mahālakshmī,[3] slaying the buffalo-demon. It takes back the worship of the goddess to at least the fifth century A.D. We have no definite evidence of an earlier date for the cult of the goddess.

Thereafter, the worship of the goddess spread far and wide in India. G.H. Khare, who has carefully surveyed the temple of Mahālakshmī at Kolhāpur, and studied the inscriptions there, states his opinion that the temple does not probab-

1. D.C. Sircar, "The Śākta Pīṭhas" (*J.R.A.S.B.*, Vol. XIV. p. 69).
2. Mirashi, *Studies in Indology*, Vol. II, pp. 200 f.
3. *Vikrama Volume*, pp. 411 f.

ly go back to an earlier age than Śaka 900 (A.D. 978).[1] Its *garbha-gṛiha* (sanctum) and the *sabhā-maṇḍapa* (hall) may be slightly earlier, says he. However, he has himself drawn, attention to the following verse in the Sanjān plates dated Śaka 793 (A. D. 871) of the Rāshṭrakūṭa king Amoghavarsha I, which refers to the goddess :—[2]

सर्पं पातुमसौ ददौ निजतनुं जीमूतकेतोः सुतः
श्येनायाथ शिबिः कपोतपरिरक्षार्थं दधीचोऽर्थिने ।
तेऽप्येकैकमतर्पयन् किल महालक्ष्म्यै स वामाङ्गुलिं
लोकोपद्रवशान्तये स्म दिशति श्रीवीरनारायणः ॥

Once upon a time during the reign of this Amoghavarsha a fell epidemic spread through his kingdom and took a toll of hundreds of lives. Then on the advice of his astrologers, the king offered his left little finger to the goddess Mahālakshmī to ward off the public calamity. This is recorded in the aforementioned verse. It says that (Jīmūtavāhana), son of Jīmūtaketu, offered his body (to Garuḍa) to save a serpent (Śaṅkhachūḍa). King Śibi made over his body to a hawk to save a pigeon. Dadhīchi did the same at the request of the suppliant (Indra). But this Vīra-Nārāyaṇa (Amoghavarsha) offered his left little finger to Mahālakshmī not to save only a single life like them but to protect (hundreds and thousands of his subjects) from a public epidemic.

As stated before, the Sanjān plates which record this epidemic are dated Śaka 793 (A. D. 871-72). The goddess Mahālakshmī mentioned in this record must be the homonymous goddess of Kolhāpur; for none else of that name was then so famous. Her temple at Kolhāpur must have been farfamed; otherwise a great Emperor like Amoghavarsha I would not have gone to the length of cutting of his finger and offering it to her. It may not have been in its present form, but in any case there must have been a shrine at Kolhāpur dedicated to her at the present site.

1. G. H. Khare, महाराष्ट्राची चार दैवते, p. 96. Khare has not discussed who constructed this temple.
2. *Ep. Ind.*, Vol. XVIII, p. 246.

The present temple of Mahālakshmī is also old. It may have received additions in later times, but its *garbha-gṛiha* and *maṇḍapa* at least are old. It is star-shaped on the outside, its outer walls being decorated with innumerable images of hermits, nymphs and dancing girls. Such temples built in the period from the ninth to the eleventh century A.D. still exist at Mārkaṇḍī in Vidarbha and Ambarnāth near Kalyāṇ in Northern Koṅkaṇ. The temple at Kolhāpur is perhaps older than some of them; because it has a less number of decorative images on its outer walls.

Such temples were not built without royal patronage. So we shall next proceed to consider who were ruling in the Kolhāpur region in the ninth-tenth centuries A.D., who could have built this great temple.

In ancient times this region was comprised in the country of Kuntala. The ancient history of it is still mostly unknown. It was included in the empire of the Sātavāhanas till *circa* A.D. 250. Thereafter, it came under the control first of the Vākāṭakas and then of the Early Rāshṭrakūṭas. The latter were known as *Kuntaleśvaras* (Lords of the Kuntala Country). Their capital was at Mānapura (modern Māṇ in the Sātārā district). These Rāshṭrakūṭas were contemporaries of the Early Guptas of North India. A tradition recorded by Rājaśekhara, Bhoja and Kshemendra tells us that the great Sanskrit poet Kālidāsa was sent as an ambassador to the court of the contemporary Rāshṭrakūṭa king by the Gupta king Chandragupta II—Vikramāditya. We have discussed this tradition fully elsewhere.[1]

The Early Chālukyas of Bādāmī conquered this country in the seventh century A.D. Pulakeśin II placed his younger brother Kubja-Vishṇuvardhana in charge of it for some time.[2] But later, he gave him the kingdom of Andhra and annexed the Kuntala country to his own dominion. The later history of this country is not definitely known.

1. Mirashi, *Studies in Indology*, Vol. I, pp. 1 f.
2. His early grant has been found at Sātārā, showing that he was then ruling over Sātārā-Paṇḍharpur territory. *J. B. B. R. A. S.*, Vol. III. pp. 11 f.

After overthrowing the Early Chālukyas, the Rāshṭrakūṭas must have extended their sway to this territory, but like several other countries, they must have placed it under the rule of some feudatory. We have no definite information on this point, but have some basis for conjecture.

A Sinda feudatory chief named Īśvara (known dates A.D. 1165 and 1172) describes himself in his grants as *Karahāṭa-pura-varādhīśvara* (Lord of Karahāṭa, modern Karhāḍ, the best of towns).[1] This epithet does not indicate that he was then ruling from Karahāṭa but that he originally hailed from Karahāṭa. It is now known to epigraphists that similar epithets, *e.g. Ujjayinī-pura-var-ādhīśvara* of the Guttas, *Māhishmatī-pura-var-ādhīśvara* of the Southern Kalachuris, *Tagara-pura-var-ādhīśvara* of the Śilāhāras of Koṅkaṇ and Kolhāpur have to be interpreted in a similar manner. So we can infer that the Sindas were originally ruling from Karahāṭa (Karhāḍ).

But have we any evidence of the Sinda rule in Kuntala? We now proceed to state it below.

Many years ago a single plate of a copper-plate grant was obtained by G.K. Chandokar, a well-known researcher of Mahārāshṭra. Another plate of the same grant was found deposited in the Bhārata Itihāsa Saṁshodhak Maṇḍal of Poonā. The grant to which these plates belong was probably of three plates. These two plates were edited by M. G. Dikshit and myself in the *Epigraphia Indica* (Vol. XXV, pp. 164 f.), thirty-five years ago. Though incomplete, this grant sheds important light on the present question.

These plates record a grant of the Sinda king Ādityavarman which he made to the Ṛigvedī Brāhmaṇa Navaśiva while he was at Junninagara. The object of the grant was the village Kiṇihikā included in the larger village of Paṅgarikā comprised in the *vishaya* (district) of Rāmatīrthikā-84. The grant is dated Śaka Saṁvat 887, Krodhana Saṁvatsara, Chaitra amāvāsyā. It was made on the occasion of a solar eclipse. The date is perfectly regular. The cyclic year corresponding to Śaka 887 was Krodhana, and there occurred a solar eclipse on Chaitra

1. Fleet, *Pāli Sanskrit and Old Kanarese Inscriptions*, No. 119.

amāvāsya of it. The corresponding Christian date is the 6th March A.D. 965.

Ādityavarman, who made this grant, belonged to the Sinda family. The plates name his father Muñja and his grandfather Bhīma. The earlier ancestors, who must have been named in the earlier plate are now unknown. Ādityavarman is said to have obtained the right to the five *mahāśabdas*. He was born in the *Phaṇīndra* (or Nāga) family and had a golden lion on his banner.

Though the exact find-spot of this grant is not known, we can identify the donated village Kiṇihikā from the *layaṇa-giri* and the Indra river mentioned in stating its boundaries. This Indra river is the Indrāyaṇī which flows in the north of the Poonā district. The donated village Kiṇihikā is probably modern Kinhai near Śelārvāḍī in that district. To the west of it lies a hill which has a few caves. It is the *layaṇa-giri* of the grant. Junninagara where the king was staying at the time of making the grant is probably modern Junnar, north of Poonā. These identifications show that king Ādityavarman was ruling over Poonā-Sātārā-Kolhāpur territory. He calls himself *Mahā-sāmanta*. He was probably a feudatory of the Rāshṭrakūṭas.

The grant does not mention the capital of this king, but from the epithet *Karahāṭa-pura-var-ādhiśvara* of the Sinda kings, it was probably at Karahāṭa (Karhāḍ) in the Sātārā district.

This grant is dated A.D. 965. It mentions two predecessors of Ādityavarman, *viz.* his father Muñja and grandfather Bhīma. As the previous plate or plates of this grant are now lost, we cannot say how many rulers of the family preceded them. But this grant shows that this Sinda family was ruling over the Kolhāpur-Poonā region in the ninth-tenth centuries A.D. The temple of Mahālakshmī was famous in this very period as shown above from the reference to Mahālakshmī in the Sanjān plates. So it would not be wrong to infer that it was built by some Sinda king in the eighth or the ninth century A.D.

M.G. Dikshit informed me many years ago that another copperplate grant of the Sinda family dated Śaka 933 had been discovered at Nārāyaṇgaon near Junnar.[1] It is not known what has become of it. It deserves to be published. It will throw important light on the later history of this family.

This Sinda family seems to have been ousted soon after Śaka 933.[2] The Śilāhāras then conquered this territory and established themselves at Karahāṭa. The *Vikramāṅkadevacharita* of Bilhaṇa (cantos VIII and IX) describes graphically the *svayaṁvara* of the princess Chandralekhā of a king of Karahāṭa (*Karahāṭa-paṭi*)[3] who married Vikramāditya VI of the Later Chālukya dynasty. This Śilāhāra king was probably Mārasiṁha (A.D. 1050-1075).

Mārasiṁha calls himself the lord of Karahāṭa and Kuṇḍi Belgaon) *vishayas*. He was soon obliged to shift his capital from Karahāṭa to Kolhāpur. All later inscriptions of the family have been discovered either at Kolhāpur or in its vicinity. These Śilāhāras proudly mention in their grants that they had won the boon of the goddess Mahālakshmī. The last Śilāhāra king of this branch Bhoja II was overthrown by the powerful Yādava king Siṅghaṇa in *circa* A.D. 1212. One of his inscriptions is incised in the temple of Mahālakshmī.[4]

The foregoing discussion has shown that the temple of Mahālakshmī dates back to at least the 9th century A.D.[5] and that it was probably constructed by some Sinda king ruling from Karahāṭa.

1. *Ep. Ind.*, Vol. XXV, p. 164, n. 1.
2. Fleet, *Dynasties of the Kanarese Districts*, *Bom. Gaz.*, Vol. I, part ii, p. 577.
3. Bilhaṇa does not name this Śilāhāra king.
His inscription there is dated Śaka 1140 (A.D. 1218-19). See G. H. Khare, महाराष्ट्राची चार दैवते, p 63 f.
5. K.G. Kundangar has stated the story that the temple was built by some king named Karṇa in the sixth cen. A.D. For its refutation, see G.H. Khare, *loc. cit*, p. 63 f.

XXVI. THE DATE OF THE MĀRKAṆḌĪ TEMPLES

(Plate V)

Mārkaṇḍī is now a small village on the bank of the Waingaṅgā, 40 miles east of Chāndā in the Chāndā or Chandrapur District of Vidarbha. At the Census of 1961 it had a population of 476 persons. It is also known as Mārkaṇḍadeva. The place is regarded as very holy as the sacred river Veṇā or Waingaṅgā, which generally flows from North to South, takes a northward bend there. As Cunningham has observed, "Mārkaṇḍī was once a large place on the open plain to the west, but the frequent inundations have driven most of the people away." There were, in Cunningham's time, not more than 20 occupied houses.

I visited the place forty years ago in 1935, in company with several members of the Vidarbha Saṁshodhan Maṇḍal such as Dr. Y.K. Deshpande, Shri A.R. Deshpande and Prof. S.P. Chaturvedi. We had to travel in a bullock cart and cross the Waingaṇgā twice in knee-deep water. We were all highly impressed by the grandeur of the temples and the innumerable beautiful images on the walls of the main or Mārkaṇḍeya temple. Later, while editing the Anjanvatī plates of Govinda III in the *Epigraphia Indica*, Vol. XXIII, pp. 8 f., I put forward the suggestion that Mārkaṇḍī might be identical with Mayūrakhaṇḍī, mentioned as the place of residence (and probably the capital) of that Rāshṭrakūṭa king in his several grants.

Cunningham visited the place in 1873 and has given a fairly detailed account of the group of temples at Mārkaṇḍī. Later, in 1902-03. Cousens also paid a visit to the place and has described these temples. Several other officers of the Archaeological Survey of India have seen these temples and published their notes on them. Cunningham thought that it was the most picturesque group of temples that he had seen. He has remarked that the general style of these temples—especially that of the main or Mārkaṇḍeya temple—is that of the Khajurāho temples, but they have not attracted the attention of art-critics as they should have done. Percy Brown's *Indian Architecture* (Buddhist and Hindu), for instance, does not even mention these temples. Recently, the Nagpur University has published a detailed illustrated monograph called *Markaṇḍī Temples* on them by Dr. S. B. Deo, University Professor of Ancient Indian History, Culture and Archaeology.

In this monograph Deo has given detailed information about these temples and has described and illustrated their architecture and sculpture with beautiful plates on art paper. He has discussed in detail the special features and beauty of the images and has identified them. He has cited references to them in his work, which enable the reader to identify them with ease. Cunningham had generally described the sculptures of these temples, but had not illustrated them. Deo's illustrations, finely executed, will enable the reader to appreciate the beauty of these sculptures in his study.

We shall first give a brief description of these temples, which will help the reader to understand the subsequent discussion.

The temples are enclosed in a quadrangle 196 ft. long from north to south, and 118 ft. broad from east to west. The wall of the enclosure is 3 ft. 9 in. broad at the base, with sloping sides and a rounded coping stone, 2 ft. thick. It is 9 ft. in height. Cunningham thought that this wall of the enclosure must have been older than the temples inside. Its entrance is through a two-storeyed structure on the south, probably intended for the *Nagārkhānā* (quarters for musicians). Besides this, there are two small openings in the wall of the enclosure, one towards the river in the east and the other towards the village on the west.

Deo says that there are now eighteen temples in the enclosure. In the time of Cunningham their number was more than twenty, nearly twenty-four. Some of these are in the form of platforms, the structures over them having disappeared. Of the existing temples, only those named after Mārkaṇḍeya, Yamadharma, Mṛikaṇḍu, the father of Mārkaṇḍeya, and Śiva are noteworthy. Two other shrines—one called Viṭṭhala-Rukmiṇī temple and the other Daśāvatāra temple—also deserve notice, as we shall have to refer to them later. Besides these, there are some monolithic pillars and a high *Vīrgaḷ* (hero-stone). They have inscriptions on them. They also will figure in our subsequent discussion.

Of all these temples, that named after the sage Mārkaṇḍeya is the largest and is known for its magnitude, architecture and elaborate sculpture. The fame of these temples is mainly dependent on it.

The temple of Mārkaṇḍeya faces east. It has now no *jagatī* or platform, but Deo thinks that originally it had one, which is now not open to view as a large area round the temple is covered with bricks cemented in mud mortar. In any case it has no high *jagatī* such as the Chandella temples at Khajurāho have.

The temple had porches on the east, north and south, but now only one of them is extant. It has four parts, *ardha-maṇḍapa* (or porch), *maṇḍapa*, *anatarāla* and *garbhagṛiha*. They all had their separate pinnacles (*śikharas*), but nearly two hundred years ago, the *śikhara* on the *garbhagṛiha*, being struck by lightning, collapsed on that of the *maṇḍapa*, which also crashed down in consequence. The roof of the *maṇḍapa* was subsequently repaired in a rude manner by a Goṇḍa king, 'whose architect introduced huge piers with radiating arches inside the principal room.' They are an eye-sore to the visitor. They should be replaced and the roof repaired in a becoming manner.

These piers and also some niches in the *antarāla* have some images subsequently inserted. They also require to be removed.

On the *jaṅghā* of the temple there are three rows of beautiful images of gods and goddesses, hermits, heavenly nymphs, guardians of quarters and *vyālas*, in different poses. Cunningham counted 409 of them. About half of them are of

Śiva and Pārvatī. Some describe the exploits of Śiva such as the slaying of the Andhaka demon. Some others are of the naked Bhairava. Some sculptures are of Chāmuṇḍā holding the *khaṭvāṅga*, while others are of dancing Gaṇapati, the seven Divine Mothers (*Sapta-mātṛikās*), Sarasvatī *etc.* Besides the images of Śaiva cult, there are others of the Vaishṇava cult such as those of Lakshmī-Vishṇu and Gaja-lakshmī, and the eight *dikpālas etc.* Again, there are numerous subordinate figures of females engaged in various activities such as dancing, talking to a parrot or feeding it, replacing the slipped foot-ornament or the girdle, looking in a mirror, applying antimony to the eye-lids, playing on musical instruments like the flute or the lute, standing below a mango-tree holding its branch, removing a thorn from the foot, writing a letter to a lover *etc.* There are several statues of hermits also. Some depict the scenes from the *Rāmāyaṇa* and the *Mahābhārata* such as Rāvaṇa's fight with Jaṭāyu, that of Vālin and Sugrīva, and of Bhīma and Duryodhana. The sculptures are so numerous that one is tired of seeing them, but their series does not end.

Cunningham says that some female statues are naked. Perhaps they are meant to be represented as dressed in diaphanous garments. Sanskrit poets describe these garments as *niḥśvāsa-hārya* (blown away by mere breath). See *Raghuvaṁśa*, XVI, 46. But the sculptures are nowhere obscene. Cunningham says, "Several of the statues of Śiva are naked, and so are some of the female statues ; but they are simply nude figures, without any suggestive indelicacy such as is only too prominent in the obtrusive bestiality of the Khajurāho sculptures."

We shall next proceed to discuss the age of this magnificent temple of Mārkaṇḍeya.

On the evidence of three rows of sculptures on the outer walls of this temple, several scholars have taken it to be of the same age as the Chandella temples at Khajurāho. The latter temples were built in the period from A.D. 900 to A.D. 1100 by the Chandella kings Yaśovarman (A.D. 915-950), Dhaṅga (A.D. 950-1000), Gaṇḍa (A.D. 1000-1010) and Vidyādhara (A.D. 1010-1035) as indicated by the inscriptions incised on them and other evidence. So Cunningham thought that this temple of Mārkaṇḍeya might at most date back to the tenth cen. A.D. He noticed there a piece of evidence to substantiate this date. It is as follows :—

On the jamb of the south door occurs the following inscription—*Magaradhvaja Jogī* 700. Identical inscriptions have been noticed in several other places such as Kelod in the Nāgpur District of Vidarbha. Potenār in the Bastar District and Borāmdev in the former Kawardhā State in Chhattisgarh, Bilhari in the Jabalpur District, Māndhātā in the Nemāḍ District, Amarakaṇṭak in the Maṇḍlā District—all in Madhya Pradesh, besides such far-off places as Khajurāho, Orchhā and Chitoḍ in North India. This number 700 cannot refer to the Vikrama or the Śaka era, for it would then correspond to A.D. 644 or A.D. 778, but these temples do not appear so old. So Cunningham thought that the number might refer to the Chedi or Kalachuri Saṁvat. It would, in that case, denote A.D. 950, which, Cunningham thought, was probably the approximate date of these temples.

Deo also has discussed the problem of the date of these temples. He dates them in the late 11th cen. A.D. on stylistical and other grounds. These temples stylistically resemble the Chandella temples at Khajurāho. Deo has enumerated the following characteristics of the latter temples.[1]—(1) a *jagatī* or platform for the temple ; (2) a moulded *adhishṭhāna* or basement ; (3) three rows of sculptures on the *jaṅghā* ; (4) a plethora of *sura-sundarīs* and *vyālas*; (5) the *sāndhāra* plan of the main temple; (6) a piramidal type of *Śikhara* over the *Sabhā-maṇḍapa* and (7) the motif of miniature *śikharas* to decorate the main lofty *śikhara*. Deo thinks that the main Mārkaṇḍeya temple resembles the principal temples at Khajurāho in all these respects. According to Dr. Sarasvatī[2], the Khajurāho temples cannot date before A.D. 1050, while Krishna Deva[3] would place them between A.D. 950 and A.D. 1100.

1. *Mārkaṇḍī Temples*, p. 30.
2. *H.C.I.P.*, Vol. V, p. 465.
3. *Ancient India*, No. 15, p. 49.

Deo thinks that the Mārkaṇḍeya temple is stylistically inferior to the later temples at Khajurāho in respect of 'proportions, elaboration of plan, the vertical magnificence of the Śikhara, and the suppleness and graceful liquidity of human form. So they are of a later age. Besides, the Mārkaṇḍī temples are free from erotic sculptures. So they belong to a later age when the influence of the Śakti cult had declined. The Daśāvatāra temple at Mārkaṇḍī is a degenerate copy of the Yoginī temples at Khajurāho and Bherā Ghāṭ. If it was contemporary with the main temple at Markaṇḍī, then also the complex of temples there has to be referred to a later age. Finally, the inscriptions on the Mārkaṇḍeya temple cannot be dated earlier than the 11th century A.D. For, all these reasons, Deo would date these temples in the late 11th century A.D. They stand midway between the Khajurāho and full-fledged Yādava temples.[1]

Stylistic evidence is not always unimpeachable. It should be substantiated, where possible, by inscriptional evidence. There are some early inscriptions at Mārkaṇḍī, but they are not connected with the temples there. Hence, their evidence has not been taken into account by both Cunningham and Deo. We shall discuss it later. But even on stylistic grounds the Khajurāho and the Mārkaṇḍī temples can be shown to be dissimilar.

As stated before, Deo regards the following as the characteristic features of the Khajurāho temples such as that known as the Kandariā Mahādeva temple there :—(1) a high *jagat* (platform) ; (2) four parts of the interior of the temple, *viz. ardha-maṇḍapa, maṇḍapa, mahā-maṇḍapa, antarāla* and *garbhagṛiha*, (3) three rows of images on the outer walls ; (4) the *sāndhāra* (i.e. provided with the *pradakshiṇā-patha*) form of the *garbha-gṛiha* ; (5) the association of the main śikhara with *aṅga* or minor śikharas ; and (6) balconied windows of the *mahā-maṇḍapa*. The Mārkaṇḍeya temple is not, however, just like the Kandariyā Mahādeva temple at Khajurāho. (1) It has no clear *jagatī* (platform). Deo's statement that its original *jagatī* has now disappeared as the surrounding place is covered

1. *Mārkaṇḍī Temples*, p. 21.

with bricks set in mud mortar is not convincing. In any case, it has no high *jagatī* like that of the temples at Khajurāho. I have seen the latter temples. They have a high *jagatī*, which gives them a majestic appearance. Such a *jagatī* is not noticed at Mārkaṇḍī. (2) The Mārkaṇḍī temples have no *maṇḍapa* after the *ardha-maṇḍapa* or the porch. They consist of only four parts like several other temples of an earlier and a later age in Mahārāshṭra. (3) The Mārkaṇḍeya temple has, no doubt, three rows of sculptures on its outer walls, but this is not an invariable characteristic feature of the Khajurāho temples; for the Lakshmaṇa temple there has only two rows of such sculptures.[1] Many early and late temples in Mahārāshṭra such as those at Kolhāpur and Ambarnāth have only one row of such sculptures. The Markaṇḍeya temple has three such rows, because, as shown later, it was constructed by a great ruler of a large kingdom. (4) The Mārkaṇḍeya temple has no *pradakshiṇāpatha*. It is of the *nirandhāra* type, differing from the Khajurāho temples. (5) The *śikhara* of the Mārkaṇḍeya temple has now fallen, but its remnant on one side shows that it was previously decorated with *aṅga-śikharas*.[2] It was not, however, covered with such *śikharas* from top to bottom unlike the temples at Khajurāho. (6) Unlike these latter temples, again, the Mārkaṇḍeya temple has no balconied windows in the *Mahā-maṇḍapa*.

The Mārkaṇḍeya temple with its four parts resembles several other temples in Mahārāshṭra and Koṅkaṇ such as that at Ambarnāth. Its plan need not have been copied from those of the temples at Khajurāho. The same can be said of the mouldings on the *adhishṭhāna* and the decoration with *sura-sundarīs* and *vyālas*.

The Mārkaṇḍeya temple has some Nāgarī inscriptions of the 11th cen. A.D., but they may have been incised later. The epigraph *Magaradhvaja Jogī* 700 does not indicate that the Jogī visited the place in the Kalachuri-Chedi year 700 (A.D. 950); for the same inscription is noticed on buildings in such distant places as Khajurāho in the north and Potenār in the

1. *Ancient India*, No. 15, p. 54.
2. *Mārkaṇḍī Temples*, p. 8.

Bastar District in the south. Magaradhvaja could not have visited all these places in the same year A.D. 950. As Hiralal has shown from a Ms. discovered in Ratnapur in the Bilāspur District, this Jogi was a contemporary of the Kalachuri king Jājalladeva II (A.D. 1165-1170). He used to visit different places with his 700 disciples and used to get the identical inscription mentioning him and the number of his disciples incised there. The number 700 does not denote any date.[1]

An insuperable objection to the view that these temples were erected in the late eleventh cen. A.D. is that there was in that age no great king ruling in Vidarbha who could have erected them at Mārkaṇḍī. Such grand and magnificent structures were generally built by powerful kings ruling over a large and prosperous kingdom and they were generally situated in or near their capitals. Such was not, of course, the case with ancient caves. They had to be excavated in hills suitable for the purpose, though they may have been distant from the seat of the then government. It is therefore, not surprising that a minister of a Vākāṭaka king of Vidarbha got a cave excavated at Ajaṇṭā, far off from the then capital Vatsagulma (Bāsim in the Akolā District). Sometimes structural temples were erected at holy places; but they too were not generally far away from the then capital of the builder. The Ambarnāth temple, for instance, is not far away from the capital Sthānaka of the Śilāhāras of North Koṅkaṇ. The Chandella kings erected all their principal temples at Khajurāho, which was their capital at the time. The Paramāra king Udayāditya constructed the temple of Nīlakaṇṭheśvara at his capital Udaipur. The Pallavas of Kānchī are similarly known to have constructed several grand temples at their capital Conjeeveram.

Let us next review the political condition in the Deccan in the 11th century when these temples are supposed to have been built. In A.D. 974 Tailapa overthrew the last Rāshṭrakūṭa king and established himself as the Supreme Ruler of South India. Though he ruled at first from Mānyakheṭa, the seat of Government was later removed to Kalyāṇa (District Bidar in Karnāṭaka). The Later Chālukya kings ruling in the eleventh

1. *Ind. Hist. Quart.*, Vol. III, pp. 408 f.

century A.D., *viz*. Someśvara II and Vikramāditya VI, were also ruling from the same place. Kalyāṇa is several hundred miles south of Mārkaṇḍī. It does not seem likely that a Chālukya king ruling at Kalyāṇa would undertake the construction of such a large and magnificent temple as that of Mārkaṇḍeya at Mārkaṇḍī. Such temples were not completed in a few years. They, in some cases, are known to have required more than one generation of rulers for their construction. For instance, the temple of Śiva at Ambarnāth near Kalyāṇ was begun by the Śilāhāra king Chhittarāja, but it could not be completed by him. Its construction continued in the reign of his younger brother Nāgārjuna and it was finally completed during that of Mumuṇirāja, the latter's brother and successor.[1] Similarly, the magnificent, temple of Koppeśvara in the Kolhāpur District was commenced by the Śilāhāra king Gaṇḍarāditya, but it was not completed even during the reign of his grandson Bhoja II and has since then remained in an incomplete state till now. So the construction of the Mārkaṇḍeya temple at Mārkaṇḍī is not likely to have been undertaken by a Later Chālukya king ruling at Kalyāṇa in the 11th cen. A.D. There was no other great king ruling in Vidarbha at the time.

A more reliable evidence for determining the date of any structure is that furnished by an inscriptional record, if one is available. Two types of inscriptions have been found at Mārkaṇḍī. Some of them are in what is known as *kuṭila-lipi* or acute-angled alphabet as Bühler has named it; while some others are in the *Nāgarī-lipi*. Inscriptions of the former type are referred to the 6th cen. A.D. by Cunningham and Deo, but from the shape of their characters they appear to be of the eighth or ninth cen. A.D.[2] Since these inscriptions were not noticed as affixed to the temples at Mārkaṇḍī, their evidence has not been taken into account by both Cunningham and Deo. There is no evidence that these inscriptions were incised two or three centuries earlier than the main temple at

1. See Ambarnāth Temple Inscription of Mummuṇi, dated Śaka 982.
2. See the Añjanavatī plates of Govinda III, dated Śaka 722. Some of the letters like *ra* and *ya*, however, appear early.

Mārkaṇḍı. In the case of one of them, there is reason to connect it with the temple of Mārkaṇḍeya. Their evidence also must, therefore, be considered in fixing the date of these temples.

Two of these inscriptions have been noticed by Cunningham. He has given their eye-copies and imperfect readings in his *Report*.[1] Deo has reproduced both in his monograph. He has not given his own readings.

One of these inscriptions is incised on three sides of a monolith column. In fact, it is not one inscription, but three records incised on the three sides of the monolith. Cunningham has given their eye-copies. Only one of these is now extant. Deo has published its estampage.

Cunningham has given his own readings of the inscriptions, but they make no sense. Cunningham also has admitted it, but he has remarked, "I can make nothing of them ; but so little is lost that I believe the whole may be deciphered by a competent Sanskrit scholar."[2] But none has attempted their reading during the last hundred years. I could read only a few words of them as given below :

(1) Inscr. on the left side—(1) *nistīrṇa(m) sapadi.* (2) (*a*) *mala-yaśo-bhuja-śrīr-yo. .sya.*

(2) Inscr. on the centre—(1) *Svasti śrī-saumya. .* (2) *ṅkula . .* (3) . . . (4) . . .*ā-chandra-sūryya.* (5) . . *śriya. .*

(3) Inscr. on the right side—(1) *nabu . . .* (2) *vyāpāra . . .* (3) *ṇṇāradiya ga . . .* (4) . . .

It is risky to decipher and interpret records from their eye-copies ; but the middle one seems to express the hope that (the fame of some one) would endure so long as the moon and the sun continue to shine. These inscriptions do not seem to belong to any temple. On the evidence of palaeography they may be referred to the eighth or the ninth cen. A.D.

There is another inscription on a monolith pillar noticed by Cunningham. It consists of three *aksharas* only, which were

1. Cunningham, *Archaeological Survey of India Report* (*C A.S.I.R.*), Vol. IX, plate XXX.
2. *Ibid*, Vol. IX, p. 150.

read as *Prayāśrī* by Cunningham[1]. The correct reading of it is *Prāya-śrī*. It appears to be the Sanskritization of a Prakrit record. In Prakrit, the honorific epithet *śrī* (*siri*) comes after a name. See *Chanda-siri* (*Chandra-śrī*) used with reference to Chandragupta Maurya in a Prakrit speech in the *Mudrārākshasa*. The genealogical lists of kings given in the Purāṇas are Sanskritized versions of the original Prakrit ones. See, for instance, the name *Yajña-śrī* which occurs in them.[2] So the name Śrī-Prāya seems to be intended here. But who was this illustrious Prāya ? This record does not provide an answer to this question ; but there is another record at Mārkaṇḍī itself which throws some light on it, as shown later.

As stated before, this short inscription is incised at the top of a monolithic pillar. Cunningham has described the figures on it as follows :—"The letters are near the top of the stone ; and below there is a male figure with four arms, carrying a battle-axe, and attended by two females. A snake encircles his waist, which may perhaps serve to identify the figure with Śiva ; but there is no other trace of that god, so far as I could see."[3] Though the battle-axe is one of the weapons of Śiva, he is generally shown with his trident (*tri-śūla*). So the figure may be the god of the Nāgas. The caves of South India were excavated by the Nāgas. So their gods and kings are seen sculptured in them. See *e.g.* the image of the Nāga king and his consort near Cave XVII at Ajaṇṭā. Hence this figure on the aforementioned monolith may be of the Nāga god.

Since Cunningham's time another inscription has been discovered at Mārkaṇḍī. The stone bearing it was found 'lying in the rear of the Mārkaṇḍeśvara temple.' The record is incised in the acute-angled alphabet.[4] Deo has given its impression in his monograph. Several years ago, a Superintendent of the Archaeological Survey had sent me an estampage of it,

1. *C.A.S.I.R.*, Vol. IX, p. 149.
2. See एकोनविंशति राजा यज्ञश्रीः सातकर्ण्यथ । Pargiter : *Dynasties of the Kali Age*, p. 42.
3. *C.A.S.I.R.*, Vol. IX, p. 149.
4. See the plate attached.

to which I could pay no attention then. Now, in connection with the date of the temples at Mārkaṇḍī, I have studied it with some care.

Deo could not decipher this record completely. He has given its reading as follows—

1. *Anurāga . . ya prabhu* (?)
2. *Bappanāgaśrī.*

He has not interpreted this record. He refers it to the end of the fifth or the beginning of the sixth century A.D. I read it as follows :—

1. *Anurāgastha-Prāya-Pūrṇṇa-*
2. *Bappa-nāga-śrī.*

This also is the Sanskritized version of an originally Prakrit record. So it contains a place-name like Anurāga, which *prima facie* appears rather queer. The Prakrit original name may have been *Anore* or *Anūra.* And it is noteworthy that a village named Annūr still exists in the Rājurā tāluka of the Chāndā District. (See the *Alphabetical List of the places in Mahārāshṭra* pub. by the State Government.)

The present record mentions Prāya Pūrṇabappa-nāga. This appears a queer name ; but names like it were current in ancient times. See the *Pūrṇahari* in the Kānheri inscription dated Śaka 765 (A.D. 843).[1] This Pūrṇabappa Nāga is called Prāya. So *prāya* probably means 'an architect.'

There are, besides, some other inscriptions on the mouldings of the Mārkaṇḍeya temple, which were not noticed by Cunningham but have been given by Deo.[2] They are of the 11th or 12th cen. A.D. They have no relevance to the present discussion.

One noteworthy thing concerning these records is that they are all engraved on the doors or the *adhishṭhāna* of the temple of Mārkaṇḍeya. The aforementioned inscription mentioning Pūrṇa-bappa-nāga also may have belonged to the same temple. As stated before, the inscribed stone was found 'lying in the rear of the Mārkaṇḍeśvara temple.' Some two hundred years ago when the spire of that

1. *Ind. Ant.*, Vol. XIII, p. 136.
2. *Mārkaṇḍī Temples*, plate LVI.

temple was struck by lightning, several stones of it were scattered round about. The present inscribed stone seems to have been one of them.

Pūrṇabappa-nāga seems to have been a *Śilpin* (architect) of the temple. Like several persons, he may have desired to have his name incised on the temple. He seems to have got it written in Sanskrit which he engraved on a slab built into some part of the temple of Mārkaṇḍeya. In ancient times several *Śilpins* are known to have done this. See *e.g.* the names of *śilpins* engraved on the temple of Somanāthapur in Karnāṭaka.[1]

If this conjecture is acceptable, the temple of Mārkaṇḍeya may have been constructed in the eighth-ninth cen. A.D.

We shall next proceed to show how the political condition in the Deccan in that age was favourable for the construction of such a magnificent temple in Vidarbha.

The Rāshṭrakūṭas were then ruling over Vidarbha. Some scholars believe that they originally belonged to Karnāṭaka.[2] That this is incorrect can be easily shown. The following verse occurs in several early grants about Dantidurga, the founder of the Rāshṭrakūṭa Imperial power :—[3]

काञ्चीशकेरलनराधिपचोलपाण्ड्य-
श्रीहर्षवज्रटविभेदविधानदक्षम् ।
कार्णाटकं बलमनन्तमजेयमन्यै-
र्भृत्यैः कियद्भिरपि यः सहसा जिगाय ॥

This verse refers to the army of the Early Chālukyas defeated by Dantidurga as *Karṇāṭaka bala* or Kannaḍa army. If Dantidurga himself had hailed from Karnāṭaka, he would not have referred to the hostile army of the Chālukyas in this manner. He was, therefore, not a Kannaḍiga but a Mahārāshṭrīya.

1. *The Keśava Temple at Somanāthpur*, p. 5.
2. Altekar, The *Rāshṭrakūṭas and Their Times* (1934), pp. 21f. They became Kannaḍa-speaking after their capital was moved to Mānyakheṭa in the reign of Amoghavarsha I.
3. *Ep. Ind.*, Vol. XXIII, p. 14.

Several early inscriptions of the Rāshṭrakūṭas have been found in Mahārāshṭra. The wonderful Kailāsa cave-temple at Ellorā was got excavated by the early Rāshṭrakūṭa king Kṛishṇarāja I. A copper-plate grant of this king has been discovered at Bhāndak in the Chāndā District of Vidarbha. The places mentioned in it can still be identified in that district as shown by Dr. Y.K. Deshpande.[1] Some scholars believe that his capital was situated somewhere near the Ellorā Cave-temples.

Several copper-plate grants of Govinda III, who belonged to this family and flourished towards the close of the eighth cen. A.D. have been discovered in Vidarbha. Three of them, *viz.* those found at Añjanavatī,[2] Sīsavai and Lohārā[3] have been edited by me. One more, *viz.* the Jharikā grant[4] has been published by Dr. Kolte. Govinda III is known to have made several of his grants at Mayūrakhaṇḍī, which seems to have been his capital. This place has not yet been identified. Some take it to be the Morkhaṇḍ fort in the Nāsik District ; but as Bühler has remarked, ancient Indian kings did not rule from hill-forts. Several years ago, while editing the Añjanavatī plates of this king, I put forward the suggestion that it may be identical with Mārkaṇḍī. Mayūrakhaṇḍī-Morkhaṇḍī-Mārkaṇḍī appear to be the likely changes in its name. The existence of magnificent temples at Mārkaṇḍī suggests that there was a capital of a great and prosperous kingdom there or in its vicinity. The only great king who was then ruling in Vidarbha was Govinda III (A.D. 793-814) of the Rāshṭrakūṭa family. He was the most powerful ruler of his age. He raided North India up to the foot of the Himālaya and defeated Pratīhāra and Pāla kings. He then returned to the bank of the Narmadā and made several kings of Central India acknowledge his supremacy. He next proceeded to the south and vanquished all kings up to Siṁhala-dvīpa. The Rāshṭrakūṭa family produced no greater ruler than he.

Govinda III was a man of religious temperament.

1. See *Vidarbha Saṁshodhan Mandal Varshika* 1969, pp. 29f.
2. *Ep. Ind.*, Vol. XXIII, pp. 16f.
3. *Ibid.*, Vol. XXIII, pp. 206 f. and pp. 218 f.
4. *Ibid.*, Vol. XXXII, pp. 157f.

The Sañjān plates of his son Amoghavarsha I describe him as follows :—[1]

कुर्वंन्धर्मान्कीर्तनैः पुण्यवृन्दै-
रध्यष्ठात्तां स्वोचितां राजधानीम् ॥

(Accumulating religious merit by the construction of holy temples, he ruled from the capital worthy of his rank.)

He had made several *mahā-dānas* such as *Tulā-dāna, Hiraṇyagarbhadāna etc*. Such a great and pious king must have naturally thought of immortalising himself by erecting a magnificent shrine of the type of the Mārkaṇḍeya temple. No other great king of his type flourished in Vidarbha after the age of the Vākāṭakas. It is, again, noteworthy that the donee of the Jharikā grant which he made at distant Alampur on the bank of the Tuṅgabhadrā on the occasion of a solar eclipse in the course of his victorious southern campaigns was a Brāhmaṇa resident of the Chāndā District itself.[2] This indicates his close connection with that district.

The Rāshṭrakūṭa kings were devotees of both Śiva and Vishṇu. See the following *maṅgala-śloka* which occurs in the beginning of their grants.[3]

स वोऽव्याद्वेधसा धाम यन्नाभिकमलं कृतम् ।
हरश्च यस्य कान्तेन्दुकलया कमलङ्कृतम् ॥

This verse invokes the blessings of both Vishṇu and Śiva. The same religious catholicity is noticed in the temples at Mārkaṇḍeya. We find there shrines of Śiva like those of Mārkaṇḍeya and also one of Vishṇu, *viz*. the Daśāvatāra temple.

A possible objection against our identification of Mayūrakhaṇḍī with Mārkaṇḍī may be considered here. It may be asked, 'How is it that one of the temples there is mentioned in an inscription as the temple of Mārkaṇḍeśvara,[4] if the original name of the place was Mayūrakhaṇḍī ?' It is not difficult to answer this question. This name occurs in an inscription in the Nāgarī characters of the thirteenth cen. A.D.

1. *Ep. Ind.*, Vol. XVIII, pp. 245 f. *Kīrtana* means 'a temple' in such passages.
2. *Ibid.*, Vol. XXXII, pp. 157 f.
3. *Ibid.*, Vol. XXIII, p. 13.
4. See Chitrao Sāstrī—*Bhāratavarshīya Prāchīna Charitrak osha*, p. 648.

That record is, therefore, nearly five hundred years later than the age of the temple of Mārkaṇḍeya, fixed above. Owing to their lack of historical sense, the people had in the meanwhile forgotten all about the original constructor of the temple. A similar instance is that of the Buddhist caves near Nāsik which are now known as the Caves of the Pāṇḍavas. Another case of this type occurs at Mārkaṇḍī itself. The temple now going by the name of the Viṭṭhala-Rukmiṇī Mandira was originally a Śaiva shrine as is indicated by the image of Gaṇapati on its lintel and the presence of Bhairava on its *jaṅghā*. The worship of Viṭṭhala and Rukmiṇī was not in vogue in the ninth century A.D.

Besides, the sage Mārkaṇḍeya could not have been associated with any of the temples there. From the *Mārkaṇḍeya-purāṇa*, we learn that his hermitage was in the Himālaya[1] and not on the bank of the Veṇā. So his name seems to have been associated with the temple at Mārkaṇḍī after Mayūra-khaṇḍī was corrupted into Mārkaṇḍī.

Even if the identification of Mayurakhaṇḍī with Mār-kaṇḍī is not accepted, it will not affect the date (*circa* ninth cen. A.D.) of the temples fixed here ; for it was only in that age after the time of the Vākāṭakas that there was a great and powerful king ruling in Vidarbha such as could have built the magnificent temples at Mārkaṇḍī.

If the date of the Mārkaṇḍī temples fixed here is accepted, it will have an important bearing on the evolution of the Deccani style of architecture. Very few temples of the Rāshṭra-kūṭa age are still extant in the Deccan. So the fourth Volume of *the History and Culture of the Indian People* published by the Bhāratīya Vidyā Bhavan has no chapter on the architecture and sculpture of that period. At present the earliest temple of the Deccani style is supposed to be the Śaiva shrine at Ambarnāth. It belongs to the middle of the eleventh cen. A.D. (A.D. 1060). The Mārkaṇḍī temples would be about 250 years earlier. The chief features of the Deccani style,[1] *viz.* four parts of the shrine—*ardhamaṇḍapa*, *maṇḍapa*, *antarāla* and *garbhagṛiha*—, three doors with a porch in front of each, a

1. Krishna Deva, *Temples of North India*.

vertical band decorated with *chaitya* windows or geometrical figures serving as the spine of the *śikhara*, and the Śukanāsikā —these are common to both the Mārkaṇḍeya and Ambarnāth temples. But whereas the *maṇḍapa* and the *garbhagṛiha* of the Mārkaṇḍeya temple are square-shaped on the outside, those of the Ambarnāth temple are star-shaped. The *maṇḍapa* of the Mārkaṇḍeya temple is square-shaped and is attached to the similarly shaped *garbha-gṛiha* and the *antarāla*,[1] but that of the Ambarnāth temple is diagonally attached to it. So the Ambarnāth temple seems to be later stylistically. That temple was completed in A.D. 1060. So the Mārkaṇḍeya temple cannot be referred to the late eleventh cen. A.D. It could not have been imitated from the Khajurāho temples; for their plans are different.

The Mārkaṇḍī temples are not widely known. There is no *pacca* road to the place from Mūl, which is the nearest place of approach. The river Waingaṅgā has to be crossed twice while going to Mārkaṇḍī. The place can be a popular tourist centre if facilities of communication with and residence at Mārkaṇḍī are provided. There is no other place in Vidarbha which can vie with it in respect of magnificent architecture and sculpture. I would, therefore, invite the attention of the Ministry of Tourism to the potentialities of this place as a centre of Tourist traffic.

1. See the plan of the temple in O. P. Verma's *Hemāḍpantī Temples*.

XXVII. THE AYYAṆA-VAṀŚA-CHARITA—A FAKE SANSKRIT HISTORICAL KĀVYA[1]

(Plate VI)

About the middle of June 1973 Shri Devisimha Chauhan, a renowned researcher of Mahārāshaṭra, quoted verses 34-35 and 39 of Canto IV of this *kāvya*[2] in a letter to me and asked me how the author of it could get information about the envoy of Khushru, the ruler of Persia, at the court of his contemporary Pulakeśin II of the Early Chālukya Dynasty of Bādāmi. He also stated casually in that letter that he was going to edit that *kāvya* with a Marathi translation. I was greatly surprised to read that letter. I had not read those verses before, but *prima facie* they appeared to be spurious. I communicated my suspicions to Shri Chauhan. Thereafter, he wrote a detailed article on that *kāvya* in No. 37 of the *Itihāsa āṇi Saṁskṛti*, a research quarterly in Marathi, which further increased my curiosity. As I had known of some fake Sanskrit poems and plays published during the last fifty years, I obtained a copy of the book from the Nāgpur University. Its perusal confirmed my suspicions. My purpose in writing the present article is to warn students of ancient Indian history against believing the descriptions and statements in that *kāvya*.

This *kāvya*, the full title of which is *Srī-Chālukyarāja-Ayyaṇa-vaṁśa-charitaṁ Kāvyam*, has been edited with a Hindi translation by Pandit Vishvanath Shastri Bhāradvāja. It was

1. *Journal of Indian History*, Vol. LII, pp. 317 f.
2. The relevant verses are as follows :

वर्षे तु षोडशे तस्य राज्यस्येरानदेशत: ।
खुस्रोनृपस्य दूतश्च विशिष्टोपायनै: सह ॥३४॥
समागच्छद्राजसभां पत्रं राजाङ्कमुद्रितम् ।
दत्त्वा संस्थापयामास मैत्रीं तस्य च तेन च ॥३५॥
चीनयात्री हुएन्त्संगस्तस्य राज्ये समागत: ।
लिखितं वर्णनं तेन स्वयात्रावर्णनेऽद्भुतम् ॥३६॥

published in the Sanskrit Series of the All-India Sanskrit University, Delhi, in 1966. It has been dedicated to Shrimati Indira Gandhi, the Prime Minister of the Indian Union.

Though nearly eight years have passed since the publication of the book, I have not seen it reviewed anywhere. I have, however, seen it referred to in the recently published *History of Karnāṭaka* by Dr. P.B. Desai and others.[1] Hence it requires to be examined critically.

The Chālukyas were one of the foremost ancient Indian ruling families. Two branches of this family are well known The earlier of them ruled from Vātāpi, modern Bādāmi in the Bijāpur District, from *circa* A.D. 500 to A.D. 750. The last known king of this family, Kīrtivarman II, was overthrown by the Rāshṭrakūṭas in *circa* A.D. 750. Thereafter, the Rāshṭrakūṭas ruled supreme in South India till *circa* A.D. 970, when they were superseded by the Later Chālukya king Tailapa II, who ruled over a large part of the Deccan. The present *kāvya* derives its name from Ayyaṇa, the grandson of this Tailapa. This edition of the work gives in an Appendix the names of all members of the family from the beginning down to Shri Sabajirao Chalukya and his two sons. It contains a plate illustrating some past members of the family.

This *kāvya* purports to have been composed by Śyāmabhaṭṭa Bhāradvāja in Śaka Saṁvat 1737 (A.D. 1815). (See the *Kavi-praśasti*, verse I.) This work contains a complete genealogy of as many as 62 generations right from Vijayāditya, the founder of the Chālukya family, to its present members, the aforementioned Shri Sabajirao *alias* Appasaheb and his two sons, Shri Mularaja *alias* Jaishivrao and Shri Kamadeva *alias* Viravijaya. This genealogy extends over as many as 12 pages of the Volume.

The Editor, Pandit Vishvanatha Shastri, has stated in the Introduction that Śyāmabhaṭṭa, the aforementioned author of the present *kāvya*, was descended from the family priest of the Chālukyas and that he was his own ancestor. So Pandit Vishvanatha Shastri has done this laborious work of editing and translating the present *kāvya* in right earnest.

1. P.B. Desai (Ed.), *A History of Karnāṭaka*, p. 160.

There is a deplorable lack of historical works in Sanskrit. Except for the *Rājataraṅgiṇī*, there is not a single work in Sanskrit which can be called truly historical. There are, no doubt, Sanskrit works like the *Harshacharita*, *Vikramāṅkadevacharita* and the *Navasāhasāṅkacharita* which have historical subjects, but they have more of *kāvya* than of history in them. Even in the *Rājataraṅgiṇī* the portion dealing with the period before A.D. 800 does not bear critical scrutiny. Shri Devisimha Chauhan, however, thinks that the *Ayyaṇavaṁśacharita* is a really historical work, dealing with the age of the Chālukyas and in a lesser degree with that of Shivaji. Usually Sanskrit historical *kāvyas* do not contain any definite dates. None of the so-called Sanskrit historical works such as the *Harshacharita*, the *Vikramāṅkadevacharita* and the *Navasāhasāṅkacharita* mentions a single definite date. But the *Ayyaṇavaṁśacharita* contains not one or two but as many as 92 dates, from which Shri Chauhan infers that its author Śyāmabhaṭṭa must have had access to such source material as inscriptions on stone and copper-plates, MSS. on birch-bark, historical documents and, above all, the historical work of Ferishta, 'the king of historians'. It is no wonder, therefore, that Shri Chauhan has cordially thanked both Shri Sabajirao and Pandit Bharadvaja for publishing this *kāvya*.

The present work does not deal only with the history of the ancient Chālukya family but also with events that occurred down to A.D. 1815, that is three years before the British annexation of the Maratha kingdom. It must, therefore, be critically examined.

(1) The first and main reason for doubting the genuineness of this *kāvya* is that the author Śyāmabhaṭṭa of this work is not likely to have had reliable and detailed information about the fifty-five generations and the long period of 1355 years which elapsed from Śaka 358 (A.D. 436) when the Chālukyas established their power in South India till Śaka 1713 (A.D. 1791) when Mankoji bravely resisted the Peshwa's looting of the Śṛiṅgeri Maṭha. No ruling family in the whole world is known to have existed in unbroken succession for such a long period. Let us, for instance, take the case of this very Chālukya family. Two of its branches are historically well

known—the earlier one of them was ruling from the capital Vātāpi (modern Bādāmi in the Bījāpur District), while the later one, which rose to power two hundred years after, had its seat of government at Kalyāṇī in the Bidar District. For clear comprehension of the subsequent discussion, I give here the complete genealogy of the first family and the relevant portion of the second.

The Vātāpi Branch

Jayasiṁha
|
Raṇarāga
|
Pulakeśin I
|
Kīrtivarman I, Maṅgaleśa

Kīrtivarman I
|
Pulakeśin II
|
Vikramāditya I
|
Vinayāditya
|
Vijayāditya
|
Vikramāditya II
|
Kīrtivarman II

The Kalyaṇī Branch

Tailapa II
|
Satyāśraya, Daśavarman

Daśavarman
|
Vikramāditya V, Ayyaṇa II, Jayasiṁha II

Jayasiṁha II
|
Someśvara I
|
Someśvara II, Vikramāditya VI, Jayasiṁha

The last known date of Kīrtivarman II is A.D. 757 and the first known year of Tailapa II is A.D. 973. No inscriptional records have been found for the intervening period of 216 years. In the early inscriptions of the Kalyāṇī branch, its connection with the earlier branch of the family is not stated. In some later inscriptions of the Kalyāṇī branch, the two branches are shown connected by inserting the names of the following princes who are said to have ruled in the intervening period.

Bhīma I
|
Kīrtivarman III
|
Tailapa I
|
Vikramāditya III
|
Bhīma II
|
Ayyaṇa I
|
Vikramāditya IV

As no records of these kings have been found and they are named only in very few early inscriptions of this branch, Dr. R. G. Bhandarkar had serious doubts about their rule. He says,[1] "There must have been several branches of the Chālukya family and it is even a question whether Tailapa sprang from the main branch. I am inclined to believe that he belonged to quite a collateral and unimportant branch, and that the main branch had become extinct. For, the princes of the earlier dynasty always traced their descent to Hārīti and spoke of themselves as belonging to the Mānavya race ; while these Later Chālukyas traced their pedigree to Satyāśraya only, and those two names do not occur in their inscriptions except the Miraj grant and its copies, where an effort is made to begin at the beginning. But evidently the writer of that grant had not sufficient materials at his command, since, as above stated, he places six princes[2] only between Kīrtivarman and Tailapa. There is little question that there was no continuity of tradition. The titles Jagadekamalla, Tribhuvana-malla *etc.*, which the Later Chālukyas assumed, mark them off distinctly from princes of the earlier dynasty, who had none like them." If this is the state of things when the intervening period is only of about 200 years, one can well imagine what must be the state of things when the gap is of not less than 1300 years !

(2) The second reason for my suspicion is that there is

1. R.G. Bhandarkar, *Early History of India* (Collected Works, Vol. III). p. 109.
2. As a matter of fact, they are seven as shown above.

apparently no justification for naming this family as *Ayyaṇa-vaṁśa* (the family of Ayyaṇa). The Chālukya family produced several great kings known for their valour, liberality and other good qualities, like Pulakeśin II, Vikramāditya VI *etc.* Bilhaṇa has made one of them, *viz.* Vikramāditya VI, the hero of his *kāvya.* Ayyaṇa, after whom the present *kāvya* is named, was the second king of that name in the Later Chālukya family. He may have ruled only for a very short time if he ruled at all. Many grants have omitted his name, while one grant calls him self-willed.[1] Bilhaṇa also does not name him while describing the predecessors of Vikramāditya VI, the hero of his *Vikramāṅkadevacharita.* Śyāmabhaṭṭa, however, describes him in the beginning of the eighth *Canto* as religious-minded, truthful, generous and learned. He ruled only for six months and then made over the kingdom to his rebellious younger brother, and himself repaired to a forest for practising austerities. All this description is purely imaginary, as it has no basis. Ayyaṇa is said to have written a work on astronomy, which, Śyāmabhaṭṭa tells us, was translated into Sanskrit by the Pandits of Vārāṇasī.[2] All this is a figment of imagination, as no such work was known even to such a well-informed scholar as Sh. B. Dikshit. Shri Chāuhan thinks that it may have been in Marathi; but Marathi was not sufficiently developed in Śaka 976 (A.D. 1054) when Ayyaṇa is supposed to have written that scientific work. The first known Marathi inscription, *viz.* the Dive Āgar plate, is dated Śaka 982. The Marathi language appears in an elementary state in that record. So all this description of Ayyaṇa II, the progenitor of the family, is imaginary.

(3) The third reason for my suspicion is that in the time of Śyāmabhaṭṭa (Śaka 1737 *i.e.* A.D. 1815) no materials for the writing of such a history of the ancient dynasty were available. Shri Chauhan has observed that while writing this

1. *Ind. Ant.*, Vol. IV, p. 208.
2. Śyāmabhaṭṭa gives its name as *Ayyananaśā* (?) and says that its Sanskrit rendering is known as *Sūryasiddhānta.* He tells us further that Ayyaṇa's great-grandson tells us (where ?) that the work was translated into Sanskrit by the Pandits of Vārāṇasī. See Canto VIII, verses 15-17. All this is imaginary.

kāvya its author Śyāmabhaṭṭa had access to copper-plate grants, manuscripts on birch-bark, historical documents of a later age and the work of Ferishta, but he too could not understand how Śyāmabhaṭṭa could have had information about the visit of the Persian king Khushru's envoy to the court of the Early Chālukya king Pulakeśin II. So he had asked me to throw light on this question in his letter referred to in the beginning of this article. The reference to this visit became known for the first time when Fergusson pointed out that it occurs in the work of the Muslim historian Tabari. This was in his article in the *Journal of the Royal Asiatic Society* of April 1879, *i.e.* full 64 years after the composition of the present *kāvya*. Śyāmabhaṭṭa could not have even dreamt of it.

From the following hemistich of Verse IV, 27 of this *kāvya*.

ग्रामाणां नवनवतिसहस्रेण समन्वितम् ।
देशं महाराष्ट्रसंज्ञं स वशे कृतवान् कृती ॥

Shri Chauhan has inferred that Śyāmabhaṭṭa had knowledge of the Aihoḷe stone inscription of Pulakeśin II, which contains a similar description of Mahārāshṭra almost in the same words. As a matter of fact, not only this description of Mahārāshṭra but the whole account of the *digvijaya* of Pulakeśin II in the present *kāvya* has been borrowed from the aforementioned Aihoḷe inscription. But was that inscription deciphered before A.D. 1815? Dr. Fleet published the first reading of it together with an English translation in the *Indian Antiquary*, Vol. V, published in 1876, more than sixty years after Śyāmabhaṭṭa finished this *kāvya*. Three years later, in 1879, he published a revised edition of it in the same Journal (Vol. VIII, pp. 237-245). Finally, in 1900 Dr. Kielhorn edited it in the *Epigraphia Indica*, Vol. VI, pp. 1-12. How could Śyāmabhaṭṭa copy that inscription in his *kāvya* composed sixty years before it was known and deciphered?

As stated before, the so-called historical *kāvyas* in Sanskrit contain no definite dates. The *Ayyaṇavaṁśacharita*, however, has as many as 92. These dates have become known by the painstaking researches of European and Indian scholars during the last two centuries. Though the Asiatic Society of Bengal was founded as early as 1784 during the time of Warren Hastings, not much progress in historical research was made in the first hundred years. After the *Indian Antiquary* was started in 1872, it gave a fillip to research work in various branches of Indology as it provided a forum for the publication of historical material such as stone inscriptions, copper-plate grants, coins etc. In 1888 the *Epigraphia Indica* was started for the accurate editing of such original material with illustrative plates. Thereafter, our knowledge of ancient Indian history began to make real progress. Ancient Indian historical records are dated in the various eras which were then current in India. Their epochs were not definitely known. It took scholars more than fifty years to determine the exact epoch of the Gupta era. The epochs of the Kalachuri-Chedi and Gaṅga eras have been determined only recently after the strenuous efforts of several scholars for more than a century. All this knowledge is now readily available in the Volumes of the *History and Culture of the Indian People* published by the Bhāratīya Vidyā Bhavan. Pandit Vishvanath Shastri Bharadvaja, the Editor of this *kāvya*, has referred to this Series. He has easy access to all this material, but it could not have been available to his ancestor Śyāmabhaṭṭa. If such historical source material as stone inscriptions, copper-plate grants, coins *etc*. had been known as early as 1815, scholars like Kielhorn, Bühler, Hultzsch, Sten Konow and Bhandarkar would not have been obliged to make the strenuous efforts they did for its discovery and correct interpretation.

(4) One more reason for my suspicion is that the coins, the photographs of which were sent to me for decipherment by Shri Sabajirao, do not appear to be genuine. He sent me three coins illustrated here (Plate VI, No. I to III) as those issued by ancient Chālukya kings. Of these, Coin No. I had already been published by Dr. H.V. Trivedi of Indore in the *Journal of the Numismatic Society of India*, Vol. XX, p. 219. From the description given by him, it appears to be of copper. It has the legend *Śrī-Jayāśraya* with the crescent above and a figure like x below on the obverse and the figure of the elephant with the trunk hanging and bent inside on the reverse.

He has not published the reverse side of this coin. He thought that the coin was issued by some ruler of the second century A.D., but admitted that no such ruler is known to have flourished in that period.

When I saw the plate of the obverse of the coin with the legend *Śrī-Jayāśraya*, it reminded me of the prince Vinayāditya Maṅgalarasa Jayāśraya, son of Dharāśraya Jayasiṁha, who was himself a son of Pulakeśin II. His grants of Śaka 613[1] and 653[2] have been published, which show that he was ruling in North Koṅkaṇ towards the close of the seventh and the beginning of the eighth century A.D. It was for the first time that such an old coin of a prince of the Early Chālukya Dynasty of Bādāmi had been found. I wrote a note on this coin, identifying its ruler. It was published in *J.N.S.I.*, Vol. XXI, pp. 135-36.

Shri Sabajirao's first coin is exactly of this type so far as its obverse is concerned. On its reverse, however, it shows a boar facing left instead of an elephant. I asked Shri Sabajirao to send me the coin for examination, but he expressed his inability to do so as he had kept that and other gold coins locked up in his *Koṭhī* at Kalyāṇī on account of the Gold Control Order !

I regard this coin as spurious. If it really has the legend *Śrī-Jayāśraya*, it must be of the Chālukya prince Maṅgalarasa Jayāśraya. But then, how has it a boar on its reverse, not an elephant as on the coin of Dr. Trivedi ? Again, how is it that the boar is exactly like that on the two other coins of later times described below ? It seems to me that some one seems to have suggested to Shri Sabajirao after my note on the coin was published in *J.N.S.I.* that it might be a coin of one of his ancestors. Dr. Trivedi had not published the reverse of his coin containing the figure of an elephant. So the figure of a boar seems to have been substituted in its place. But how does that boar bear such a close resemblance to that which appears on two other coins issued several hundred years later? This coin, therefore, appears spurious.

1. *Ep. Ind.*, Vol. XXVIII, pp. 17 f.
2. *J.B.B.R.A.S.*, Vol. XVI, pp. 5f.

Coins Nos. II and III also appear false. Coin No. II has on the obverse the moon and the sun in the centre and the legend *Śrī-Āyaṇadeva Kalyāṇeśvara* encircling them, and on the reverse the figure of a boar in the centre, with the word *Śāku* above and the date 937 below. This coin is supposed to have been issued by Ayyaṇa in Śaka 937 ; but the figures 9 and 7 had not assumed this form in that age.[1] Besides, this supposed date for Ayyaṇa belies the description in the present *kāvya*. In Canto VII, verse 25 Śyāmabhaṭṭa tells us that after Vikramāditya V died in Śaka 940, Ayyaṇa ruled only for five or six months. Thereafter, he became disgusted by the rebellion of his brother Jayasiṁha, and relinquished the throne for practising austerities. If this description is correct, how could he issue this coin in Śaka 937, three years before his accession ?

Coin No. III has the name *Śrī-Kāṁvādeva Mahāmaṁḍaleśvara* on the obverse, and *Kalyāṇa-puravar-ādhiśvara* on the reverse. The coin purports to have been issued by a ruler of Kalyāṇa, but no such ruler is known from the genealogy of the Chālukyas of Kalyāṇī.

There are other reasons also for taking these coins as spurious : (1) The gold coins of the Later Chālukyas are very thin. They have the figure of the boar in the centre and the legend punched round it in small circles. Their reverse is blank. See the coin in Plate III, No. 79, in Elliot's *Coins of Southern India*.[2] (2) As the Later Chālukyas were ruling in the Kannaḍa country, the legend on their coins is in Kannaḍa characters, not in Nāgarī as on Coins Nos. II and III illustrated here.

So, like the *Ayyaṇavaṁśacharita*, these coins also appear to be spurious.

For the reasons stated above, the *Ayyaṇavaṁśacharita* cannot have been as old as A.D. 1815. It seems to have been composed by some one recently after the Volumes of the *H.C.I.P.* were published by the Bhāratīya Vidyā Bhavan. It is written

1. For the figure of 9 and 7 in this period, see Table IX B of Bühler's *Indischen Palaeographic*.
2. See coin No. IV in the attached plate.

in simple *anushṭubh* verses such as can be composed without much effort. But its author, whoever he was, seems to have been well informed. Otherwise, he could not have utilised for his purpose the afore-mentioned coin of Jayāśraya published in *J.N.S.I.* as lately as 1959, by adding a fake reverse.

Some of the information given in the *Ayyaṇavaṁśacharita* is correct and some erroneous. Shri Chauhan has pointed out the inaccuracies in the data collected from Ferishta's work. The ancient history of India has many dark spots. The author of this *kāvya* has tried to throw light on them by supplying imaginary details. For instance, the author, in order to show that the Later Chālukyas were connected with the earlier branch of Bādāmi, has given an imaginary genealogy from Maṅgaleśa to Tailapa II. It has no basis. Similar defects in the history of the Marathas given here can be easily pointed out by the experts of that period.

In his aforementioned review of this work in the Marathi Quarterly *Itihāsa āṇi Saṁskṛiti*, Shri Chauhan has wondered why the Editor Pandit Vishvanath Shastri has not given any other readings, if he had at his disposal two MSS. of the *kāvya*. The Editor has explained this in his Preface, p. 9. He tells us that after making the press copy of this *kāvya* he obtained from Shri Sabajirao another MS. of it. He took it to his home in Vārāṇasī for comparing it with his own MS. He kept them both tied together in a piece of cloth. Some time after, when he wanted to refer to them, he found that the MSS. in the bundle had been eaten by white ants ! No comment is necessary.

The attempts to circulate such fake works date back to very early times. Hence we find that Vyāsa is supposed to have himself composed all the eighteen Purāṇas. Kālidāsa is credited with the authorship of numerous later works including the *Jyotirvidābharaṇa*. Recently the *Bhavishyapurāṇa* was shown to contain references to events of the Gupta age, but it was pointed out by Dr. R. C. Majumdar that the portion must have been composed by some one who had knowledge of recent historical researches. Some years ago *Rajavaidya* Jivaram Kalidasa Shastri of Saurāshṭra caused agitation among scholars by publishing the *Yajñaphala* of Bhāsa, the *Kṛishṇacharita kāvya* of Samudragupta, the *Pūrva-Pāṇinīyam* and the *Bhojapatrī Gītā*. But these works have been shown to be fake. Pandit Gopaladatta Shastri revealed that he had himself composed the *Yajñaphala-nāṭaka* and passed it under the name of Bhāsa. Dr. Belwalkar has shown how the *Bhojapatrī Gītā* is a fake work. Similarly, some one seems to have composed this *Ayyaṇavaṁśacarita Kāvya* recently in order to show how Sardar Sabajirao Chalukya is a direct descendant of the ancient Chālukya family. We regret to say that the attempt has not been successful.

Sanskrit Pandits would be well advised not to mislead people by composing such spurious works. The truth will be out sooner or later.

INDEX

(The figures refer to the pages and *add.* to additions and corrections. The following abbreviations have been used : *au.*—author; *ch.*—chief; *co.*—country, *com.*—Commentary; *dy.*—dynasty; feud.—feudatory; *k.*—king; *lo.*—locality; *m.*—male; *tit.*—title; *wk.* work.

A

B

W

Y

ERRATA

Page	*Line*	*Incorrect*	*Correct*
45	12	Kolhāpur	Herle
70	4	केलितः	केलिदः
127	26-28	(Recently a stone inscription of Aparāditya I, dated Śaka 1070 has been discovered at Āgāshī in the Ṭhāṇā District. It shows that Aparāditya I was ruling for some years after the issue of the Panhāle plates of Śaka 1061.)	
147	7	Devarasa	Revarasa
149	7	Devarasa	Revarasa
197	18	VII	XXVII

Plate I

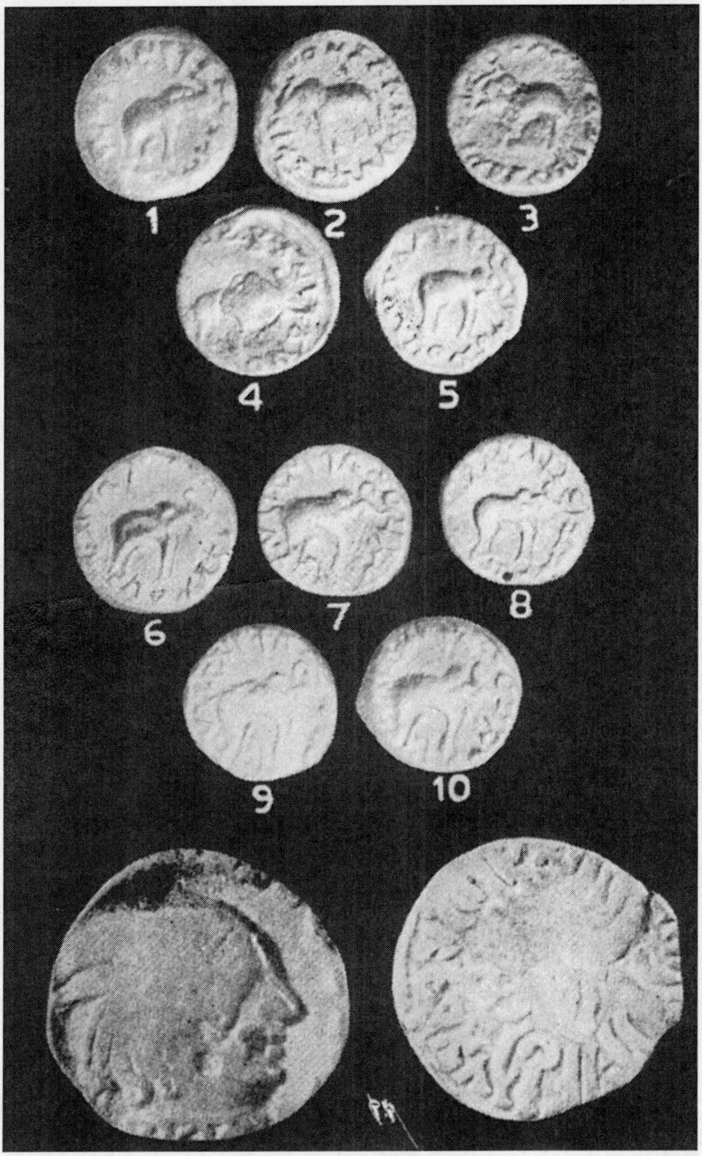

Nos. 1 to 5 - Lead Coins of Vāsishṭhīputra Puḷumāvi
Nos. 6 to 10 - Lead Coins of Vāsishṭhīputra Skanda Sātakarṇi
No. 11 - Silver coin of Western Kshatrapa Viśvaseṇa
(Enlarged Size)

Plate II

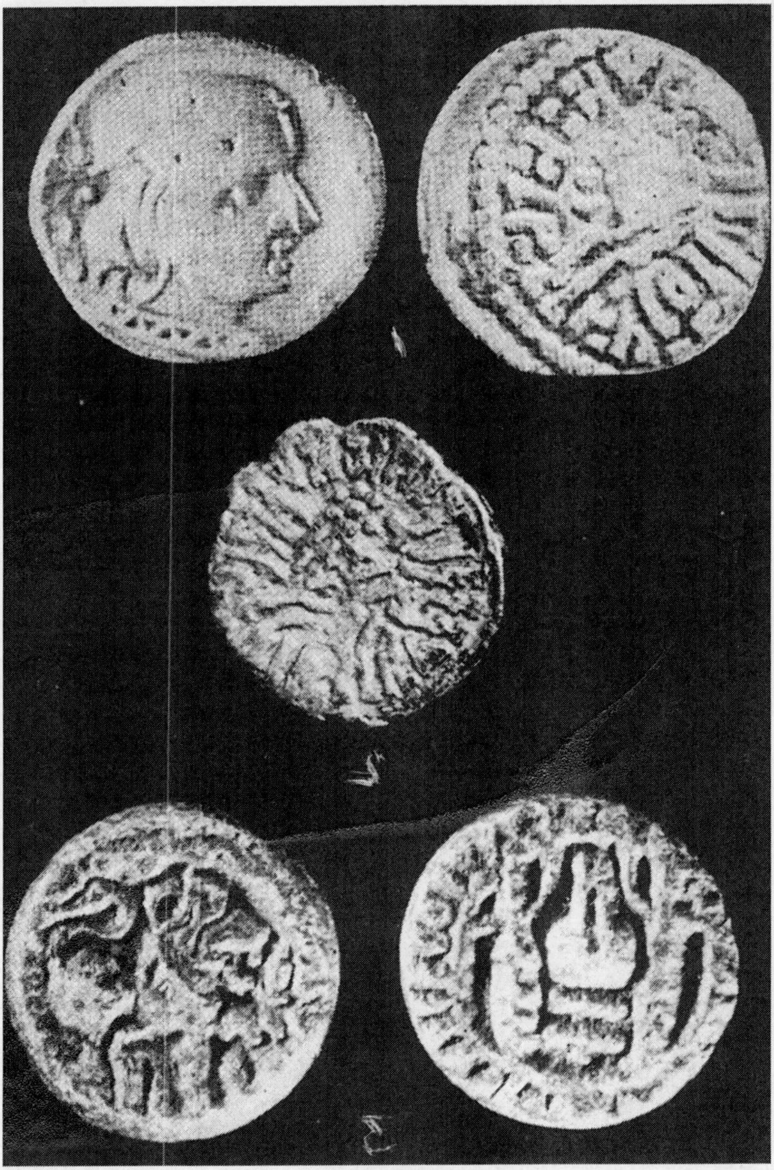

1

2

3

No. 1 - Silver Coin of Western Kshatrapa Rudrasena III
No. 2 - Silver Coin of Western Kshatrapa Saṅgadāman
No. 3 - Vishnukundin Coin from Nagpur
(All in enlarged size)

Plate III

1

2

3

Nos. 1,2,3 - Coins of Śaka King Māna Mahisha

Plate IV

Image of Pārśvanātha in Cave II at Dhārāśiva

Plate V

A Stone Inscription at Mārkaṇḍī

Plate VI

2

Fake and Real Coins of the Western Chālukyas 3

Plate VI

4

Fake and Real Coins of the Western Chālukyas

Plate VI

4

Fake and Real [illegible]